The World of
Perversion

SUNY series in Psychoanalysis and Culture

Henry Sussman, editor

The World of
Perversion

Psychoanalysis and the
Impossible Absolute of Desire

James Penney

State University of New York Press

Published by
State University of New York Press, Albany

© 2006 State University of New York

All rights reserved

Printed in the United States of America

No part of this book may be used or reproduced in any manner whatsoever
without written permission. No part of this book may be stored in a retrieval system
or transmitted in any form or by any means including electronic, electrostatic,
magnetic tape, mechanical, photocopying, recording, or otherwise
without the prior permission in writing of the publisher.

For information, address State University of New York Press
194 Washington Avenue, Suite 305, Albany, NY 12210-2384

Production by Marilyn P. Semerad
Marketing by Anne M. Valentine

Library of Congress Cataloging-in-Publication Data

Penney, James, 1971–
   The world of perversion : psychoanalysis and the impossible absolute of desire /
James Penney.
      p. cm. — (SUNY series in psychoanalysis and culture)
   Includes bibliographical references and index.
   ISBN 0-7914-6769-4 (hardcover : alk. paper) — ISBN-13: 978-0-7914-6770-1
(pbk. : alk. paper)
   1. Psychoanalysis. 2. Sexual deviation. 3. Desire. I. Title. II. Series.

BF175.5.S48P46 2006
150.19'5—dc22   2005019597

ISBN-13: 978-0-7914-6769-5 (hardcover : alk. paper)

10 9 8 7 6 5 4 3 2 1

For my parents, Claire and Doug.

*And for Justin: Welcome to the world—May it be better
when you leave it than when you arrived.*

Contents

Lacan, ce n'est pas gai.

—*Catherine Clément*

Acknowledgments

No doubt this is merely a fantasy, but I have caught myself thinking during these last few years that things must have been easier—back then, before my time—for serious psychoanalytic critics. By this I mean the ones who, when presented with the inevitable "Yes, but of course we need to break with Freud in order to do x" insist that in fact it is not necessary, that you ultimately learn more by going back, by sticking to the spirit of the texts already there. Freud knew (as did Lacan) that psychoanalytic knowledge and the kind institutionalized in the academy are two very different things. Today's corporate university, tethered more than ever to the logic of capital and the disciplinary mummification of inquiry (often under the very guise of "excellence" and "interdisciplinarity"), has only made this contrast in values all the starker.

Now that I have secured an apparently reliable toehold in the academy, I have the luxury of looking back to recognize the parties who helped make happen what had begun to seem unlikely. Much of the thought which has made its way into this book goes back to my graduate student days at Duke in the late 1990s. Fredric Jameson and Toril Moi, as well as Philip Stewart, Michèle Longino, and Helen Solterer (for Gilles de Rais) provided inspiration and constructive criticism in equal measure during that time. Aisha Karim and Svetlana Mintcheva helped me cope with life in an institution which, to my "provincial" Western Canadian eyes, bore a closer resemblance to a Disney plantation than a real (read: public) university. The Social Sciences and Humanities Research Council of Canada provided helpful fellowship support; and the Mellon Foundation and Society for the Humanities made possible a stimulating postdoctoral year at Cornell.

While revising the manuscript I realized that my interest in Diderot's *Rameau's Nephew* was on some level an anticipation of the harsh realities of the university and the academic job market. In this light I also wish to thank warmly all those who have opened doors, or even helped keep them slightly ajar, along the way, especially Nasrin Rahimieh, Dianne Chisholm, Christopher Lane, Dominick LaCapra, Mitchell Greenberg, Tim Dean, Clive Thomson, Joan Copjec, Judith Still, Diana Knight, and Ian McLachlan.

Earlier versions of portions of chapters 2 and 3 were originally published in *Perversion and the Social Relation*, edited by Molly Anne Rothenberg, Dennis Foster and Slavoj Žižek and *Paragraph: A Journal of Modern Critical Theory* 24, no. 1 (2001) respectively; I gratefully acknowledge, again respectively, Duke University Press and Edinburgh University Press. James Penney, "Beyond Atè: Lacan, Ethics, and the Real," *Journal for the Psychoanalysis of Culture and Society* 7.1 (2002), Ohio State University Press is reproduced in modified form with permission of Palgrave MacMillan.

Chapter One

Epistemologies of Perversion

> Desire is essentially a *perverse desire*.
>
> —Julia Kristeva, *Le temps sensible*

Perversity and Perversion

That desire is essentially perverse is one of two main points I wish to argue in this book. The other, however, is that desire is not perversion, and neither is the drive. My position will be that there is no antinomy between these two propositions. For this to be so, a fundamental conceptual distinction must be drawn between desire's essential *perversity* and *perversion* as such; between desire's *generic* excess over its own law and a *particular* response of the subject to this excess—a specific subjective structure, in other words. Indeed, the only way of making sense of Freud's discourse on perversion is to uphold this distinction, which implies a surprising paradox: More fundamentally than "sexual differ- ence" or "the mother's castration," *what the pervert disavows is the essen- tial perversity of desire*—its constitutive deviation from a genital or phallic norm which nonetheless remains psychically operative as a sine qua non of subjectivity properly speaking.

Apart from Freudian psychoanalysis and its Lacanian formalization, there are two additional discursive contexts which traverse this study. The first is queer theory. Too heterogeneous and variously determined to be distilled into a single orthodoxy, queer theory has nonetheless virtually unanimously endorsed the historicist reduction of perversion

1

to normative instantiations of power. One of my goals will therefore be to spell out the consequences, in particular the political ones, of the introduction into antihomophobic criticism of the distinction I have just drawn.

The second context furnishes a conceptual historicization of perversion. Throughout the vicissitudes it has endured since its derivation from the Latin *perversio*, the meaning of the term has pivoted around a notion of a deflection from a right or true course. Abstracted from its original military connotations into moral, indeed theological, ones, and acquiring in early modernity the properly sexual denotations from which sexology and psychoanalysis would eventually inherit, perversion suggests a deviation which, notably, is logically dependent on the norm from which it deviates. This observation makes intelligible my underlying wager: The disjunction between the *object* and the presumptively reproductive *goal* of the Freudian libido is rigorously analogous to the disjunction which haunts the moral and theological discourses of early modernity. In consequence, it is possible to say that the psychoanalytic concept of perversion in the theory of sexuality inherits directly from the concept's previous incarnations in the related terms "sin," "concupiscence," and indeed "evil," all of which, naturally enough, depend on the idea of a Good from whose respectable course they reliably depart.

By beginning selectively to trace the antecedents of the distinction psychoanalysis posits between desire's perversity and perversion properly speaking, I will try to show how psychoanalysis not only presents a properly dialectical theory of sexuality which splits the subject between a norm and a deviation or transgression, but also how psychoanalysis insists that the effort to suture this split produces the ethically, and indeed politically, problematic perverse structure. Because so much of the current opposition to the psychoanalytic discourse on perversion finds its inspiration in the work of Michel Foucault, *The History of Sexuality*, historicist in methodology and relativist in implication, will serve as a propitious place to begin.

Perversion as Power

Joan Copjec has already rigorously argued through Lacan against Foucault's historicist reduction of the Freudian unconscious.[1] Still, it will be helpful briefly to revisit *The History of Sexuality* with the goal of determining precisely how Foucault's definition of perversion as power not only departs from the psychoanalytic argument, but also shares a worrisome affinity with the concept of perversion as psychic structure refined by Lacan. We recall that in 1976 Foucault made the aegis-inaugurating claim that perversion is a fabrication of "sexuality"—the panoply of discourses originating, depending where in the text one looks, sometime during the seventeenth or eighteenth century. Foucault adduced to this claim the idea that these perversions witnessed their most influential classificatory and theoretical elaboration during the nineteenth century in sexological and psychiatric writing, as well as in the early texts of psychoanalysis. The approach of *The History of Sexuality* to the problematic of perversion is radically nominalist: There were no perverts, Foucault advances, until they were invented by such sexological luminaries as Krafft-Ebing, Ellis, Moll, and Legrain.[2] Moreover, the invention of perversion played a determining role in a general strategy of power which produced the perversions it attempted to control through this production itself. If sexology constructed the entire baroque panoply of perversities, in other words, it did so only to indulge all the more decadently in the enjoyment of their regulation. By inaugurating a theory of sexuality premised on the idea of a repressive law, modern bourgeois science, including specifically psychoanalysis, perpetuated its disciplinary hegemony through what Foucault terms a "polymorphous incitement to discourse."[3] The discourse of sexuality functioned as a strategy of surveillance which aimed to lure subjects into seeking their truth through the disclosure of sexual experience. This is of course the "repressive hypothesis" Foucault attempted not so much to refute, but to qualify, in an allegedly more accurate and antinormative fashion. Where, in Foucault's view, the psychoanalytic concept of repression predicates itself on the negative delimitation of a field of transgression—on prohibition, in other words—the "productive" model of sexuality redescribes this instance of repression as itself positive, as producing the very discourse which leads subjects to seek their truth through sex and sexual disclosure.

My own view is that Foucault's gesture was noble but ill advised. The relatively recent, predominantly Anglo-American phenomenon of queer theory has only underscored how after centuries of legitimately oppressive forms of state and church control over the sexual sphere, control which of course continues to varying degrees today, it stands to reason that these "regimes" would eventually be unmasked for what, unquestionably, they really were: means of marginalizing, criminalizing, and regulating nonnormative modes of sexual behavior. The stubborn reappearance and perpetuation of premodern sodomy laws in a number of jurisdictions, notably in the United States but also in the Muslim world and elsewhere, serves as proof positive of the complicity between power and a voyeuristic, indeed perverse, desire for sexual regulation and surveillance. But at this point a number of skeptical questions must be posed. By qualifying it as *causal*, does Foucault's productive model of sexuality not misconstrue the relation between the discourses these regimes or state apparatuses enunciate and what I would call "the real of sex"—actual sexual behaviors in concrete sociohistorical situations? Is sex, in other words, not precisely what is unavailable to the epistemophilic sexological gaze which—one can on this point agree with Foucault—reached its greatest level of classificatory intensity near the end of the nineteenth century? Further, is it not more accurate to posit as the *cause* of the incitement to discourse of which Foucault so eloquently speaks precisely the impossibility of regulating sex, of conjoining the real of sex to its figuration in discourse or power? Finally, is *The History of Sexuality*'s evocation of power as perversion not tantamount to a properly perverse disavowal of the disjunction between discourse and sex?

The frustration of both the various post-Freudian revisionist models of sexual "liberation," most influentially those of R. D. Laing and Wilhelm Reich,[4] and the jubilatory *soixante-huitard* effort to inscribe these models onto the real of history, likely led Foucault to wonder about late modernity's failure to found a new era of sexual "happiness," or to explain why we all, when not succumbing to more severe psychical disruptions, are still afflicted not only by versions of the same neurotic symptoms which plagued Freud's "repressed" patients, but also by what Julia Kristeva has memorably called the "new maladies of the soul."[5] Indeed, it is precisely in the form of Foucault's response to the frustration of the liberation model of sexuality that one should situate the properly symptomatic dimension of his intervention. Not coincidentally, I wish to argue, this response features dangerously reactionary political implications. For surely the strongest thesis expressed in *The History of Sexuality* is the one which asserts that if the subject remains unable, at the postliberatory moment, to translate its notion of a full enjoyment onto the level of experience, it is because of an omnipotent agency of power which cannot be localized, one which alienates—appropriates, even— the subject's enjoyment at the very moment it presents itself on the horizon of possible experience. Indeed, I would suggest that the desire to overcome the traumatic, all-seeing invasiveness of power's agency is precisely the motivation which causes the Foucauldian subject to seek an alternative, falsely corporeal, liberation through the abandonment to power of the category of the subject as such. In other words, the truth of the Foucauldian desire to escape power's production of subjective experience is precisely the subject's properly perverse enslavement to power's obscene jouissance; this subject's refusal of the risky, self-expropriating agency of an excess pleasure alien to the forms of knowledge.

To do justice to Foucault's memorably rendered argument, however, it will be necessary to examine in greater detail the precise terms of his claims. Given especially that in so much contemporary queer theory Foucault's late premises are simply assumed, the fundamental questions in my view need to be reposed. What are the theoretical pre-suppositions informing the critique of sexuality discourse Foucault frames in the terms of an analytics of power? What precisely is the content of Foucault's concept of power, a concept which figures so centrally not only in the entirety of his later work, but also in so many of the more recent texts on sexual politics this work directly inspired? We recall that for Foucault, the nature of contemporary power is such that what he calls the "juridico-discursive" model may no longer accurately describe it. Classical political theory's location of the exercise of power on the formal level of the state and its multiple apparatuses and discourses— of the institutions of civil society, indeed of the panoply of notions which gravitate around the term "democracy," all of which conceptually de-pend on an idea of abstract political or discursive representation—fail to take account of the diffuseness of a contemporary power which cannot be pinned down.

As a result, the work of late modern or postmodern power is more accurately evoked through a nonsemiotic vocabulary of vectors and forces derived from the physical sciences. In this connection, one also notes that Foucault's criticism of what he takes to be the psychoanalytic un-derstanding of "the law" presupposes that the conceptual edifice of psy-choanalysis belongs to this modern or bourgeois representationalist understanding of the field of power and its effects. Along with the spi-raling disciplinary capabilities of the increasingly bureaucratic and regu-lated quality of life in late bourgeois capitalism comes the diffusion of the sphere of power well beyond what formalized legality may legiti-mately be taken to evoke. Gilles Deleuze concisely renders this notion of power's outstripping of form when he writes with regard to Foucault's framework that "there is no State, only state control."[6] Power in late modernity is no longer localized, concrete, or traceable; its efficacy has become diffuse, plastic, and elusive.

Foucault links the law of sexuality he attributes to psychoanalysis to the earlier classical idea of an identifiable source of political legitimacy to which everyone is subject through the symbolic authority of a mon-arch or representative legislative body. Implicit in Foucault's critique of psychoanalysis is therefore the idea that it features a fundamental con-ceptual archaism—that its concept of law is inextricably tied to a histori-cally surpassed administrative or governmental constellation. Because during the last two centuries or so the modus operandi of power has become increasingly complex and heterogeneous, the idea of law which psychoanalysis presupposes no longer obtains. Like the entire complex of the repressive hypothesis on which it rests, this concept of law relies, Foucault advances, on "a representation of power which, depending on the use made of it and the position it is accorded with respect to desire, leads to two contrary results: either to the promise of a 'liberation,' if power is seen as having only an external hold on desire, or, if it is constitutive of desire itself, to the affirmation: you are always-already trapped" (83).

The importance of this passage is immeasurable because it concisely renders the two variations on the law-of-desire paradigm Foucault deems to stem from the repressive hypothesis he reads into psychoanalysis. In Foucault's view, of course, both variations rest upon naive and disenabling assumptions. First, when the law is viewed to be an outwardly imposed limit on desire—an imposition on the subject of a concrete or localizable source of political discipline—one is tempted by a fascinating utopian belief in liberation, in the possibility of accessing an enjoyment which the law puts out of reach. Second, if the limit to desire is considered to be self-hindering—if desire refers to an external prohibition to make manifest an "internal" or inherent impossibility— then one is left with the familiarly melancholic logic of the "always-already." If subjects legislate desire themselves, then they are condemned forever to suffer from its inherent capacity to regulate the sexual domain, to stake out and defend specific, acceptable paths for desire. Crucially, in Foucault's view this latter understanding of desire as internally limited makes the assumption that this limitation is responsible for the subject's endlessly frustrated effort, markedly complicit with power, to uncover its truth through sex.

It may be too early to state at this juncture that the difficulty with Foucault's contention lies in its faulty formulation of the notion of a self-legislating, self-limiting desire. Though I will return to this contention shortly, I wish at this point to bring out something of the paradoxical nature of the properly political dimension of Foucault's project. For despite the fact that Foucault appears to intend his analytics of power as a postutopian model of erotic practice centered on "bodies and pleasures" (157), the final result of Foucault's conception of perversion as power is to put to ruin the subject's sovereignty, to smooth over the disjunction between the exercise of normative power and the function of the subject as psychoanalysis defines it. My suggestion, in other words, is that this gesture *exacerbates* the subject's dependency on the lure of subjective truth which, Foucault is correct to assert, the discourse of sexuality deceptively holds up.

A number of the more striking examples of Foucault's description of power's agency in *The History of Sexuality* illuminate the logic of subjective self-instrumentalization I wish to connect to the psychoanalytic concept of the perverse structure. What is especially remarkable about the textual moments in question is their evocation of the alienation of pleasure from the embodied subject, indeed the attribution to power of the power to extract pleasure from the body and to make use of it to its own ends. Foucault describes, for example, a disembodied faculty of seeing whose power is intensified through physical contact with the (subject's) body. The eye of power performs an "examination and insistent observation" exercised by means of "a physical proximity and an interplay of intense sensations" (44). Power makes use of the human body as a means of converting its abstract or potential power into concrete, lived pleasure-power. Thus, power "sets about contacting bodies, caressing them with its eyes, intensifying areas, electrifying surfaces, dramatizing troubled moments . . . [and] wrapping the sexual body in its embrace" (44). Power becomes sexualized to excess; it obscenely invades our bodily intimacy to prolong and intensify a pleasure the text attributes not to the subject-body, but rather to the noncorporeal faculty of seeing which quite literally colonizes the body. In other words, Foucault ascribes the experience or consciousness of the intensities of pleasure which traverse the body not to an embodied subject, but rather to a nonsubstantive and nonsubjective faculty of power. Indeed, Foucault underlines this externalization of the consciousness of pleasure when he refers to power's "polymorphous conducts" (47) which, as he puts it, "actually extracted from people's bodies and from their pleasures." These pleasures, Foucault continues, "were drawn out, revealed, isolated, intensified, incorporated by multifarious power devices" (48). Foucault's striking language conjures images which compare the relation of power to the subject to that of an agriculturalist to his land: Power implants itself into the earth body in order to intensify a quantity of pleasure which can later be harvested at maturity. In this way the body functions as an instrument of power's will to pleasure. Like the infant whose lack of mobility and language renders it defenseless against the (retroactively traumatic) bodily stimulations occasioned by its caregivers, the Foucauldian subject is subjected to pleasures assumed for the benefit of power. The subject thereby becomes the bodily extension of the substance-consciousness of power.

We can now retrace our steps and revisit my previous claim that Foucault makes his fatal error when he misconstrues the two available paradigms for the law of desire as an irremediably complicit double bind. For is it not the case that the second idea of a self-limiting desire only presents itself to us as a recipe for inescapable entrapment if we are still in the thrall of the first idea of a law externally imposed by power?

More precisely, Foucault's specific formulation of the two modes of the law betrays the truth that the first understanding remains presupposed in the second. In order to proceed from the premise that desire is self-hindering to the conclusion that one is, as Foucault puts it, "always already trapped," one must necessarily have already situated oneself in the position of what Lacan described as the subject's fundamental fantasy. In other words, one must necessarily believe that what the law prohibits is possible or realizable, that the premise of an internally limited desire leads not to the conclusion that desire has no adequate object, but to the ideological fantasy that the law works in tandem with an obscene instance of power which sadistically withholds or extracts from the subject its enjoyment. In this sense the perverse structure can be described as a particular mode of escape from this traumatic fantasy of the Other's jouissance. Whereas the neurotic holds fast to this fantasy as a means of postponing or delaying its own self-expropriation in the experience of enjoyment, the pervert transfers its division from jouissance onto the Other, adopting the role of enabler of a jouissance from which it can remain at a comfortable remove. The neurotic suffers from the disjunction between possible knowledge and the experience of jouissance; in political terms, this means that the neurotic is painfully aware of power's separation from itself, its tendency to act in violation of its law. The pervert, in contrast, effects the reconciliation of power with knowledge, seeking to attribute to transgression the consistency of a new law unmarred by contradiction, by a lack of knowledge of its own effects. Foucault's reading of the law-of-desire paradigm shies away from the paradox that the law imposes an interdiction on an impossibility. Far from producing a melancholic defeatism, however, this paradox opens up an empty, impossible space in the social field which provides the subject with the capacity to measure the ethical and political value of actually existing laws.[7]

Foucault's analytics of power enters the realm of perversion, I wish to suggest, when it moves from the identification of the dissimulated interests that concrete, disinterested laws express to a descriptive aesthetics of the relations between forms of discipline exercised by abstract, nonrepresentational vectors of power stripped of determinate attributes and therefore untraceable to the vested interests of identifiable social groups, classes, and constituencies. We can take as an example the modern reincarnation of the medieval laws against sodomy to which Foucault alludes in *The History of Sexuality*. Of course, these laws caused alleged perverts to suffer fiery deaths at the stake and today absurdly allow for the criminal prosecution of subjects who freely engage in specific consensual sexual behaviors.

The proper psychoanalytic approach to this question, in my view, would seek to inquire after the dependence of the law's power on disavowed knowledge of its transgression. That is to say, the attitude of obedience with respect to the law against sodomy is complicit with an unconscious or disavowed homoerotic libidinal dynamic circulating, for example, among the members of a coterie of church fathers for whom sexual desire between men is the enabling but excluded principle of their form of social organization. In contrast, the Foucauldian directives require the critic to move beyond such a concrete identification of interest: They oblige us to displace the surreptitious satisfaction I just attributed to the religious leaders to a power viewed as pure abstract interest, an interest which always transcends its concrete representatives and whose final purpose is the intensification of its own enjoyment. More concretely, we lose the capacity to argue that the law against sodomy is unjust on the grounds that it expresses the disavowed libidinal interest of members of the church hierarchy, or even, in the contemporary context, of the patriarchal figurehead of the bourgeois nuclear family. In sum, Foucauldian power is *intentional*—it encounters no limit or obstacle to its realization, no unconscious which would divide it from itself—but *nonsubjective*—it instrumentalizes the agents through whom it acts, subsumes them under its agenda of disciplinary intensification.

If the law against sodomy is an expression of power *tout court*, then the critical intellectual is left with the modest task of demonstrating how this law is linked to other laws, and these laws to mechanisms of surveillance, and these mechanisms to yet other discourses and knowledges, all of which mutually contribute to the intensification of an elusive power complex's satisfaction. The paradoxical conclusion to be drawn here is that the detection of political interests in discourse requires the deployment of a notion of disinterest. The point, of course, is not that a genuinely disinterested law could ever be written. Rather, the concept of disinterest—the vanishing point of politics which constitutes the horizon of sociality, the very limit or lack of totality which characterizes the social field—must be retained so as to allow for a reasoned demonstration of the covert political interests which actual laws both dissimulate and defend.[8]

Foucault's narrative of power's intensification can be helpfully expressed in terms of the shift from the paradigm of modernity to postmodernity. According to Foucault's historical model, for example, the development of a codified public law at the end of the Middle Ages was the inaugural step in power's evolution from its rigidly determinate, vertical configuration in feudalism toward the modern, diffusely lateral technologies we are viewed to know today. In other words, the idea of historical process here at work foregrounds power's uninterrupted intensification and abstraction, its progressive reinvention of itself as ever more pervasive and complex vectors of force. Foucault participates in the unfortunate theoretical regression to the postmodernist ethos when he proceeds from the legitimate premise that in late modernity the relation between instances of power and localizable forms of political agency has radically increased in complexity to the *conclusion* that it is no longer possible to establish any connection whatsoever between these instances and interests. Rather than insistently demonstrating how the modernist, liberal universalizing notions of justice, freedom and rights necessarily fail to articulate the disinterest they purport to uphold, and thereby working toward the continual expansion of the terrain of democratic universality, the concept of universality as such is jettisoned from the Foucauldian framework in favor of a gradualist, reformist politics of particularism which assumes that the very forms of political representation function as repressive instruments of power.

More precisely, the difficulty with the Foucauldian reduction of the public sphere to pure, abstract political interest does not consist in its postulate that the universal Good necessarily harbors a particular will it dissimulates beneath a cloak of generality. My objection is rather that Foucault equates the public good with will as such, with a disembodied, deconcretized and nonsubjective mechanism of power which transforms the entire field of social relations into an instrument for its own disciplinary enjoyment. The protoparanoid, properly postmodern aspect of Foucault's later work therefore consists in its formulation of a radically post- or antidialectical political theory, one which casts away as metaphysical archaisms the conceptual tools required to distinguish between interest and power, between the efforts of concrete constituencies or classes to achieve hegemony in a particular social field, and an abstract disciplinary force delinked from concrete collective interests which acts on the social body from everywhere and nowhere. This properly perverse idea of power exacerbates the ideology of victimization, indeed the very defeatist melancholy Foucault wishes to escape, by deconcretizing political agency, by delegitimating the utopian option of calling into question the disavowed dividends in enjoyment which allow a regime of power to function in the first place. Foucault's idea of power tries to persuade us that our oppression stems not from forces we can trace to specific socioeconomic, legislative, and juridical structures, but from power as such—from a transcendental, nonsubjective intentionality which saturates and disciplines these structures from a place at a remove from the libidinal economies of any concrete actors in the social world.[9]

Perversion as Structure

I have argued that Foucault's definition of perversion dangerously tends toward a subjective orientation which instrumentalizes the subject with respect to the instances of power. The late Foucauldian paradigm ultimately suggests that there is no escape from perversion in its complicity with power abstractly defined. Indeed, the subject becomes the very embodiment of power's perverse jouissance, and this gesture of desubjectivation is finally what Foucault has to offer his reader when he recommends an exploration of "bodies and pleasures," which, in light of his previous contentions, can only be attributed to power itself. But a question immediately presents itself: If, as Foucault is nonetheless surely correct to contend, the discourse of perversion has largely functioned throughout its modern history as a means of policing and pathologizing nonnormative sexual behaviors and relationships, how might it be possible to recuperate a concept of perversion without relegitimating its phobically normative history? My suggestion will be that in its zeal to denounce the complicity of the discourse of perversion with a genuinely oppressive exercise of power, queer theory has thrown the baby out with the proverbial bathwater. More precisely, my insistence that perversion is still a legitimate concept—in clinical psychoanalysis as well as its broader expansion onto political and cultural terrain—need in no manner detract from the ambitions of an antihomophobic critical project. Indeed, the recuperation of the concept of perversion from its phobic analytic baggage may be precisely what is required to recontextualize the concerns of queer theory within a broader, genuinely political project.

From the initial groundbreaking theses of the *Three Essays on the Theory of Sexuality* to the later association of perversion with the notions of fetishism and ego splitting, the development of Freud's theory of sexuality provides the rudiments of an alternative approach. The more recent theoretical contributions of Lacanian discourse bring further conceptual precision to the idea Freud began to seize upon of perversion as psychic structure. It should go without saying that a genuinely antihomophobic engagement with psychoanalysis must object to any a priori connection of the strong sense of perversion with homosexuality. Therefore, it will be of particular interest to inquire after the intricacies and contradictions of Freud's discussion of what is known as "object choice" in its relation to perversion. This line of inquiry, I will contend, leads to two surprising conclusions. First, the biological sex of the object-partner is a question of relative indifference to the drive (though this is surely not true in the case of desire properly speaking); in consequence of this assertion, psychoanalysis quite radically calls into question the discourse of sexual orientation as we know it today. Second, for the biologically male subject, the perverse structure is to be linked not to the choice of a phallic(ized) male sexual object, but rather to the defense against such a choice, in other words to a form of resistance against homosexual desire.

The *Three Essays* contains Freud's first extended meditation on the question of perversion. It lays the groundwork for all his later attempts to elucidate the problematic of sexuality and its link with unconscious desire. In this text Freud makes use of the sexological classifications laid down before him to problematize the rigid differentiation of normative sexuality from perversion. As I will suggest, however, Freud's effort to recast the categories by means of which sexual practices are normalized is fraught with contradiction and distorted by assumptions which remain unhelpfully implicit. Moreover, since its original publication predates Freud's later, properly metapsychological work, the *Three Essays* succeeds in recognizing neither the implication of sexual difference in the structure Freud would later evoke under the term "fetishism" nor the link between the perverse structure and the vicissitudes of the drive. In spite of its failure to lay the groundwork for the structural theory of perversion which was Freud's ultimate ambition and Lacan's signal accomplishment, the *Three Essays* nevertheless establishes the fundamental motifs of the psychoanalytic discourse on perversion. For this reason it merits careful consideration here.

In his discussion of what he terms the sexual "aberrations," Freud's first move is to endorse Krafft-Ebing's distinction in his work *Psychopathia Sexualis* between deviations of sexual object and deviations of sexual aim. In the first group Freud places what the sexological vocabulary of the day referred to as "inverts," along with those who practice what are now known as bestiality and pedophilia. Each of these subjects commonly chooses a nonnormative sexual object, the norm for object choice here figuring as an adult human subject of the opposite sex. In the second category of sexual deviation Freud variously groups fetishists and romantic lovers, voyeurs and exhibitionists, sadists and masochists; members of each of these groups manifest either an "extension" of erotic investment beyond the genital areas of the object or a "fixation" of sexual activity on what Freud called a "preliminary" aim.[10] Freud's suggestion is that these subjects arrest the erotic encounter at a point prior to what is conventionally viewed to be its goal—the one, obviously enough, which renders conception possible. Crucially, Freud links only the second group—the aim deviations—to perversion properly speaking.

One of the more striking consequences of Freud's differentiation of object and aim deviations is to separate out, at least superficially, what is generally called homosexuality from the set of perversions as Freud here defines them. Indeed, the most radical general ramification of this particular figuration of perversion is to deemphasize the importance of the sexual object's attributes. This unusually consequential feature of Freud's theory is brought to the fore in the assertion that "the sexual drive is in the first instance independent of its object" (48). Additionally, as Arnold Davidson is right to underline, Freud's association of perversion with deviations of sexual aim effectively severs the connection between perversion and the rhetoric of physiological and genetic degeneracy which constituted one of the fundamental ideological biases of mid- to late nineteenth-century psychiatric discourses.[11] Though, as we will see, other aspects of his formulation beg crucial questions, Freud nonetheless decisively disengages the problematic of perversion from biological and genetic concerns. On one level at least, "perversion" in psychoanalysis begins to designate simply an interruption of the "normal" course of the sexual encounter: a particular variation, in other words, on ordinary sexual relations.

The 1905 definition of perversion, left unaltered after the last set of revisions Freud brought to the *Three Essays*, runs as follows: "Perversions are sexual activities which either a) extend, in an anatomical sense, beyond the regions of the body that are designed for sexual union, or b) linger over the intermediate relations to the sexual object which should normally be traversed rapidly on the path towards the final sexual aim" (150). As is quite evident, this definition restricts the sphere of perversion to sexual activity, and only to those activities which deviate from a rigorously defined and explicitly teleological genitality, or from an efficiently realized and equally genitally conceived aim. Though it is easy to protest at the overwhelming generality of his definition, we should note that Freud himself was the first to grasp the unsettling consequences of the idea of normal sexuality that his definition implies. Indeed, the set of perverse sexual behaviors overlaps to such an extent with the presumptively normative ones that Freud is forced to go to great lengths to prevent one from collapsing entirely into the other. At this inaugural moment of Freud's theory of sexuality the epistemological stakes of clinical diagnosis which would haunt all subsequent psychoanalytic thought about perversion become immediately apparent. Given that all sexually active subjects participate in one manner or the other in practices here defined as perverse, then to what criterion does the clinician make reference to diagnose an instance of perversion?

The figuration of homosexuality in Freud's discourse brings to light the weakness of the definition of perversion as a deviation of the sex act's aim. Though the object/aim distinction's overt consequence is to remove the object's attributes, in particular its biological sex, from the set of criteria which define the perverse, the careful reader of the *Three Essays* cannot help but notice that the avowedly conventional rhetoric of genitality which intersperses Freud's discussion renders the status of homosexuality less than clear-cut. Indeed, most sexual activity between same-sex partners does not unambiguously lead to the "normal" sexual aim when this "aim is regarded as being the union of the genitals in the act known as copulation" (149). Yet, as we have already seen, the notion of inversion—that is to say of object deviations—was to differentiate the sexual act with a nonnormative object from the properly perverse, aim-deviant one.

Clearly, several problems arise at this point in Freud's classification of the sexual deviations. First, Freud uncritically recirculates the contradiction implicit in the notion of inversion that he inherits from the sexologists. More precisely, he fails to decide whether inversion designates homosexual desire proper—in other words the desire for sexual relations with a partner of the same biological sex—or rather what one might problematically call "gender nonconformity," in other words feminine behavior performed by, or character traits inherent in, a male subject. Does inversion, in other words, relate to the subject or the object of desire? Though Freud clearly emphasizes the latter, the concept of inversion in the *Three Essays* swings indecisively between its unambiguous reference to same-sex object choice and its significantly less clear designation of the masculinity or femininity of the invert's mind and body. Freud in fact argues against the crude notion attributed to Karl Heinrich Ulrichs that the male homosexual subject features a feminine brain in a male body. "A large proportion of male inverts," Freud writes with conviction, "retain the mental quality of masculinity" (144). Of course, Freud's assertion begs the question what is meant by "mental quality," not to mention the vexed problem of the precise sense of the term "masculinity" which is here put to work.

But there is a second, more conceptually significant, ambiguity in Freud's classification of the sexual deviations. For though Freud will claim that "the union of the genitals" is the norm to which the perversions are referred, the inversion concept presupposes by implication or by default a vague notion of orgasmic relations as a norm for sexual union. The relation between inversion and perversion in the Freudian system is thus fundamentally asymmetrical: We can imagine perversion without inversion (in the instance, for example, of heterosexual anal intercourse); yet it remains impossible to conceive of inversion without perversion if we posit a sexually active subject and a conventional meaning—the one which was almost certainly Freud's own—for his phrase "the regions of the body designed for sexual union."

Of course, Freud's reconfiguration of perversion's epistemology in the *Three Essays* was unambiguously radical with respect to the contemporary medical and sexological contexts. But insofar as the normative concept of sexuality against which perversion is defined presupposes a smooth and perfect integration of the drives into a full genitality—a norm which Freud elsewhere, with relative consistency, explicitly problematizes—the inversion/perversion distinction tends toward incoherence, losing in the process any rigorous epistemological value in the context even of the more general theory of sexuality Freud also offers in the *Three Essays*. With admitted generosity the Freudian attitude toward perversion prior to the metapsychological developments can be expressed in the terms of a tolerance for ambiguity. The analyst avers that sexuality is essentially perverse, yet will retain a clinically operative notion of perversion in spite of the difficulty, indeed the apparent impossibility, of defining it with reference to the particularities of the object and aim of sexual relations. What is clear is that the Freud of the *Three Essays* remains unable to coin a satisfactory theoretical definition of perversion on the empirical level of the classification of sexual behaviors. Indeed, as I will now move on to explore, the emergence, however embryonic, of the notion of perversion as structure draws less on the particularities of the subject's sexual comportment than on the more properly metapsychological dimension of the Freudian project.

The presentation of what Strachey rendered as "component instincts"—the concept Lacan would later develop under the term *pulsions partielles* (partial drives)—helps to redress the impasse toward which the object/aim classification of the *Three Essays* leads.[12] In 1915 Freud attempts to shed light on what he then considered the murkiest area of psychoanalytic inquiry: drive theory. "Instincts and Their Vicissitudes" identifies four attributes and four destinies of the drive; none of these attributes or destinies makes reference to an attainable genital or reproductive norm. Consequentially situating them on "the frontier between the mental and the somatic," thereby casting aside the conceptual baggage of a pseudo-Cartesian mind/body dualism, Freud defines the drives with reference to the "pressure" they exert on the psychic apparatus; the "aim" they reach by decreasing somatic excitation; the "object" they choose with the utmost variability; and the somatic "source" from which they derive energetic stimulation.[13] Notable here is the greater level of precision brought to the terms "aim" and "object" with respect to the earlier classification. Also, Freud specifies that the drives themselves are not only "numerous," but they "emanate from a great variety of organic sources, act in the first instance independently of one another, and only achieve a more or less complete synthesis at a later stage" (122).

As we will see, this last formulation is far from unproblematic. Still, "Instincts and Their Vicissitudes" has the tremendous merit of spelling out Freud's conception of the drives as fragmented and partial, emanating not—or rather, not exclusively—from the genital areas, but rather from privileged limit zones: points of contact between a corporeal inside and a noncorporeal outside, points which are scattered across the body's surface. The mouth and anus, for example, are the organic sources which name two of the drives that Freud's work develops in greatest detail. The drives begin as partial drives, then, and it is only at a "later" point, as Freud vaguely contends, that an event occurs which unifies them into what he equally vaguely calls a "more or less" coherent whole. Before exploring in greater detail what Freud here casts as an act of precarious or imperfect drive unification, however, it is crucial to note a second consequence of his outline of the drive's attributes. For Freud decisively installs a disjunctive *miss* at the endpoint of the drive's trajectory. More precisely, he insists on distinguishing in a contrasting fashion the drive's object from its aim: The drive's course is disconnected—untethered—from its object. Whereas in the earlier dead-end classificatory formulation "object" confusedly referred to the partner's anatomical sex, here the term is depersonalized—de-sexualized, even—and reconceived as a kind of body part or organ associated with, but also somehow detachable from (and therefore irreducible to), the partner's body. The corollaries of Freud's theoretical turn are equally crucial: Not only are the object's specifiable attributes qualified as contingent with respect to the drive's action, but the decrease in psychical tension which constitutes drive satisfaction on Freud's understanding depends, as I have just intimated, on a missed encounter. The temporary return to psychical equilibrium—the criterion of the drive's very success—stems directly from its failure to meet the object on its course.

By now it has begun to become clear how Freud's characterization of the drives reflects what I have referred to as the inherent *perversity* of sexual desire as psychoanalysis formulates it. In our discussion thus far, however, we have encountered no hint of a link between the drive and *perversion* properly speaking. This observation would appear to confirm my second main thesis, namely that neither desire nor the drive is properly speaking perverse. Yet "Instincts and Their Vicissitudes" features extended discussions of the perversions, including sadism and exhibitionism, and this fact presents us with at least the semblance of a

✳ —see p. 1

contradiction. My suggestion as to how to deal with this problem is this: It is possible to read this same essay retrospectively from a Lacanian perspective to discover a latent or embryonic theorization of the perverse structure. To this end, it will be necessary to examine Freud's delineation of the drive's four possible "vicissitudes": the available means by which it can attain satisfaction. They run as follows: The drive can turn into "its opposite"; choose the subject's "own self" as its object; or else undergo either "repression" or "sublimation" (126). My contention here will be that Freud's discussion of the first two vicissitudes is one likely source for Lacan's elaboration of his concept of perversion as psychic structure. Two basic characteristics emerge from Freud's consideration of them: a shift from what he terms "activity" to "passivity," and a reversal of the functions subject and object. These formulations of Freud's are surely not the best ones. Yet they begin to formulate what would later become Lacan's main thesis concerning perversion qua structure, namely that the pervert renounces his function as subject of the drive in such a manner that he apprehends his own satisfaction *in* and through the body of his object. In more specifically Lacanian terms, the pervert becomes the "passive"—we will see precisely what this slippery term implies—object-cause of a jouissance in his Other, an Other who in consequence becomes the veritable subject of the drive.

But before inquiring after the details of Freud's emergent understanding of this subjective transfer and how it is put to work in the specific perversions, it will be helpful to clarify my earlier contention concerning the problematic Freudian motif of the drive's "unification" or "synthesis." This motif is connected elsewhere in Freud's writing to the notion of the 'resolution'—never unambiguous or indeed convincing—of the Oedipus complex. To be sure, Freud's approach to this issue is ambivalent. On the one hand, the argumentative thrust of "Instincts and Their Vicissitudes" identifies an antimony between the holistic, unifying, properly narcissistic energies of the "ego-instincts," and the divisive, shattering, or parceling effects of the "sexual instincts" (that is, the drives proper). On the other, however, Freud's idealistic—and indeed idealizing—discourse on love in that same essay misleadingly introduces the prospect of a phenomenon he formulates as a "synthesis of all the component instincts of sexuality under the primacy of the genitals and in the service of the reproductive function" (138). Startlingly, Freud fails in this instance to heed the lesson of his own analysis of emotional ambivalence, that is to say, love's propensity to transform dialectically into its opposite. Indeed, far from leading to the paradise of genital-reproductive integration, love—here understood as the attempt to synthesize the partial drives—inevitably leads, as experience consistently shows, to hate. In the terms of Freud's own analysis, then, the integrative forces of love give rise to the very same tendency toward "the exercise of violence or power on some other person as object" (127) which Freud chooses to provide as his definition of sadism. Worryingly, Freud remains seemingly blind to the manner in which his latent investment in an idea of the drive's normalization aligns itself conceptually with the very ethically troublesome—and in my view properly perverse—vicissitudes of the drive.

In a welcome gesture Lacan decisively reverses this unfortunate and muddled Freudian revisionism; in so doing he recuperates the authentically subversive quality of Freud's own deep thesis about the instinct's bifurcation from its object. "With regard to the biological finality of sexuality, namely reproduction, the drives . . . are partial drives," Lacan declares, suggesting that the libido can only ever go partway toward its presumptively (purely) reproductive goal; and indeed implying that conception can only ever be an accidental outcome of the drive's circuit.[14] Lacan here understands reproduction—or more precisely the very particular and ideal act of eroticism which could hypothetically be stripped down purely to that function—as the nonexistent or unrealizable whole to which the sum of the partial drives will never add up. This explains why Lacan decides to present the partial drive series through the analogy of the montage technique in surrealist collage: In its endless possibilities for juxtaposition, the sequence features no endpoint—no "finality" (169), as Lacan says—and the elements which make it up exhibit no rational, no determinate relation to one another, be this relation conceived as "historical"-temporal, or be it one of logical "deduction" or causal "genesis" (180). Lacan's happy clarification of the Freudian "component instincts" reacquaints us with the dialectical reversal which, as I have been arguing, is the most consequential ramification of the psychoanalytic theory of perversion: The drive is already perverse, already subject to a deviation from its alleged biological-reproductive goal. What is more, the effort to normalize this deviation is in fact the ambition of the pervert. "In perversion," Lacan concisely summarizes with reference to the elusive normative goal (which of course reveals itself to be anything but reproductive), "the target [of the drive] is reached" (182).

We can now return to Freud's own discussion of the perversions to discover how they contain the seeds of Lacan's more precise formulations. As I have already intimated, what "Instincts and Their Vicissitudes" presents as the perversions' two characteristic features—the switch from what is described as an active to a passive aim, together with the reversal of the instinct's content (sadism to masochism, or scopophilia/voyeurism to exhibitionism, for example)—are doubtless better conceptualized as an attempt to suture the disjunction, to heal the wound to which they bear witness. In other words, the pervert puts his project into effect by means of a transfer of the subjective function, including the traumatic psychical loss which is its necessary consequence, onto the object of the drive. Perversion in the strong sense is therefore less a function of the kind of dialectical reversal in which Freud tends to frame his conceptualization of the drive's perversity than a refusal of the splitting between the two poles of the couplet between which each partial drive oscillates. "Analytic observation," Freud offers by way of illustration, "leaves us in no doubt that the masochist shares in the enjoyment of the assault upon himself, and that the exhibitionist shares in the enjoyment of [the sight of] his exposure" (127).

As Freud's examples illustrate (as opposed to his theorizations), though perhaps less than perfectly clearly, the pervert is placed within his psychic configuration as at once the subject and the object of jouissance. More precisely, perversion provides the opportunity to experience enjoyment outside oneself, as contained within one's victim/partner, while at the same time allowing one to function as the cause or agent of this enjoyment. The perverse scenario features the added benefit of keeping the subject comfortably ensconced at a reassuring psychical remove from the scene of passion. To be sure, the essence of the perverse structure is more paradoxical than Freud's dialectical rhetoric would suggest. For the structure effectively allows the subject to cause his own enjoyment in the Other, and thereby to function at the same time, however vicariously, as both sadist and masochist, scopophiliac and exhibitionist, all the while managing to shield himself from the threat of castration which would prevent him from in effect *witnessing himself enjoy.*

The pervert's successful evasion of the immediate consequences of castration—the fact that, in the context of the visual field, for example, the drive pushes him to make himself seen (by the Other qua gaze), but without permitting him to see himself being seen—is made clear in Freud's evocation of what we might legitimately call the "synthesis" of scopophilia and exhibitionism. A step-by-step examination of Freud's formulation of this synthesis will spell out more clearly what renders it perverse. Freud first describes scopophilia as "an *activity* directed toward an extraneous object." At a second moment he evokes a process by which the subject in effect identifies with the gaze—externalizes its own agency of looking, in other words—and proceeds to present "a part of [its] own body" as the object of its own disembodied look. At a third moment the "partial" voyeuristic and exhibitionistic drives are unified into what, I wish to argue, is a perversion properly speaking. Here there occurs what Freud describes as "the introduction of a new subject to whom one displays oneself in order to be looked at by him" (129).

What had been in the second moment a merely abstract agency of seeing with which the subject identifies, but whose look will threaten to stray elsewhere, now becomes subjectivized. This new subject is of course the pervert's victim—the "extraneous person," to use Freud's expression, who is of course also the pervert himself—through whom the pervert achieves what for the neurotic must remain an unrealizable unconscious fantasy: He sees himself being seen as the possessor of the object–cause of jouissance. Naturally, this jouissance is at least vicariously his own, but it is also, most importantly, comfortably externalized in the (embodied, subjectivized) Other. Thus the pervert succeeds in carving out for himself an experience of enjoyment which does not compromise, as it must necessarily do for the neurotic, his command over the visual field. More precisely, this configuration preserves the pervert's immunity from the agency of the gaze, which would otherwise threaten to reveal the shameful secret of his (disavowed) castration, in other words his failure to assert his look seamlessly over the entirety of the visual field.

For all its evocative but somewhat confused hinting at the theory of perversion as psychic structure, however, "Instincts and Their Vicissitudes" never makes explicit the distinction I have drawn between desire's perversity and perversion as such. For help on this issue we can turn once again to Lacan, whose refreshingly clear gloss on Freud's presentation of the scopophilia/exhibitionism couplet brings a greater level of conceptual precision to the problematic of perversion. In essence, Lacan seizes upon Freud's intimation of the subjectivization of the object-partner to define perversion as the transfer of the splitting constitutive of subjectivity onto the Other. Whereas the neurotic, himself subjected to symbolic castration, submits to a division between a communicable network of signifiers in the utterance and a repressed, nonsignifying, perverse residue of unconscious desire, the pervert works to precipitate this division in the Other and to present himself as the object which will enable the Other's self-reconciliation. Returning to the example of the visual field, Lacan stresses how castration has the effect of disrupting perverse voyeuristic pleasure by making manifest an uncanny agency of seeing—the gaze—which the voyeur necessarily fails to locate in space. "The other surprises [the voyeur]," Lacan asserts, "as [an] entirely hidden gaze." The voyeur becomes a pervert properly speaking when he succeeds in occluding the gaze, in subjectivizing it in such a way that he becomes "situated . . . at the culmination of [the drive's] loop" (182). The pervert becomes the target which the drive reaches; he succeeds in seeing himself from the impossible point of the gaze, thereby suturing the void in the visual field that impedes the perfect dyadic self-reflection of narcissism.

We can now see why Lacan chooses to define what he calls "the structure of perversion" as "an inverted effect of the fantasy." More precisely, the formula for fantasy (S <> a) is flipped around (a <> S) in perversion's "matheme." For Lacan, the latter formula signifies that in perversion "the subject . . . determines himself as object in his encounter with the division of subjectivity" (185). Though Lacan's formulation no doubt clarifies some of the ambiguity of Freud's consideration of the question, it similarly leaves implicit or obscure the fact that the pervert's instrumental passivity is earned only by actively causing the victim's splitting from itself. In other words, the pervert successfully avoids the consequences of castration only by castrating the Other, and it is precisely this aggression and violence which he jettisons from consciousness. As a result of the pervert's nonsubjectivization of his own agency in the perverse scenario, he experiences his own activity as a compliant response to the Other's demand. In this sense, the pervert is anything but an agent: His ethically questionable activities are undertaken on behalf of the Other; in other words, the pervert responds to an unconditional imperative to execute what for him is his victim/partner's sovereign will.

Fetishism, Sexual Difference, Homosexuality

Freud's essay "Fetishism" (1927) postdates by twelve years his work on the instincts' vicissitudes. Its importance accrues not only from the examples it provides illustrating these last vexatious aspects of perversion, but also from the way it introduces the problematic of sexual difference into the discussion. I have claimed that queer theory's resistance to the concept of perversion in psychoanalysis is primarily motivated by its presumption of an intimate link in this discourse between perversion (in the strong structural sense) and homosexuality. I would like to suggest to the contrary that Freud's discourse on fetishism, which is indeed one of the perversions, links the fetishistic structure not to the manifestation of homosexual desire, but rather to the defense against it. From the perspective of queer theory, the truly shocking conclusion to be drawn from "Fetishism" is not that the male homosexual is a failed (perverse) man, but rather the opposite, that the fetishist is a failed homosexual. More rigorously put, the fetishist is the subject who first refuses the challenge of phallic castration and then resists the consequences of its feminine alternative. Thus the fetishist, and by extension the pervert, does not so much "deny sexual difference"—that vague phrase one often comes across in even the most suggestive and open-minded clinical literature—as resist the process of sexuation in both its masculine and feminine versions.

But before paying closer attention to this crucial feature of Freud's discussion, it will be helpful to explore the way the essay finally brings to the fore the disquieting, and properly misogynistic, aggressiveness with which the pervert provokes the manifestation of the Other's castration. As is well known, the fetishist is distinguished by his ability mentally to entertain simultaneously two contradictory propositions, namely that the woman is, and is not, castrated. This implies that the gesture through which the fetishist will induce castration in his Other is the very one which will be disavowed. As we have already seen in our general consideration of perversion, this disavowal paradigmatically takes the form of the fantasy that the fetish's construction is commanded by the Other. Freud's first example is that notorious denizen of grade school classrooms, the *coupeur de nattes* (the braid cutter) whose act in Freud's view "contains [with]in itself . . . two mutually incompatible assertions" (157).[15] Though Freud does not spell out his contention, the reader infers that the subject's cutting of the girl's hair dramatizes the fantasy of the father's castration of the woman, whereas the opposite fantasy is secured by the assertion that the girl's hair will grow back, or else perhaps by a disavowal of the act itself. Freud's second example is the old Chinese custom of foot wrapping. The paradox here at work is that the mutilation of the girl's foot through the prevention of its natural growth at once enacts and dissimulates female castration. "It seems," Freud writes, "as though the Chinese male wants to thank the woman for having submitted to being castrated."[16] Yet this reverential gratitude of course dissimulates a nastier truth: The woman's impaired mobility renders her all the more vulnerable to the fetishist's ambition of sexual control.

Having established how the pervert jettisons from consciousness his own active involvement in his partner's victimization, we can now turn to a more detailed look at Freud's account of fetishism and its relation, or lack thereof, to male homosexual desire. As has often been remarked, fetishism is for Freud a principally masculine perversion. It functions to present the male subject with a substitute for the maternal phallus of infantile fantasy, and it is this fantasy which allows him at once to accept and to disavow the mother's castration. Freud claims more specifically in "Fetishism" that a disturbing perception can trigger the male subject's repressed memory of the sight of the female genitals, a memory which sometimes proves too much to bear. In consequence, he will invest a significant sum of libido in a substitutive object which stands in for the maternal phallus, an object which effectively functions as a screen which staves off a full, traumatic encounter with female "lack." To illustrate this thesis Freud tells the story of an analysand brought up in England who migrates to Germany, loses his mother tongue, and begins to fetishize women with "shiny noses." Remarking that the German word for "shine" (*Glanz*) is a homonym of the English "glance," Freud concludes that this subject associates the nose with (a recollection of) the sighting of the female sex organs. The compensatory fetish object more or less successfully performs two functions: First, it defends against the realization that the woman's or mother's desire is not exclusively directed at her partner or son, and therefore that the latter is not, at least exclusively, the former's privileged object; and second, it wards off this realization's disquieting corollary, namely that the fetishist's phallic appendage could meet the same horrific fate. The fetish object thus embodies the castration that the subject himself fails to undergo—or as Freud expresses it, the fetishist "treats [his object] in a way which is obviously equivalent to a representation of castration."[17]

Freud's observations underline how the phenomenon of fetishism, and indeed of perversion more generally, bears witness to the fragility of the fantasy structure at the moment of the subject's confrontation with the absence which haunts representation, in other words its sociosymbolic world. The intimate link between the perception of sexual morphology and the problematic of representation is indeed one of the underlying insights of the psychoanalytic discourse on perversion: For the speaking subject, the traumatic void which separates linguistic structure from itself, as well as the "master signifier" whose function is to dissimulate this separation, is intrinsically tied to infantile libidinal curiosity, to what Freud termed the subject's "sexual researches." More specifically, the perception of female "lack" is a direct consequence of the fundamental impasse against which the forms of consciousness—signifiers—run up in their effort to communicate the demands of the drive to the psyche. Crucially, this problematic link bears no relation to culture or history, in the precise sense that any cultural system in any historical period will necessarily encounter this same impasse of sexual difference.

In Freudian terms there is a traumatic gap between the instinct and reality; Lacan expresses this same dehiscence through the notion of an antagonism between the drive and the signifier. By assuming its symbolic castration the "normal" male subject will effectively accept the Lacanian axiom that "the phallus is a signifier"—that it refers to a properly imaginary object barred from signification, absconded behind the curtain of prohibition's "no." My suggestion is that apart from psychosis there are two alternatives to conventional masculine sexuation for the male subject. The first is of course perversion: Instead of tarrying with the difficulty of masculine sexuation, which would subject the would-be fetishist to (the perception of) irremediable loss, the fetishist transposes the fantasy of the maternal phallus onto a substitutive object, often another part of the female body, which serves to represent castration. This transposition allows the fetishist not only to maintain that the mother at once is and is not castrated, but also to avoid the consequences which would result from his own castration—the sacrifice of what Lacan, after Shakespeare's Shylock, called "the pound of flesh." But there is also a second alternative. To be sure, what is rarely noted in analyses of fetishism is that the psychical reconciliation of contradiction it makes possible also prevents the fetishist from locating the phallus in fantasy *on the male body*, a gesture which logically leads to the advent of what would appear to be a properly homosexual desire. In other words, the would-be fetishist can undergo an "other" castration, one which not only assumes an acceptance of the axiom "the phallus is a signifier," but which also links this signifier with an Other embodied in accordance with a morphologically male phallic ideal. In short, the (anatomically) male subject takes, or tends to take, another male subject as his sexual object.

It is indeed Freud himself who makes explicit the possibility of this alternative to phallic castration. The fetish object, he avers, "saves the fetishist from becoming a homosexual by endowing women with the characteristic [a phallus] which makes them tolerable as sexual objects."[18] Freud's comment unambiguously forces the conclusion that the fetishistic pervert is homophobic in the most literal of senses: The crucial portion of his unconscious motivation stems from a visceral aversion to the libido's homoerotic canalization. It would appear, then, that the perverse structure is adopted by the male subject who not only refuses to accept the loss required by the masculine form of castration, but who also rejects the possibility of undergoing a different castration associated with the advent of a desire for a male object incarnating the phallic ideal. Confronted with the anxiety-producing specter of virile loss, the fetishist resists this other castration which would effectively implant the phallus in fantasy on an anatomically male object. Thus the fetishist who resists masculine sexuation also refuses to undergo an alternative "feminine" castration which Freud associates with homosexual desire. Here we again encounter the notion that the perverse structure results from the subject's failure to assume the consequences of the forced choice between what Freud calls "masculinity" and "femininity."[19] The male subject is therefore not simply either conventionally masculine (on the level of his castration) or a pervert. There remains a third way, if one can put it this way, one which features a direct relation to the male subject's tendency to develop what is known as a homosexual desire.

The dominant trend in psychoanalytic writing on male homosexuality, including to some extent that of Freud himself, has been to view this orientation as a consequence of a failed masculine castration. In this view, the male homosexual's desire is determined, like the fetishist's, by a nostalgia for the phallic mother—for an object, in other words, which combines maternal omnipotence with the desired phallicized body.[20] Quite evidently, however, this model presupposes that masculine sexuation is the only one undergone by male subjects. If one proceeds from the assumption that sexuation only occurs in accordance with the subject's biological sex, male homosexual desire can only appear as a perversion of the phallic model. If, however, at least some male subjects who tend to choose male objects actually undergo what Lacan calls a "feminine" sexuation, the picture changes radically. Lacan himself draws our attention to this phenomenon I have referred to as *cross-sexuation*.[21] "Let's take the side where the man positions himself," Lacan says in *Encore*, alluding to the "male side" of what he calls the "phallic function." "Ultimately, one positions oneself by choice—women are free to place themselves there if it pleases them. . . . Everyone knows that there are phallic women, and that the phallic function does not prevent men from being homosexual."[22]

Two observations should be made concerning Lacan's key utterance. First, if women are free to place themselves on the male side, and men on the female side, of the phallic function—if, as "everyone knows," some subjects are cross-sexuated—then biological sex does not always determine the form of the subject's sexuation. Second, Lacan links female homosexuality to phallic sexuation and male homosexuality to the feminine. Homosexuality as Lacan here describes it therefore cannot be connected to the perverse structure concept since the castration undergone by these subjects is identical to the normative one. The only element which distinguishes these subjects from the "normal" (that is, more or less heterosexual) neurotic male and female is the disjunction between their biological and psychical sexes.

To be sure, one is hard pressed to find credible clinical treatments in the Lacanian field (or any other, for that matter) of this question of the relation between sexuation and homosexual desire. Still, the work of Belgian clinician Serge André is exceptional in that it attempts to distinguish between what he considers two forms of male homosexuality, one which participates in the perverse structure, and another which conforms to the structure of neurotic repression approximating normality. Both forms of male homosexuality in André's view depend on the male subject's failure to adopt the relation to the phallic signifier associated with conventional masculine sexuation. What André terms an "excessive imaginarization of castration"[23] occasions the normal neurotic male homosexual structure; patently, this contention offers itself for comparison to my hypothesis concerning the relation between feminine sexuation and male homosexual desire. But a question immediately presents itself: What is the meaning of André's notion of an imaginarized castration? And further: In relation to what—to cut to the chase—does he view this castration as "excessive"?

We recall that in his analysis of the feminine Oedipus complex Freud underlines the immediacy of the young girl's experience of castration. "She behaves differently" from the boy, as Freud puts it. "She makes her judgment and her decision in a flash. She has seen it and knows that she is without it and wants to have it."[24] Whereas the boy's castration is potential and deferred, a dangerous threat which hangs over what Freud frames as his narcissistic investment in his virile member, the girl is forced to come to terms more radically with the actuality or tangibility of her anatomical lack. In her case, in other words, loss has always already occurred. In the light of this account of sexual difference, the castration of André's paradigmatic neurotic male homosexual may be viewed as excessive only in relation to that of Freudian boy, that is to say to the subject who will become, on my hypothesis, either basically conventionally heterosexual or fetishistically perverse. Thus André's notion of an excessive castration may most fruitfully be read as implying that this subject does not situate himself as the representative of the phallic signifier as does the one who adopts the phallic variety of sexuation. By extension, the boy's anatomical equipment will not necessarily cause him to identify as or with the one who has (or rather should have) the phallus. Rather than resist the loss which gains access to the phallic position, in other words, this "other" male subject undergoes a castration which, in its clarity and immediacy, more closely resembles that experienced by the Freudian girl.

André's paradigm of neurotic male homosexuality is therefore to be distinguished from that of both the normative woman and the normative man, although it is much closer to the former than to the latter. "The principal trait of the homosexual's imaginary filiation," writes André, "relates to the paradox of his masculinity. He is without a doubt male, but he is male only through the power of a mother or a lineage of women."[25] Unlike the male-to-female transsexual, for example, the male homosexual does not feel trapped in a woman's body; he does not bear witness to a sense of dispossession or estrangement with respect to his masculine embodiment. Rather, the structure of identification connecting him to the maternal line is coupled with a corporeal schema which does not feature the same, properly phallic, narcissism informing masculine sexuation, which is of course not to say that he will be immune to an idealization of the masculine bodily form.

The only difficulty in my view with André's nonetheless invaluable analysis is the link it posits between the male homosexual's castration and Lacan's register of the imaginary. I concur with André's decision to connect the advent of male homosexual desire to an identificatory structure associated with the mother or the maternal line. Yet the castration which produces this desire can be no less symbolic than that of any other subject; in other words, the "inversion" of the structure of filiation André connects to male homosexuality by no means necessarily compromises the experience of castration as such. Indeed, I would suggest that André's notion of imaginarization is more properly to be associated with a specifically male homosexual symptomatology which, due to the morphological identity of the subject's and the object's masculine embodiment, may render him more vulnerable to the corporeal idealization of the object of desire. In general terms, however, André's analysis implies that the castration of the male homosexual is similar to that of the heterosexual woman. As a result, he is forced to tarry with the disjunction between the manner in which culture feminizes the position from which he desires and his concrete biophysiological situation in a male body. Indeed, it is not difficult to appreciate how numerous aspects of gay culture—from drag to gym culture—attempt to negotiate the particular challenges of this incommensurability.

The clinical understanding of male homosexuality will only advance to the extent that the male subject's sexuation is not automatically presupposed to conform to what Lacan called the "male way." In consequence, it is not legitimate to presuppose a priori that the structure of the male subject who will bear witness to a manifestly homosexual desire is failed on the level of his castration. At any rate, it should be noted in this connection that the notion of failure is essential to Lacan's concept of sexuation. Indeed, it is the pervert whose sex is not marked by failure and it is precisely this feature of his psychical economy which renders it problematic. But one additional comment is required. Though in the current institutional climate the politically urgent gesture is surely to underline the actual existence of a nonperverse, generally neurotic male homosexual structure, it is equally necessary to refuse the temptation of advancing to the politically correct conclusion that there is no relation whatsoever between forms of male homosexual desire and the perverse structure. Indeed, it is the very lack of such a critical perspective in the queer theory tradition—namely one which identifies and condemns the multiple perverse tendencies in contemporary homosexual subcultures—which is urgently needed in the field of sexuality theory today. At the present moment the authentically ethico-political stance for any member of that rare species of psychoanalytically inclined queer theorist is twofold: to underline in clinical and cultural analysis the normality of (some forms of) homosexuality; and to bring to light the properly perverse forms of complicity in homosexual subcultures in the self-identified queer and sexually progressive theoretical circles. The time has come, in other words, for nonheterosexual men and women to muster up the courage to withstand the clamorously superegoic accusations of "internalized homophobia" emerging from sectors of the various sexual minority communities, and to proceed to a form of queer autocritique—to the founding of an authentically critical gay and lesbian theory decisively severed from the perverse vectors of corporatism, hyperconsumerism and neo-Foucauldian pseudopolitical self-fashioning and self-discipline in which they are at present dangerously mired.

Worlds of Perversion: A Reader's Guide

When the mid-nineteenth-century sexologists whose discourses Foucault loved to evoke began to use the term "perversion" to describe deviant sexual behaviors, it was clear that their classificatory systems articulated moral judgments in spite of the intentions of the most enlightened to adopt a disinterested, scientific tone. These judgments, in other words, are simply embedded in the history of the term. This contention would suggest that the expansion of perversion's semantic field onto the late-modern terrain of sexuality discourse did in fact fill a disciplinary function. From this point of view Foucault's hypothesis on sexuality would seem to be correct: Just as perversion from the fourteenth century onward served to legislate moral correctness through the concept of sin and the institution of the confession, perversion in its sexual usage functioned to enforce the normality of particular sexual behaviors through the discursive constructions of nineteenth-century sexology and psychiatry.

When these claims are subjected to closer scrutiny, however, one discovers that they are not entirely correct. For if perversion's modern usage is fundamentally linked to a notion of a Good from whose course we have deviated, a particular lineage of this usage describes this deviation as constitutive, as the condition of possibility of (moral) consciousness as such. From this second perspective, the normative Good appears not as an imposition of power which constrains the subject from outside, but rather as an internal, properly structural agency of accountability situated at the level of the subject's self-relation. As I indicated at the outset, this is the tradition which I argue informs the Freudian discourse on perversion, and it will be the task of the next four chapters to link up, through the study of concrete cultural cases, the presexological and prepsychoanalytic moral and ethical etymology with the conceptualization of perversion in Freudian psychoanalysis. As we will see, for a number of modern thinkers belonging to this latter tradition, each indebted to particular Judeo-Christian formulations of original sin and radical evil, the normative ambitions of constructs of moral goodness necessarily fail. In consequence, such constructs cannot unambiguously indicate the proper course for ethical action. As the following chapters will repeatedly show, this is so because moral goodness simply exceeds the capacities of thought: What we ought to do remains, like desire itself, both indeterminate and undeterminable.

And if, unheeding of the historicists' prohibitions, one advances through the centuries from the metaphysical explorations of morality in early modernity into the late modern era of sexuality, one notes that Freud makes an analogous gesture in his landmark interrogation of perversion. The theory of sexuality cannot finally define sexual normality because sexuality, in its essence, is perverse. Just as we continually fail to incarnate the absolute disinterest the moral law commands, so are we inherently incapable of keeping the libido on the course of the proper genital object. Perversion, in both its moral and sexual usages, here demarcates the dehiscence between the subject's multiple conditions—historical, cultural, political, in sum discursive—and its ineradicable sense that these conditions fail to incarnate an elusive, absolute Good. The main task ahead of us will therefore be to describe the structure of this failure, highlighting the properly psychical level on which it operates, and to identify the tradition to which this structure belongs as tragic, dialectical and, ultimately, psychoanalytic.

In contrast to the late Foucauldian position, which links the sexual usage of perversion to a normative deployment of discourse, psychoanalysis—and the intellectual traditions from which it inherits—instead describes the moral and sexual spheres as constitutively split between an inherent human perversity and an insidious categorical absolute which calls the subject to moral perfection and immunity to desire. Where Foucault links that which hinders the accrual of sexual intensities to the normative force of power, psychoanalysis posits, in contrast, an internal, properly psychical limit tied to the elements of mental representation which produces a necessary illusion—a fantasy—of its beyond. From this latter perspective Foucault's critique of the repressive hypothesis begins to appear as a futile—and politically disastrous—effort to suture this structural gap which prevents us from realizing in our everyday practice the principles which guide our actions, and from acquiring that elusive normative self-intimacy which would finally disclose in full the frustratingly impenetrable enigma of desire.

"Perversion," writes Serge André, "is much more than a clinical entity: it's a way of thinking."[26] This proposition is correct provided one understands the last phrase along the lines of the term "discourse," but crucially in Lacan's—not Foucault's—sense. For Lacan did not believe that discourse is a positive and determinate system of subject-production which brings to fruition the intentions of abstract power. Discourse for Lacan is rather a form of the social relation—a way of organizing a collective subjective function around a traumatic void of nonknowledge—and perversion can be understood as a particular form of this social relation, one which offers a specific way of coping with power's dehiscence from knowledge by means of the disavowal of this dehiscence. Indeed, the psychoanalytic tradition contributes most valuably to the theory of perversion when it renounces the sexological attempt to classify sexual behaviors in favor of the description of the clinical and political implications of a particular libidinal economy which rests, ultimately, on a particular self-instrumentalizing relation to the sociosymbolic Other and its inherent void. The psychoanalytic concept of the perverse structure serves to elucidate our tendency to refuse to tarry with the enigma of desire by arriving at an overhasty conclusion as to what the Other wants of us, and consequently to fashion ourselves—our speech, our actions—as its object of satisfaction.

The clamorous post-Foucauldian call enjoining us to engage in a thoroughgoing depathologization of the discourse of perversion finally offers an elitist and subjectivist project which paradoxically depoliticizes sexuality through its very hyperpoliticization. This tendency advances as an ideal for praxis a relentless and surely doomed pursuit of ever more intense forms of erotic or corporeal pseudotransgression. As Juliet Flower MacCannell has cannily observed, the blasé reception in mainstream popular culture of the new consumerist culture of perversion demonstrates an alarming degree of complicity with respect to the ethic of overproduction and obsessional hyperactivity increasingly commanding labor relations and conditions in the new high-tech economy. That the new tourist-friendly fetish clubs and the so-called Multimedia Gulch of software firms inhabit the same South-of-Market San Francisco neighborhood, she bravely suggests, is no mere coincidence.[27] But MacCannell's prescient contention additionally features in my view a more general corollary: One should not fail to note the suggestiveness of the historical coincidence of, on the one hand, the Foucauldian critique of sexuality and subjectivity and, on the other, the unprecedented liberation of the forces of market capitalism—in other words the heretofore unforeseen colonization by capital of even the most traditional, remote, "backward" life-forms.

Capitalism has never been particularly homophobic; homosexuality as such has never functioned as an obstacle to the commodification of everyday life and the subsuming of social relations under the drive for profit. The radical post-Oedipal deterritorialization of sexuality—the growing obsolescence of the nuclear family in the advanced economies, the decline of paternal authority, the synergistic collusion of the sex trade and the new media, for example—has exposed marginal sexual cultures to the full effects of market capitalism on the level of its current unforeseen expansion. Or perhaps Deleuze and Guattari were right when they framed the issue the opposite way: The liberation of global capital has caused the symptoms of today's sexual deterritorialization, and these symptoms—the recently fashionable proliferation of pseudosubversive forms of gender performativity, the paradoxical coincidence of sexual hypervisibility and erotic entropy, the nostalgic or even reactionary truth of numerous officially anarchorevolutionary forms of resistance to ultraliberal economic globalization—are part and parcel of the logic of late capitalism. On the level of the mainstreaming of homosexual cultures and their integration within the structures of the global market, phenomena such as the gay glossy fashion magazine, the gay holiday cruise, and the gay network sitcom, not to mention the endless multiplication of internet pornography pages and paid dating services, trenchantly call into question the capacity of minority sexual cultures to resist the increasingly unlimited expansion of capital. Indeed, it is highly probable that this expansion has itself produced the very notion of the minority sexual culture as lifestyle option, as a featured entrée on the menu of available modes of conspicuous consumption.

Meanwhile, on the level of the institution of theory, Foucault's impact on sexuality studies has strongly discouraged the analysis of nonheterosexual social formations in their relation to the larger political and economic totalities. Indeed, Foucault's influence has led many of the discipline's most influential figures not only to adopt an unambiguously hostile posture with respect to all concepts of the state, but also to recommend that all cultural initiatives on behalf on nonheterosexual subjects forego the liberal rhetoric or rights and liberties in favor of the construction of autonomous minority sexual communities entirely severed from (what is left of) the general public sphere. At the present moment it is extremely difficult, for example, to address within the confines of hegemonic queer theory the radical failure of Western homosexual cultures to

call into question the market logic which appears so utterly to have
taken them over. Virtually all valences of queer theory, from those which
espouse the politics of identity to those which call for its radical
deconstruction, implicitly presuppose as their political goal a form of
recognition or integration within the current regime of power. This is
indeed the vexatious terrain to which I return in detail in the book's
concluding postscript, which functions as the other politico-theoretical
bookend for the concrete studies falling between. Indeed, those readers
most interested in contemporary queer theory may wish to consult it at
the present chapter's imminent conclusion.

That the mobilization of Foucault's later political theory tends to
premise itself on the properly cynical assumption that the modes of
political representation as such are archaic—that they are no longer the
principle means of power's expression, or rather that any attempt to
reclaim these modes in the name of popular sovereignty is hopelessly,
indeed shamefully, naive—only bespeaks the extent to which queer
theory has succumbed to the corporatist agenda. This tendency features
among other presuppositions the idea that Apple's or Microsoft's inau-
guration of domestic partnership packages indexes the progress and
achievements of queer politics. Even those aspects of the gay movement
which would appear to have a vested interest in the redemocratization
of the state apparatus—the first-world AIDS/HIV lobby, for example, on
the level of its call for increased access to immune-system-boosting drug
therapies—too often sidestep the larger picture in favor of models of
action premised on organization within the bounds of what is referred
to as the "gay community." Though very likely at its origins objectively
progressive, gay liberation has shown itself to have come at the cost of an
acceptance of the socioeconomic status quo. In the present climate of
massive mainstreaming and commercialization within nonheterosexual
cultures, the assumption that the axis of sexual orientation in cultural
analysis carries a priori political significance is no longer sufficient. What
is now required is a thoroughgoing analysis of the means by which queer
politics and identities have been granted as consolation prizes for acquiescence in the global postsocialist ersatz consensus. I should add that in
my view a preoccupation with the inflammatory rhetoric of a rabidly
homophobic religious Right, particularly influential in the United States,
objectively functions as a distraction which can only depoliticize the agenda
of an antihomophobic and explicitly socialist cultural and political project.

In an effort to address precisely these failures within the discourse
of sexuality theory, I have deemed it necessary to stress contra Foucault's
attack against psychoanalysis the importance of retaining, on the level
of theory, two concepts of perversion which I summarily reiterate here.

The first concept advances on the level of content that desire is essentially perverse because desire is infinite and impossible. Desire always exceeds its object and articulates itself transcendentally—in a manner which overflows the container of its own sociohistorical conditions of possibility. The second concept avers that perversion is also a viable notion on the level of its emergence from Freudian discourse as a term descriptive of a particular psychic structure, a specific orientation of the subject with respect to the Other's desire. I will argue in various ways through the course of the following chapters that this structure is not conducive to oppositional or progressive political praxis.

Indeed, the structure in question positions the subject as the instrument of the status quo's jouissance—as the instrument, in the terms of a different vocabulary, of power. What is more, the second, politically noxious concept of perversion depends on a disavowal of the first. The subject becomes structurally perverse, in other words, when it attempts to disguise from itself the essentially perverse nature of desire, the impossibility, in other words, of sustaining a relation of adequation between our demands—for recognition, satisfaction, love—and the possible objects of experience in the sociosymbolic world. We become perverse in the strong structural sense when we presuppose that we may fully instrumentalize our desire with respect to a principle—of reason, utility, production, or pleasure. The discourse of perversion resists the difficult truth that desire rebels against all efforts to subsume it under the command of a normative Good.

I have hypothesized that the problematic of perversion on the level of its presexological history features an intimate relation to a certain idea of tragedy and to the tradition of the dialectic. One of the main presuppositions of this book is therefore that Freudian psychoanalytic theory is to be situated in the line of these traditions by virtue of its formulation of the subject of the unconscious and its qualification of perversion in its second, structural sense as a betrayal of the necessary possibility of this subject's nonetheless unverifiable sovereignty. At its most basic level Lacan's formula for the subject (S <> a) evokes this subject's noncoincidence and nonsimultaneity with itself. This self-separation emerges as a result of this notion: though the subject is an effect of language, he or she does not exist *in* language. Lacan's *a*—this "extimate," fantasmatic object the subject must create in order to posit retroactively the cause of its desire—stands in for the absent absolute which gives substance to the lack of finitude, and hence the perversity, of desire. The paradox of *a* is that it is at once irreducible and impossible: It exists as a universal element of psychic life precisely because it does not—cannot—materially, verifiably exist.

Now though this structure of the subject condemns it to a difficult relation to the nonsubstantial or immaterial, it also guarantees that the subject will not be limited by its discursive conditions, however intimately one may wish to tie these conditions to the exercise of power. The subject will therefore feature a capacity to act with respect to the impossible, not in a manner which founds a new society bereft of political antagonism, but rather in a way which recognizes a certain impossibility within the subject itself, a certain stubborn and unchanging being which calls into question the legitimacy of all possible social formations, and which inscribes the ethical in a locus of hope in which social progress is paradoxically allied with the subject's tendency toward self-annihilation, with its very resistance to progress conceived with respect to a greater social Good. It is therefore no coincidence that this book will culminate on the topic of (a politicized) ethics: Indeed, as Lacan said, the status of the subject is fundamentally ethical. In the context of the following chapters, the axiom advancing the ethical status of the subject suggests that we must not, like Foucault, lose sight of the impossible object represented by Lacan's a. For, when we do, we tend to function as this a ourselves and, regretfully, we foreclose on the possibility of a difficult, indeed often painful, but authentic and necessary critical engagement with the social world. The ultimate paradox of the discourse of perversion is perhaps that it is only by reasserting the primacy of the tragic structure of the subject—the idea that the structure of subjectivity always fails to realize the promise of reconciliation with respect either to the self or its object—that we may avert the emergence of tragedy in the real: the end of politics as we (used to) know it, and the unqualified, irreversible victory of unlimited capital and its mortgaging of all human endeavor under the unforgiving logic of profit maximization and joyless utilitarian economic productivity.

Chapter Two

Confessions of a
Medieval Sodomite

The wicked man either counts in advance, even during the course
of life, upon this pardon so easily obtainable, or else, at life's close,
believes that it is merely a question of the claims of divine justice
upon him, and that these claims may be satisfied with mere words.

—Immanuel Kant, *Religion within the Limits of Reason Alone*

And why not say (as some people slander us by saying that we say)
'Let us do evil so that good may come'?

—Romans 3:5–8

Meet Gilles de Rais

Sodomite, pederast, homicidal criminal, and enthusiast of the black arts,
Gilles de Rais is the most infamous monster of French cultural history.
A nobleman and warrior of the early fifteenth century, Gilles distinguished himself in battle, most notably alongside Joan of Arc during the
Hundred Years War, earning the prestigious title of Marshal of France
at the precocious age of twenty-six. Orphaned at eleven, Gilles became
one of the richest and most powerful men in all medieval Europe upon
the death of his grandfather and guardian, Jean de Craon. The transcripts of the trial of Gilles de Rais, preserved through the centuries in
a Nantes archive, convey the testimonies of dozens of witnesses who
claim that the members of Gilles's entourage kidnapped, over a period

35

of about eight years, over a hundred adolescent and preadolescent children, almost exclusively boys, whom Gilles then submitted to disturbing rituals of erotic torture, then summarily murdered by strangulation, decapitation, or dismemberment.

Not surprisingly, during the centuries after his execution at the stake for the crimes of heresy, sodomy, and invocation, Gilles de Rais became the stuff of folkloric legend, frightening generations of Breton schoolchildren through his figuration in the Bluebeard tale, which nonetheless holds few resemblances to the facts that the trial documents relay.[1] After Voltaire, in his *Essai sur les mœurs*, expressed doubt about Gilles's guilt, early twentieth-century historians, most notably Salomon Reinach,[2] reawakened interest in the case when they began to question the authenticity of the documents and the legality of the trial.[3] Most recently, Pierre Klossowski's 1965 translation from the Latin of the trial's proceedings,[4] accompanied by Georges Bataille's analysis of the cultural and historical importance of Gilles de Rais, has brought the case to the attention of the contemporary public and has raised important questions about the conceptual stakes involved in our engagement with Gilles's perversion. Gilles de Rais has clearly been the source of endless fascination for over five hundred years, but one senses that the tradition of critical literature on Gilles has yet fully to come to terms with the puzzling paradoxes and seemingly incredible goings-on of the trial phenomenon.

The proceedings document the scandalous confession of a man of unsurpassed feudal privilege and unshakable faith who, accused of the most unthinkable crimes, managed nonetheless to obtain, despite his eventual execution, a symbolic pardon by the Inquisition in the form of reincorporation into the religious community. The preservation of Gilles's remains in the church of the Carmelite monastery of Nantes further demonstrates the Inquisition's counterintuitively conciliatory attitude. Compounding the strangeness of the trial is the reaction of the public who witnessed Gilles's confession. While describing his atrocious crimes before the parents and relations of the victims, Gilles managed to elicit the empathy of his audience, which followed him in a procession to the gallows and offered prayers to God for his redemption.

In the light of these remarkable details, the transcript of the confession of Gilles de Rais is crucial to any exploration of the problematic of perversion because it appends to the performance of sexual crimes a detailed first-person testimony of the subjective logic which underlies them. The case is especially germane to my argument about perversion in that it conjoins the properly sexual significations of the perverse which, though identifiable in the language used in the trial, have become predominant only since the mid-nineteenth century, with the moral and theological valences of the concept as expressed through the semantically related notions of sin, guilt, and concupiscence. The trial of Gilles de Rais nicely communicates, in other words, how perversion is above all else a discourse in the Lacanian sense I evoked in the previous chapter: a concrete manifestation of an individual or collective subject's relation to the sociosymbolic Other and its traumatic, ultimately indeterminable desire. Most contemporary readers of the trial documents would surely be willing to qualify Gilles's crimes as "perverse" in a loosely contemporary sense, meaning that they betray a disturbingly sadistic and predatory sexual violence. My contention, however, will be that the full significance of the trial only emerges when its transcript is read in the light of the precise psychoanalytic conceptualization of perversion.

Indeed, Gilles's confession exhibits an uncanny doubling of the two understandings of perversion—the structural and the universal—that the psychoanalytic tradition provides us. On the one hand, Gilles's discourse exemplifies the sacrificial, self-instrumentalizing logic associated with the perverse structure. As I will try to show in some detail, Gilles solves the enigma of the Other's desire by inverting the normal relationship between crime and atonement. On the other hand, however—and this is ultimately what renders his execution necessary in the eyes of the church—Gilles makes an unqualified claim in favor of the universal "banality" of perversion, effectively preventing the church authorities from differentiating categorically between his own spectacular deviations and those of the audience's ordinary believers. The copresence of the two notions of perversion in Gilles's confession allows for a precise formulation of the complicity of the perverse structure with concrete instances of political domination, in this case that of the church over the feudal masses of western France in the mid-fifteenth century. Before exploring in detail, however, how the confession is illuminated by the structural understanding of perversion, it will first be necessary to explore the stakes involved in the setup of the trial apparatus, and to establish how the most conspicuous available interpretation of the trial—Georges Bataille's—fails to appreciate its true significance on account of its contextualist historicism.

The Spectacle of Perversion

It is now commonly acknowledged that the medieval church required its heretics in order to construct its ideology of faith and to impose its political dominion. The Inquisition served as a political instrument through which faith became an imperative of submission to the earthly representatives of divine authority rather than to a notion of the divine will itself. One of the most striking elements of the trial of Gilles de Rais is the judicial apparatus's theatricalization of the criminal and his perversion, or perhaps more accurately the complicity of this apparatus with Gilles's own desire to create a spectacle of himself. The material circumstances of the trial not only betray the extent of the church's investment in Gilles's perversion; they also provide a taste of the dynamic of mutual facilitation between Gilles's criminality and the church's political hegemony.

The trial took place in the great room of the Tour Neuve castle in Nantes before a large and attentive audience. The transcripts of the trial vividly convey the thoroughly public character of the proceedings and highlight the scandalous juxtaposition of Gilles's graphic evocations of the infanticides with the full ceremonial deployment of the church's judicial machinery. In the text of Gilles's citation, Jean de Malestroit, Bishop of Nantes, decries the enormity of Gilles's crimes, referring to their "unheard-of perversity" and declaring that they could not be described in such august circumstances due to their utterly scandalous nature.[5] When he announced that the full extent of Gilles's transgressive acts would be "disclosed in Latin at the appropriate time and place" (150), the Bishop attempted to situate these acts on the other side of the iterable, sheltered from the impressionable ears of the vulgate-speaking audience. Jean de Malestroit's letter of citation announcing the trial of Gilles de Rais participated in this manner in a quest for the sensational: The ecclesiastical authorities tantalizingly proclaimed a coming spectacle at the same time that they nominally denounced its outré contents. What becomes apparent here is an emblematic example of a splitting in the church's position of enunciation which characterizes the entirety of its dealings with Gilles. While overtly denouncing the criminality of Gilles's activities, the church covertly participated in the transformation of the trial into a sensational event designed to consolidate the institution's ideological power over the community of believers. Indeed, the trial documents suggest that the church anticipated the tremendous seductive power Gilles would wield over the parishioners of Nantes. From the beginning of the trial phenomenon, so it would appear, the religious elites were fully cognizant of the opportunity the Gilles case provided to consolidate its political authority.

The representatives of divine justice, however, were not the only parties responsible for the trial's titillating publicity. With the aristocratic haughtiness of a grand personage accustomed to the accordance of his most capricious whim, Gilles also sought after the diffusion of the news of his crimes in an apparent, and surely counterintuitive, effort to increase the eventuality of his religious rehabilitation and divine pardon.

The fundamental paradox of Gilles's attitude with regard to his trial immediately presents itself: In spite of the seriousness of the accusations mounted against him, Gilles unfailingly considered throughout the trial proceedings the dramatization of his own brutality as favorable to his prospects for clemency on the part not only of the church authorities, but also of God himself. Subsequent to the public reading of his bill of indictment, for example, Gilles enthusiastically assented to the publication in French of the full depositions of the witnesses to ensure that these testimonies would reach the widest possible audience. Moreover, having made his initial out-of-court confession under threat of torture, Gilles confirmed the validity of his testimony when he reappeared during official court procedures, adding in the process further self-incriminating details. Menaced with excommunication and torture, Gilles decided not simply to participate in his own incrimination, but to do so in the most theatrical fashion possible.

In one of the numerous gory crescendos of his confession, for example, Gilles acknowledged having cut open the bodies of his young victims in order to delight in "the view of their internal organs" (189). According to Bataille's interpretation of the trial, a cynical desire to horrify his public, combined with an egotistical ambition to bask in his own evil glory, set the stage for Gilles's precise and clinical exhibitionism. After the judges of the Inquisition threatened him with excommunication, Gilles began his grisly evocation of the crimes in order to reveal, according to Bataille, their "horrible grandeur, that grandeur that would leave [the audience] trembling" (60, TM). At the moment when the Inquisition issued its threat, Gilles realized in Bataille's view that he had nothing to lose. Having lost the dignity of his privileged position in the feudal social structure, there remained for Gilles only the terrible spectacle of his crimes, and he certainly was not going to forego the opportunity to flaunt them in all their disturbing morbidity. Bataille's assessment of Gilles's motivation here reveals his argument's tendency toward psychologization, a tendency I will have occasion to examine more carefully in the next section.

To return to the question of the motivation for his self-incrimination, however, the evidence suggests more straightforwardly that Gilles was petrified by the prospect of being jettisoned from the community of God and thereby deprived, from his perspective, of a chance for salvation. Gilles's thoroughly ingenuous piety is the aspect of his confession which is at first glance so difficult to reconcile with the horror of his crimes. Indeed, the Inquisition's threat of excommunication is the unambiguous turning point of his confession. After it, Gilles voluntarily accepted the legal authority of the church over his indictment; this acceptance was surely an enormous blow to a personage accustomed through social standing to be an exception to the law. Surprisingly, however, it failed to occur to Gilles that the narration of his crimes could be considered grounds for the reinstitution of the excommunication (it was actually pronounced and then withdrawn subsequent to Gilles's acquiescence). Though Gilles willingly granted to the earthly power of the Inquisition the capacity to jeopardize his salvation, he nonetheless distinguished sharply between the church's power to pronounce on the criminality of his activities and the judgment of the divine authority itself.

All the evidence suggests that, in Gilles's view, his chances at absolution only increased in proportion to the morbid completeness of his confession. This is indeed what is so astounding about Gilles's depiction of his attitude toward the crimes; it is also what should turn our attention to that aspect of his confession which points to the specificity of his relation to his sociosymbolic Other, figured in his deeply religious imagination by the judgment of God. As I have already pointed out, at no point in his testimony did Gilles waver from his self-inclusion in the set of blessed believers. Though the luxury of his enormous feudal privilege no doubt facilitated his espousal of this position, the fact remains that not once during his confession did Gilles fail to consider himself, as well as the crimes he committed, as either in some manner alien to the human fabric, or else as beyond the reach of God's forgiveness.

The staunch conviction which underlies Gilles's refusal to acknowledge any extraordinary evil force at work within himself is surely what explains the trial audience's otherwise incomprehensible fascination with Gilles. While the Inquisition attempted to display the criminal in all his horrific glory in order to gain public sanction for its act of capital punishment, Gilles fully complied with his own indictment, enthusiastically amplifying the notary's accusations, while at the same time premising his confession on the hypothesis that anyone, in the proper circumstances, could be led to commit crimes as unthinkable as his own. Whatever evil force compelled him to perform the horrifically sadistic murders lies dormant, he subversively implied, in each of his confession's auditors. Witness on this point the transcription of Jean Petit, notary public, who recorded as follows this crucial aspect of Gilles's testimony:

> [T]he said Gilles de Rais, the accused, voluntarily and publicly, before everyone, confessed that, because of his passion and sensual delight, he took and had others take so many children that he could not determine with certitude the number whom he'd killed and caused to be killed, with whom he committed the vice and sin of sodomy;[6] and he said and confessed that he

had ejaculated spermatic seed in the most culpable fashion on the bellies of the said children, as much after their deaths as during it; on which children sometimes he and sometimes some of his accomplices inflicted various types and manners of torment; sometimes he severed the head from the body with dirks, daggers, and knives, sometimes they struck them violently on the head with a cudgel or other blunt instruments, sometimes they suspended them with cords from a peg or small hooks in his room and strangled them; and when they were languishing, he committed the sodomitic vice on them. (190)

Clinically and nonchalantly reported, this shocking parade of details concerning the crimes of Gilles de Rais could only have horrified, one would certainly think, the trial's audience. It is difficult to imagine five centuries after the fact the effects of this narration of the murders on the parents who, during the latter years of Gilles's crimes, accepted to hand over their children to his accomplices after the rumors of his disturbing practices had already begun to spread through Brittany and the Vendée. Remarkably, however, there is no indication in the trial records that Gilles's confession provoked an outcry among the audience members; in fact, the opposite is the case. Michel Bataille's fictionalized account of the trial plausibly depicts the audience's reaction to Gilles's confession and accords with the evidence of the transcripts. "The crowd did not reply, uttered no insult, did not scale the barriers to do harm to Gilles, did not lynch him," he writes. "But rather, in light of the enormity of facts that could be appreciated through no known criterion, the crowd fell to its knees and began, as he asked, to pray for him."[7]

The reader of the trial documents is confronted with this nearly incredible scenario: At the moment of Gilles's in-court confession, the members of the communities to which the victims belonged calmly, empathically listened to his confession as if in the presence of a patently evil but wise moral prophet. For example, the audience serenely received Gilles's moral exhortations to pay close attention to the rearing of future generations of children to prevent them from succumbing to the dark temptations to which he himself succumbed. More precisely, while laying blame for the crimes on his difficult upbringing, Gilles "entreated the parents among the auditors to impart good principles to their children and provide them with the habit of virtue during their youth and childhood."[8] An array of questions is suggested: How is it possible to explain the apparent coexistence in the minds of the audience of these two seemingly antithetical manifestations of Gilles—the detestable, homicidal monster and the sublime moral pedagogue more worthy of credence than the authorities of the Inquisition themselves? And how do we come to terms with the transference of the audience in regard to Gilles—the means, in other words, by which he is attributed with an innocent knowledge in the very presence of the ecclesiastical authorities whose moral and judicial power was at that moment in full display? Further, how are we to take account of the apparent complicity between the perverse logic of Gilles's confession and the public's desire to forgive him? And finally, how did the church authorities take advantage of this complicity between Gilles and his public? Before grappling with these questions, however, it will be helpful first to bring further detail to Bataille's interpretation of the trial as a means of identifying how his method fails to answer them convincingly.

The Tragedy of History

In spite of its tremendous historical perspicacity, Bataille's description of what he qualifies as the tragic dimension of the Gilles phenomenon unpersuasively accounts for the trial audience's willingness to forgive the criminal, and additionally works against Bataille's own effort to assess Gilles's position with respect to his own conditions of historical possibility. Indeed, in my view Bataille's inability to recognize the significance of the audience's relation to Gilles's confession symptomatically repeats the logic of fascination which accounts for the audience's sympathy in the first place. For these reasons Bataille's historicist consideration of Gilles's confession must be supplemented by an account of the dimension of desire—both Gilles's own and that of his audience—if we are properly to understand the trial event. Bataille's reduction of Gilles's subjectivity to his circumscription in and by the discourses of late-medieval France results not only in a contradictory psychologization of Gilles which portrays the criminal as at once an evil manipulator and suggestible simpleton, but also in a disturbing depoliticization of the church's manipulation of the trial in the interests of its own material gain.

Bataille's introduction to *The Trial of Gilles de Rais* presents the criminal as a grotesque monster who personifies the tragedy of a social class decadently abusing its privilege and discovering itself outmoded by the remarkable forces of a nascent bourgeois humanism. In this way Bataille's interpretation situates the importance of the trial entirely within the particular historical circumstances of the transitional period of early fifteenth-century France. In its quest to consider the case amidst the multiple and conflicting historical forces of this moment, Bataille's argument may too easily be summarized by the following historicist thesis which, though certainly not incorrect, remains nonetheless unsatisfying: The Gilles de Rais phenomenon symptomatizes the sensual decadence and warmongering violence of an outdated social class issuing a futile protest against a democratizing bourgeoisification which would increase in importance with the emergence of an urban commercial middle class during the transition to the French Renaissance.

Without denying, of course, the relevance of the trial's placement in its historical context, as well as the lucidity and richness of Bataille's evocation of it, it is nevertheless necessary to insist that it may not properly be understood without tarrying with the apparently counterintuitive transferential fascination the public showed for Gilles, as well as the properly perverse machinations of theological consciousness through which Gilles attempted to justify his actions to God—his sociosymbolic Other. Implicit in my approach, in other words, will be the assumption that the trial, considered as a historical event, is not fully reducible to the material traces which have survived it. It is possible, in other words, to read these traces as a means of describing with adequate plausibility dynamics which remain, strictly speaking, unarticulated by them, and which inform contemporary cultural dynamics in a way similar to the way they inform their own.[9]

Where Bataille explains Gilles's crimes as a determinate effect of his sociohistorical circumscription, I will instead attempt to recuperate Gilles's subjective *sovereignty*[10] by drawing conclusions from the manner in which his confession orients him with respect to the then-available representations of his actions. It is only in this manner that responsibility may be ascribed to Gilles for his crimes—that we may attribute their causation to a force other than that of a traumatic historical transition which would succeed in fully determining the desires and actions of those subject to it. By restoring to Gilles's confession this virtual dimension of desire, I wish to open a gap in the seamless continuum of Bataille's historical contextualization, a gap which has the effect of attributing to Gilles a position of enunciation vis-à-vis his own confession.

Bataille's method of analysis pivots around a particular understanding of tragedy: "The principle of tragedy is crime," he explains, specifying with reference to Gilles that "this criminal, more than any other, perhaps, was a character of tragedy" (10, TM). In the light of this comment it becomes necessary to examine in some detail how the concept of tragedy colors Bataille's depiction of Gilles. Bataille's formulation of tragedy presupposes a subject coextensive, as I have suggested, with the discourses through which it is articulated. Gilles is thus a character for Bataille: The figure of Gilles de Rais acquires his tragic cast through the tidy exemplarity with which he personifies an impotent aristocratic protest against democratizing early capitalist sociohistorical forces.

For example, Bataille takes great pains to locate Gilles de Rais among the uppermost echelons of late feudal European culture. Issuing forth from the great families of Laval-Montmorency, Craon, and Rais, Gilles's ancestors belonged to the "noblest, richest, and most influential houses of the feudal society of the time" (20). Each of Gilles's peers was a great lord, owner of vast feudal properties and opulent castles. Living in easy luxury, the society to which Gilles belonged entertained itself through the gallant quest for glory. Supplementing the tedious nonchalance of its material comfort with the manufactured dangers of chivalric antagonism, the participants in this quest sought after the strengthening of alliances, the distinction of feats of bravura in battle, and the flaunting of means and privilege through the conspicuous expenditures of mysteries and fêtes. Bataille thus describes a late-medieval social setting characterized by manifest interclan violence and enormous lordly egos, a carefree but cruel field of ambitions realized at any expense.

As Denis Hollier has pointed out, the Middle Ages represented for Bataille, who was trained as a medievalist, the historical apex of Christianity's cultural influence. The medieval period was the moment of "greatest taboo" and consequently "also the place of the most astounding crimes."[11] Through his reckless bravery on the battlefield, his aggressive provocation of feudal rivals, and his profligate spending on the accoutrements of devotion and carnivalesque spectacle, Gilles exhibits his perfect personification of the ethos of noble privilege at the late-medieval moment. In Bataille's analysis Gilles's historical circumscription causes him to perform the crimes; there is no logical solution of continuity between the circumstances surrounding Gilles's life and his being: He is fully articulated by, perfectly expressed through, the discourses through which we have access to him. In this way Bataille fails to attribute to Gilles the chance *to fail* to become a sovereign subject, to resist the temptation to act in consequence of the perverse, sacrificial logic through which he paradoxically tries to exculpate himself through crime.

Thus the notion of tragedy comes into play, according to Bataille, when the lateness of this feudal mode of being is taken into account. Throughout the French fifteenth-century, the feudal elite found itself overcome by historical forces which even the resources of its enormous privilege failed to subdue. Bataille refers, for example, to the increasingly administered approach to war: "Heavy cavalry" was replaced by "infantry and archers, arrows and pikes" (40). War was no longer a chaotically playful field open to personal distinction through feats of bravery, but rather a carefully managed activity in which the warrior was transformed into a soldier: an anonymous instrument of another's will who sacrifices his desire for glory to duty, cause, or nation. At the moment of Gilles's military distinction the act of war had already begun to lose its ludic function as it became increasingly tethered to a project of collective assertion and national identity formation.

Socialized to participate in violent conflict as a means of demonstrating his aristocratic essence, Gilles and those of his privileged ilk were suddenly stripped of their means of distinction, bereft of a medium through which to channel the force of their warmongering energies and the violent aggressiveness of their fragile narcissism. Gilles was "riveted to war by an affinity that marked a taste for cruel pleasures"; and now that war no longer existed in the way it once did, Gilles, as Bataille rather pathetically puts it, "had no place in the world" (41). The tragic nature of the case of Gilles de Rais devolves from the impact of these sociohistorical developments on one particular "type," on an individual trained to perform a historical function which had been superseded by history itself. In Bataille's view, late feudalism introduced into elite European culture an ideological conflict between the calculation, moderation, planning, and sacrifice of the emerging bourgeoisie with the daring, playfulness, spontaneity, and profligacy integral to the aristocratic style of life. With the appearance of humanism on the western European cultural scene, life itself became a value, and one was no longer required, as were the feudal nobles, to go to heroic lengths to prove oneself worthy of it.

It becomes apparent in this way how Bataille's sociohistorical methodology allows him to qualify tragedy as an essentially aristocratic mode. "Without the nobility," he asserts, "without the refusal to calculate and to reflect, . . . there would be no tragedy" (53). The tragic becomes the sole dominion of a noble class to which Gilles qua subject is effectively reduced. Bataille does not appear to be concerned by the desubjectivation of Gilles that his definition of tragedy implies. The murders have no properly psychical significance; their meaning may be reduced without distortion to "the convulsive tremblings of [the] world" which the victims' "slit throats expose." "The crimes of Gilles de Rais," Bataille summarizes, "are those of the world in which he committed them" (43). Gilles is depicted as a blank slate on which were set in motion great historical conflicts which were not simply beyond his control, but which transformed him into a vehicle for their own abstract ends. Perfectly sutured to his representation of the class to which he belonged, Gilles is deprived, at least at this level of Bataille's analysis, of even the most modest capacity for agency, of any ability to reflect upon or mediate the concrete historical circumstances through which his experience was necessarily articulated. Rather than qualify the crimes as a particular *symptom* of a traumatic, liminal historical conjuncture, Bataille considers them its very *incarnation*, the very form of the manifestation of the historical real.

As might well be imagined, the trial transcripts suggest that Bataille's carefully constructed sociohistorical diagnosis of Gilles's criminality leaves a number of things, if I can put it this way, to be desired. There is ample evidence in Bataille's own interpretation of the trial that his notion of tragedy fails to elucidate every detail of the case. For example, in biographical terms Gilles's first criminal acts coincide with the death of Jean de Craon, his grandfather, guardian, and initiator into the violent world of the feudal warrior. As Bataille himself underlines, the most obvious instigating factor in the onset of Gilles's criminal behavior is an event of primarily "personal"—the term is misleading—or psychodynamic significance, one related to the demise of the figure most likely to have represented for Gilles the agency of symbolic castration. When he makes reference during his testimony to his turbulent childhood punctuated by Craon's death, Gilles himself invites us to read his crimes psychoanalytically: as a response to a trauma indeed inscribed within a specific sociohistorical context, but additionally linked to a properly psychical predicament, to a confrontation with the Other's desire. Indeed, Gilles's self-diagnosis is so perfectly modern and spontaneous that it acquires an almost comic dimension, one which anticipates the puerile confessional ethos of North American daytime talk-show television. For in no uncertain terms Gilles blames his criminality on his screwed-up childhood—on, as he puts it, the lack of direction, discipline, and authority characterizing his overly privileged early years.[12] In the absence of any more objective insight, Gilles psychologizes his pathological behavior in a way so familiar as to require no historicization.

Revealing the latent complicity of a purportedly antihumanist contextualism with a tendency toward a decidedly humanistic psychologism, Bataille's analysis composes a contradictory portrait in which Gilles is depicted as both a type and an aberration, a historical example and an idiosyncratic perversity. Bataille himself participates, in other words, in Gilles's own psychological confessional method. For example, the French critic links Gilles to dark tendencies innate to the human fabric while at the same time presenting him as a properly monstrous negation of what he terms "human values." This difficulty is especially egregious in Bataille's assessment of the question of Gilles's agency. Flatly contradicting his depiction of Gilles as an infantile simpleton without a will of his own, Bataille occasionally imbues his subject with a redoubtable and malicious cunning, with a superhuman ability to seduce both his public and the church authorities. "The character of

Rais ... is a force that seduces and dominates," he writes. Comparing the feudal warrior class to which Gilles belonged to the Germanic Barbarian tribes, Bataille attributes to Gilles's noble essence "a violence respecting nothing, before which nothing fails to cede" (37, TM).

It is at textual moments such as this, I would suggest, that Bataille psychologizes Gilles in a thoroughly symptomatic fashion: He endows the criminal with the capacity to apprehend his desire transparently, to represent a conscious intention to himself and to bring it straightforwardly to fruition. In such passages Bataille also betrays his own transferential seduction by Gilles; indeed, it is as if he had suddenly taken a seat among the trial audience and succumbed to the logic of their ambivalent fascination. At these moments of his analysis Bataille figures Gilles as a sexually threatening, "hardened" (12) manipulator fully capable of bending his subjects to his own evil will despite remaining, fundamentally, a naive simpleton, a "*niais.*" Bataille's contradictory critical moves bear witness in this way to the ambivalence of a transferential identification: Gilles is at once an evil, manipulative genius who knows exactly what he is doing, and a patently unknowing instrument of abstract historical forces. Breaking the smooth surface of the passive tabula rasa version of Gilles that he needs to illustrate his historicist thesis, Bataille's fantasy version of the diabolical, omnipotent Gilles emerges from time to time with disastrous results for the coherence of his argument. Gilles is simultaneously an exemplary incarnation of his social milieu and an utterly singular contradiction of human nature—both an infantile, impotent simpleton adrift in necromantic fantasy and a masterful, threateningly virile manipulator of circumstance.

It is interesting to note that the properly homophobic aspects of Bataille's consideration of the trial are not unrelated to this contradictory portrait of the criminal. By way of contextualizing Bataille's comments about what would now likely be called Gilles's homosexuality, I wish to open a brief historicizing parenthesis on the topic of sexuality and late-medieval culture. First, as has been amply demonstrated during the past three decades, the contemporary concept of sexuality as a term descriptive of a subject's identity does not predate the nineteenth-century invention of sexuality discourse. As Jonathan Goldberg notes with reference to the term's usage during the English Renaissance (and one fails to see how the comment would not also apply to fifteenth-century France), "sodomy" confusedly describes illicit sexual acts—virtually anything outside of procreative sex within marriage—which are not presumed to express an essence or identity of the subject who performs them. In the presexological universe, any subject is quite capable of giving in to the temptation of sodomy. It should also be noted that, as

Goldberg suggests, the crime of sodomy emerged into visibility only on occasions when it was tethered to another act of criminality which threatened church power.[13] Indeed, the trial evidence suggests that the Inquisition was very likely only mildly interested in the specifically sexual aspect of Gilles's crimes; as I will discuss in greater detail in the final section of this chapter, the crime of sodomy was probably a convenient pretext under which the church could settle its eminently political scores with Gilles.

But to return to the trial's homosexual aspect—to the fact that Gilles was almost exclusively interested in adolescent boys and likely had sexual relations of one kind or another with a number of his male cohorts, including his Florentine invoker François Prelati—there is evidence suggesting that we should not overestimate the extent to which it would have been perceived at the time as scandalous. According to Philippe Reliquet, male homosexual activity among late feudal nobles in France was relatively common.[14] Young lords of Gilles's level of privilege habitually sponsored the company of *mignons*— adolescent male pages who often performed services of a sexual nature for their masters. Indeed, Gilles's cronies recruited the young boys who would become his victims to serve as pages in his castles.

In his analysis of the trial, however, Bataille directly relates what he considers Gilles's monstrous aberrance to this erotic preference for young male victims. What Bataille refers to as Gilles's "homosexuality" is a function of the outmoded, decadent quality of his personality, of the fact that the criminal failed to obey an imperative of civilization during his undisciplined and overprivileged childhood. Gilles thus personifies for Bataille the bloodthirsty and violent "archaic human nature" present in late-medieval culture, specifically within its homosexually inclined male nobility (14). The homoerotic networks linking Gilles with his numerous lackeys serve to highlight this depraved archaism characteristic of both Gilles and the entire feudal aristocracy. To illustrate his contention Bataille interprets Gilles's melodramatic good-bye to his cherished alchemist and likely lover François Prelati not as evidence that Gilles, despite his brutality, was also capable of that most human of emotions, namely love, but rather as proof of Gilles's infantilism and naivety, of the location of his intellect beneath the threshold of universal rationality (19–20).

For Bataille, the homosexual practices of Gilles and his male class peers were not simply another instance of their debauchery, but rather the very mode of their devolution into brutality, lawlessness, and excess. Homosexuality thus "facilitated," as Bataille puts it, the descent of the young feudal warrior into unbridled homicidal mania and self-destruction (31). Phobically, Bataille makes Gilles's homosexuality an essential feature of his criminality, a condition of possibility for the infanticides. Homosexuality becomes synonymous with transgression, to the point that it is impossible to figure crime—and hence the tragic—within Bataille's framework in the absence of its homosexual element. This is quite clearly another danger of Bataille's historicist understanding of tragedy. Since his tragic mode is shot through with concrete and particular historical content, Bataille is able to make homosexuality an essential attribute of the dislocation of late-medieval culture with respect to the ascendant vector of history—bourgeois capitalism. Bataille's argument regarding aristocratic homosexuality proceeds as if the republican revolution were somehow waiting in the wings to eliminate homosexual desire from history itself. Bataille's gesture not only implies a highly problematic historicist understanding of homosexuality which collapses homosexual desire onto its concrete historical manifestations,[15] but it also relates homosexuality in an essential or necessary way to the themes of decadence, lateness, and profligacy with which Bataille describes the feudal aristocracy of mid-fifteenth-century France.[16]

It is precisely Bataille's symptomatic othering of Gilles—the ease, in other words, with which his suggestive gesture toward a notion of a universally shared human monstrosity or perversity degenerates into an account of Gilles's idiosyncratically diabolical foreignness to the human—which prevents him, along with the vast majority of the trial documents' readers, from grasping in its disturbing nuance the significance of the audience's transference with respect to Gilles. Bataille will refer, for example, to the "insensitivity" and "indifference" which "situate [Gilles] beyond the feelings of ordinary humanity" (16, TM); such comments open a chasm which will forever separate Gilles from his confession's auditors. In order to come to terms with the consequences of this interpretative move, it will be necessary to inquire after the status of the object that Gilles constituted for his confession's auditors. Bataille, for his part, attributes Gilles's apparent seduction of the crowd to a strange power of persuasion traceable, but not perfectly reducible, to the impressiveness of his feudal authority. Of what metaphysical attribute does this charismatic supplement consist? Bataille explains the "compassion" of the audience for Gilles de Rais by claiming that its members were able, during the trial, "to realize through [their] tears that this great lord who was to die, being the most notorious of criminals, was like everyone in the crowd" (58, TM).

Though Bataille needs to argue in favor of Gilles's nonhuman monstrosity in order to avoid a confrontation with the trial's most unsettling ramifications, he asserts at other points in his analysis that the audience's relation to the criminal was mediated by a kind of empathic identification which contrasts sharply with the spontaneous, visceral disgust one would intuitively attribute to the response of Gilles's confession's auditors. At the same time that he was viewed in sheer horror, Bataille claims that Gilles was also the object of "the terrified sympathy [and] compassion of those who s[aw] him cry" (61). The attribute of Gilles with which the audience identified and empathized, according to Bataille, is his particular brand of extreme criminality: that which separates him, in other words, from what is normally allowed to be associated with the human. Bataille implies that this idea of a shared monstrosity is a function of the crowd's fully and consciously cognized representation of Gilles. When an audience member looked at the accused, in other words, he saw a deviance—a perversion—he recognized in himself.

The point of identification which makes possible this collective fascination with Gilles is a function, in this view, of a shared transgression, a community of guilt. Watching Gilles break down before the evidence of the evil inside him, the spectator could weep vicariously at the evil he sensed within himself. Bataille's argument here features an intuitive, commonsensical persuasiveness. Although I do not disagree that the libidinal dynamic motivating the public's sympathy is related to such a fraternity in transgression, it is nonetheless unlikely, however, that this transgression constituted the public's point of identification. Among the presuppositions supporting Bataille's argument is the notion that a group consolidates its identification around a consciously assumed representation of collective guilt. A return to psychoanalysis will allow us to discover, however, how it renders more complex and intellectually persuasive the trial audience's relation to Gilles's grisly confession. Psychoanalysis will enable us not only to uncover the disturbing complicity between Gilles's perversion and his public's identification, but also to discern the opportunity this complicity offered to the church to consolidate its ideological hegemony.

An Innocent Transference

The manifest and aware identification with Gilles's monstrosity that Bataille attributes to the trial's public is not only highly improbable, given in particular the extreme suffering the crimes surely brought upon the audience members, but also implicitly predicated on an improperly theorized notion of transference. The transference is put in motion by forces of resistance which distract the subject—individual or collective, indeed the logic is identical in both cases—from a traumatic confrontation with unconscious material by means of a relation to a fascinating, consoling object imbued with knowledge of desire. In a paper on the Dora case Lacan underscores how the transference halts the emergence of evidence of the unconscious when he describes it as "a moment of stagnation in the analytic dialectic."[17] Of course, Freud also underlined how the transference functions as a form of resistance to the manifestation of unconscious desire, describing it in *Studies on Hysteria* as a "false connection" or "*mésalliance*" which dissociates the content of a wish from "the surrounding circumstances that would have assigned [it] to a past time."[18] Freud would later replace this temporal notion of misconnection with a more topological one, ultimately suggesting that the transference establishes a psychical connection designed to delink the wish from its association with traumatic unconscious fantasy, thereby allowing the subject to sustain its desire by casting a veil over desire's ultimate, death-bearing object.

This is the point Lacan takes up in his seminar on the transference, in which he outlines the subject's ambivalence with respect to this fantasmatic object—how it may alternately appear as the precious, fascinating *agalma* (treasure, jewel) which holds the promise of perfect narcissistic self-reflection, or the traumatic point of the subject's "fading" from its own sociosymbolic domain.[19] The dynamic of identification constitutive of the transferential relation is therefore fundamentally narcissistic: The knowledge I suppose in the Other to whom I address myself is the knowledge which allows me to anticipate seeing myself in the way I wish to be seen. For Lacan, the Other in the transference is the well-known "subject supposed to know" about a desire I wish to recognize not as disturbingly alien, but rather as reassuringly my own. To refer back to the case of Gilles de Rais, in Lacanian terms the audience attributed to Gilles the knowledge pertaining to how one might remain innocent in light of traumatic intuitions of guilt—in other words how one might sustain a satisfying self-concept while at the same time communing in an at least partially disavowed, guilty enjoyment. By qualifying the audience's relation to Gilles as transferential, in other words, I wish to point out the means it provided to the audience of averting—of resisting—an encounter with what it refused intellectually to acknowledge, namely its willing participation in the obscene jouissance of Gilles's confession, and very likely its half-knowing complicity in his access to his eventual victims.

The logic of transgressive communion for which Bataille finds evidence in the transcripts is indeed the cement that binds the trial audience to Gilles's confession. Contra Bataille, however, this shared guilt is disavowed—jettisoned from the field of collective consciousness—and it is therefore with Gilles's enunciation of his fundamental metaphysical innocence, rather, that the audience identifies, properly speaking. Thus, we can describe the audience's relation to Gilles as a collective transference—one that exemplifies the dynamic of the Freudian "group"—because it defers a traumatic encounter with guilty, unconscious enjoyment. Readers of Freud will be aware that our most deep-seated intuitions of culpability, traceable to the murder of the primal father in unconscious fantasy, are not attributable to any concrete wrongdoing for which we could existentially assume responsibility.[20] Nonetheless, given both the length of time between the emergence of rumors of the crimes and the first actions undertaken against Gilles—not to mention the apparent facility with which most of the children were handed over to Gilles's cronies in exchange for money—it could indeed be argued that numerous audience members undoubtedly had much to feel guilty about.

On the alternative reading I am suggesting, then, Gilles acquires the attribute of transferential fascination for the crowd not through his admissions of guilt, but rather through his protestations of innocence. Or, more precisely put, the audience's seduction by Gilles takes hold as a result of the manner in which its narcissistic identification with Gilles's sense of his own innocence creates a kind of alibi for the shadily shared transgression to which Bataille refers. What was so moving about Gilles, in other words, was not the manner in which he offered an externalization of the public's guilty regret at having in some manner contributed, however unwittingly, to the children's grisly end. Instead, Gilles's uncanny charisma should be explained with reference to the means he provided to his audience to exorcise these intuitions, to eradicate them through the unfurling of a beautiful image of divinely sanctioned purity and innocence. The escape Gilles offered the public from a messy interrogation of its own complicity in the children's demise surely illuminates the apparent lack of any dissenting voices at the trial. Gilles is able to confess in such morbid detail precisely because he premises his testimony on an unshakeable belief in a properly metaphysical innocence which increases in direct proportion to the objective guilt Gilles accrues through the confessional narration of his crimes.

Thus Gilles's moral authority stems from the willingness with which the crowd attributes to him knowledge of its innocence. Here we may discern the structure of the ego ideal. The persuasiveness with which Gilles exonerates himself encourages the public to take the criminal as the point of its symbolic identification: the perspective from which it appears worthy to itself, from which it may regard itself in an approving light. This narcissistic structure also allows the crowd to shield itself from the traumatic kernel of truth in Gilles's confession, namely, that he is not, in fact, an inhuman, monstrous incarnation of radical evil, but rather a manifestation, extreme to be sure, of evil in its universal banality; of perverse, sadomasochistic tendencies operative on some level in any normal subject's libidinal economy. A crucial nuance must therefore be added to Bataille's interpretation of the audience's relation to Gilles. While it does indeed bind itself to the spectacle of Gilles's perversion in order to commune with the scandal of his crimes, the condition of possibility of this communion is not this scandal's horror, but rather the seductive pull exerted by Gilles's claims to a holy innocence. This contradictory, bivalent structure in this way allowed the crowd to experience the illicit thrill of Gilles's gruesome crimes while at the same time remaining hygienically shielded from them thanks to the Inquisition's depiction of Gilles as a despicable monster at a radical remove from the human fabric.

In *Group Psychology and the Analysis of the Ego* Freud details the relationship between the type of empathic identification which supports the trial audience's transference with respect to Gilles and the vicissitudes of moral consciousness—the subject's relation to the superegoic voice of conscience, of internalized self-surveillance and judgment. In his analysis of the logic of group formation Freud first defines identification as "the earliest expression of an emotional tie with another person,"[21] and then contrasts the identificatory phenomenon with a libidinal object cathexis, thereby suggesting that we develop a relationship of "emotional communication" with another as an alternative to taking this other as a sexual object. Here it becomes apparent how the audience's identificatory structure served to desexualize its spectatorial position in relation to Gilles, repressing into its unconscious any libidinal investment it may have had in Gilles's dangerous and transgressive sexuality. Freud's formulation thus underscores the dissociation of sexual feeling and affect in the object relation: By disavowing the libidinal component of its fascination with Gilles, the trial audience fostered an emotional relationship with the criminal, one which was surely strengthened by Gilles's talent for manipulative, melodramatic speeches. For this precise reason it is possible to qualify the crowd's reaction to Gilles's confession as defensive. In order to avoid the interrogation of its own fascination with Gilles's criminality, the audience adopted the accused's profession of innocence as the idealized perspective from which it could view itself as beyond moral reproach.

Freud argues in this way that identification puts to work a kind of egoic empathy in which the subject, in this case the collective subject constituted by the trial's auditors, "moulds" its ego "after the fashion of the one that has been taken as model."[22] In a public event such as a trial, for example, in which the discourse of an individual is given pride of place, a dynamic can emerge in which the participants fuse into a group by sharing a common point of identification, in other words by adopting a charismatic leader's ego as their own. Through this process Gilles's public manages to reconstruct itself on the foundation of the criminal's self-described noumenal innocence, in so doing constituting itself as a group in the properly Freudian sense of the term. Instead of structuring the neurotic, self-critical agency which characterizes the classical bourgeois superego, the dual-faceted structure of the group, according to Freud, extends "the original narcissism in which the childish ego enjoyed self-sufficiency."[23] The constitution of a group thereby short-circuits the ordinary structure of self-consciousness by installing a relation of complicity between enjoyment and narcissism. Whereas the ego ideal typically threatens its subject with the prospect of shame, thereby casting enjoyment under the shadow of properly moral considerations, the group dynamic fosters a sympathetic relation between the experience of excess pleasure and the mechanism of self-regard.

From a historical perspective, one could perhaps go so far as to suggest that the decline of the rigid feudal social structure at the time of Gilles's trial played a key role in this process. Insofar as the emerging capitalist mode of production during the late-medieval period began to displace the critical agency of consciousness from the external figure of the feudal superior (lord, guild master, and so on) or church authority to an internal, critical voice of bourgeois moderation and frugality (this is indeed the gist of Bataille's formulation of tragedy), it might be said that a general cultural anxiety related to the subjectivation or individuation of the voice of conscience in part contributed to the audience's inability to fashion a more autonomous, responsible relation to Gilles's confession. In this view, at the historical moment of the trial, the feudal masses, subject to increasing urbanization and greater independence with respect to the landed lords and touched by theological humanism, were confronted with the anxious hysteria to which their very (relative) freedom gave rise. Subject to the new, abstract, and unpredictable laws of commercial exchange which, for us, have long since become all too familiar, the subjects of Nantes may have come to recognize that the phenomenon of Gilles's scandalous trial could be put to use to construct a cult of personality which effectively introduced a reassuring element of moral certainty and collective identity amidst chaotic sociohistorical change, all the while dissimulating the trauma of an irresistible yet unacknowledged enjoyment.

Radically Evil?

If the audience's relation to Gilles was characterized by a transferential dynamic by means of which it disavowed unconscious intuitions of guilt, then the Inquisition's relation to Gilles may be described as informed by a politically motivated effort to subvert Gilles's pretensions to normality through a hysterical demonization of him. It is possible to illuminate the Inquisition's desire to impute a diabolical intentionality to Gilles with reference to Kant's refutation, through his development of the theme of radical evil, of the possibility of a purely malignant rationality in the moral life of man. This brief philosophical excursus will shed more light on the mechanism through which the church attempted to set up, as I have suggested, an absolute demarcation between Gilles's criminal acts and the terrain of the "human." When confronted with the scandal of the crimes, the ecclesiastical authorities showed an extreme anxiety with respect to the question of Gilles's intentionality: According to what principle of evil, they asked themselves, could acts as unspeakable as Gilles's be carried out?

The Inquisition's hysterical discomfort manifests itself through the insistence with which it wanted to discover, beneath the discursive evidence of the crimes, what Gilles actually wanted through their accomplishment. This is yet another instance of the church's radical othering of Gilles. His crimes could only have resulted from a diabolical desire— "diabolical" here understood in the properly Kantian sense which I will shortly evoke—to destroy the points of reference according to which the normal subject negotiates its actions in the world. For the church, Gilles's crimes quite simply could not be located among the possibilities for earthly conduct in the late-medieval period. Unsatisfied with Gilles's own account of his intention (or lack thereof), the authorities issued a truly proto-Stanislavskian demand for a principled account of Gilles's motivation. For the Inquisition's aggressive questioning repeatedly insinuated that Gilles must have acted with reference to an idea of evil whose presence in his moral consciousness would effectively banish him, it was maintained, to a diabolical inhumanity which could then serve as justification for his execution.

Gilles's response to the authorities' line of questioning, in its disarming simplicity, is surely the most potentially subversive aspect of his confession because it reveals how, in Kantian terms, his horrible acts resulted from an everyday inversion of the constituents of moral consciousness rather than from a radical negation of the very form of the moral law. In one of his most salient utterances, Gilles declared that he committed the crimes "according to his imagination and idea, without anyone's counsel and following his own feelings, solely for his pleasure and carnal delight, and not with any other intention or to any other end" (187). One could perhaps go so far as to say that in this utterance Gilles effectively claims responsibility for his perversion. The president of the trial, Jean de Malestroit, was clearly dissatisfied with Gilles's explanation, for he repeatedly returned, like a method acting coach, to an inquiry after the "motives," "intent," and "ends" which informed the murders.[24] There followed a telling exchange between an uncomprehending Gilles and an exasperated Malestroit. As transcribed by Jean Petit, notary of the out-of-court confession, this exchange began with Gilles's exclamation, "'Alas! Monsignor, you torment yourself and me along with you.' The Lord President responded in French: 'I don't torment myself in the least, but I'm very surprised at what you've told me and simply cannot be satisfied with it. I desire and would like to know the absolute truth from you. . . .' To which Lord President the accused responded: 'Truly, there was no other cause, no other end nor intention, if not what I've told you: I've told you greater things than this and enough to kill ten thousand men'" (187).

In his celebrated posttheological treatise *Religion within the Limits of Reason Alone*, Kant contemplates the possibility of a radical evil in human nature to which he attributes what common sense would consider two contradictory qualities: innateness and responsibility. Evil, according to Kant, is not a natural *predisposition* which inheres in the concept of humanity in such a way that it determines the actions of agents; rather, evil is a *propensity*: a function of the maxims, in other words, according to which we acquire responsibility for what we choose to do. Though evil is the subjective ground of the will, and thus the product of a freely determined choice, it is nonetheless so deeply ingrained in experience that Kant is able to claim that it is "rooted in humanity itself."[25] It was through these counterintuitive, not to mention contradictory, assertions that Kant was able to argue that evil inheres in human experience while maintaining that we freely choose evil through the adoption of a bad maxim of action. Though the moral subject is irreducibly responsible for its failure to conform to the moral law, it cannot do otherwise: A stain of evil will forever separate any humanly accomplishable act from perfect conformity with categorical duty.

Kant was careful to distinguish his notion of radical evil from previous conceptions, such as numerous Christian formulations of original sin—though not, as will be evident in the next chapter, Pascal's—which related evil to the "natural inclinations" of man's sensuous nature or to the "corruption" of a "morally legislative reason." Kant refuted the former by claiming that we do not partake of evil simply by virtue of our "merely animal being" and the latter by arguing that evil does not result from a subversion or negation of the moral law which burdens us with obligation.[26] The moral law, in the Kantian view, is a function of humanity's innate rationality; one's actions in consequence necessarily carry within themselves, as it were, a reference to it. In spite of the moral subject's inability fully to purify its will, morality's rationality remains sovereign, is not in itself corrupted by human failing. From a Kantian perspective, in other words, a subject is never capable of acting in perfect ignorance of the moral law; the more the subject attempts to evade the traumatic rationality of freedom, the more this subject accuses itself for its failure to comply with duty. But if evil for Kant is coextensive with actions resulting neither from an indulgence in a sensuous inclination, nor from a willed opposition to the form of the moral law, then . . . what is it, exactly?

Evil, like goodness, presupposes the adoption of a maxim which, due to our sensuous nature, may never be perfectly realized in a concrete, completed action. If we may not be reduced to our brute animal nature, however, neither may we renounce this nature in favor of a purely noumenal existence in which it would be possible to perform a dutiful action entirely for duty's sake. Consequently, for Kant, humanity must be neither purely good nor purely evil, and every subject will freely choose the maxim its actions in the world will presuppose. As moral agents, in other words, we are irremediably split between the sense of obligation or duty with reference to which our actions are performed and the pathological stain of self-interest which forever poisons our devotion to the moral law.

It is now possible to discern how Kant's thoughts on radical evil helpfully illuminate the trial of Gilles de Rais. For how are we to interpret the president's insistent questioning after Gilles's motivation other than by recognizing it as rhetorical: as presupposing the "correct" answer that Gilles acted not purely in accordance with a bad maxim of action which merely fails to obey the moral law without reference to sensuous self-interest, but rather, as Kant puts it, to "repudiate the moral law in the manner of a rebel"[27]—to adopt evil, that is to say, as a pure principle of action, thereby subverting the moral law's pretension to foster actions which take the highest Good as their end? The Kantian framework allows us to see clearly why Gilles's response to his interrogators is so unsettling: It reveals how (at least minimally) distant are his actions from a diabolical intentionality, from a motivation so pure in its dedication to evil that it features no determination derived from experience. "I had no end in mind," Gilles effectively and unambiguously declares, "other than my own immediate sensuous gratification."

The Inquisition quite simply proved itself incapable of entertaining the admittedly unsettling prospect that the all-too-human motive for what Gilles called his "carnal delectation" could have pushed him to commit such gruesome murders. To the dismay of the authorities, in Kantian terms Gilles proves to be evil only insofar as he "reverses the moral order of the incentives when he adopts them into his maxim."[28] Instead of first attempting to comply with the categorical moral law, and then falling into human sensuous self-interest, Gilles subsumes the law's command under his pathological, experientially determined motivation. In the Kantian framework, any action features a noumenal and phenomenal component, the former designating the supersensible, principled relation of the action to the moral law, the latter denoting the empirical, sensuous incentive which articulates the agent's self-interest. Where the good agent subordinates, without successfully subsuming, the phenomenal to the noumenal component, the ordinary evil agent, as opposed to the genuinely diabolical one (which Kant claims cannot exist), "makes the incentive of self-love and its inclinations the condition of obedience to the moral law."[29]

In Kant's vocabulary, the Inquisition's insistent questioning manifests a desire that Gilles confess to *wickedness*, when his crimes, at least on one level, demonstrate a perfectly ordinary, in the sense of universal, *perversity*. Kant defines wickedness as "a disposition . . . to adopt evil as evil into our maxim as our incentive"; in contrast, the perversity of an evil heart "may coexist with a will which in general is good," and designates merely "the frailty of human nature" before the command of the moral law or a "lack of sufficient strength" to conform categorically to duty.[30] Just as the pure-hearted agent's attempt to conform to the moral law will never succeed in perfectly separating itself from sensuously determined motives, there will always be a potentially benevolent or well-intentioned feature discernable within the effort of the wicked rebel to subvert the law in its very notion, to make evil the category of rational freedom itself.

Kant's contention concerning the impossibility or nonexistence of what he terms "wickedness" lends itself to comparison with what I have identified as the structural and universal concepts of perversion that psychoanalysis bequeaths to us. The implication of Kant's critique of radical evil for the psychoanalytic theory of perversion is that no absolute distinction can be drawn between the two concepts; if we imagine the structural and universal formulations of perversion as mathematical sets, there is at least one point at which they intersect. In other words, the subject whose discourse may be qualified as perverse (and I will indeed maintain in the next section that elements of Gilles's confession can be qualified in such a manner) does not fully succeed in escaping the universal, a priori conditions of desire. The pervert and the normal neurotic subject feature different ways of dealing with the same impasse of desire—the same impenetrable enigma in the heart of the Other. This impasse of the real, which in psychoanalytic theory causes desire to be forever estranged from itself, is conceptually analogous, I wish to suggest, to the perversity which disallows, in Kant, the existence of either a purely evil or a purely benevolent will. An irreducible libidinal dissatisfaction disallows in psychoanalysis the full normalization or genitalization of the drive, thereby rendering impossible the execution of a successful sexual act (or, put differently, the successful sexual act depends on the failure or fragmentation of the drive); in strictly parallel fashion, the malignity at the heart of Kantian practical reason renders impossible a perfect realization of duty in a moral act. Here the analogy between the sexual and moral universalist concepts of perversity becomes strikingly clear.

As is quite evident, the trial authorities tried to seduce Gilles into admitting to a properly diabolical or wicked intentionality because, in their view, such a confession would have justified a tidy execution at the same time that, more crucially, it would have put in abeyance the question of the Inquisition's own deeply pathological motivation in orchestrating the trial. By eliciting a confession of Kantian wickedness from Gilles, the church would have been able categorically to distinguish the criminal's evil motivation from its own cynically self-interested reasons for prosecuting him. By attempting to figure Gilles as the agent of a purely evil will, the Inquisition wished to appear fully justified in pursuing the criminal; this endeavor featured the additional advantage of strongly discouraging the trial audience from investigating what the ecclesiastical elites had to gain from Gilles's arrest and execution.

Paradoxically, however, because Gilles refused to succumb to the Inquisition's pressure—because, in other words, he so transparently, so naively, so responsibly, I am tempted to say, divulged the perverse logic behind his crimes—it becomes possible for us as readers of the transcripts to discern through the haze of the trial's diversionary melodrama the full extent of the authorities' political opportunism and cynical exploitation of the Gilles phenomenon. But in order to spell out more precisely the means by which the church elites were able to capitalize on Gilles's perversion, it will first be necessary to describe in detail the workings of its logic.

The Perverse Sacrifice

Of all the key turning points in his confession, Gilles's speech at the moment of the trial's climax is especially demonstrative of its perverse logic. In addition, this speech helps to convey the illicit complicity between Gilles's theatrical protestations of innocence and the guilty transgression of not only the crimes themselves, but also of the church hierarchy's manipulation of the spectacle. This passage of the transcript highlights once again how, during the entirety of the proceedings, Gilles never once vacillated from his absolute faith in both his exemplary piety and God's imminent clemency even while relaying the most shocking details of the crimes. Indeed, so great was his sense of God's love and favor that Gilles proved abundantly capable of bestowing moral counsel on his accomplices as they prepared for their own encounter with the final judgment. Notary Jean de Touscheronde recorded Gilles's final words as follows:

> [T]he said Gilles de Rais confessed and exhorted his aforesaid servants [Henriet and Poitou] on the subject of the salvation of their souls, urging them to be strong and virtuous in the face of diabolical temptations, and to have profound regret and contrition for their misdeeds, but also to have confidence in the grace of God and to believe that there was no sin a man might commit so great that God in His goodness and kindness would not forgive, so long as the sinner felt profound regret and great contrition of heart, and asked Him for mercy with a great deal of perseverance. And God was closer to forgiving and receiving the sinner in His grace than the sinner was to asking His forgiveness. And they should thank God for having shown them such a sign of love, He who required them to die in the fullness of their strength and memory, and did not permit them to be punished suddenly for their wrongs, and who gave them such an ardent love of Him and such great contrition for their misdeeds that they no longer had anything in this world to fear from death, which was nothing but a short death, without which one could not see God in all His glory. And they ought very much to desire to be out of this world, where there was nothing but misery, so as to enter into eternal glory. And thus, as soon as their souls left their bodies, those who had committed evil together would thereby meet each other again in glory, with God, in paradise. (278)

And to this declaration of faith in the imminent salvation of those united by a communion in sin, the notary appended the following passage, which has the merit of underscoring the dimension of Gilles's perversion that solicited the transferential identification so characteristic of the public's response:

> [A]fter having exhorted them thus, Gilles got down on his knees, folding his hands together, begging God's mercy, praying to

Him to be willing to punish them not according to their misdeeds, but, being merciful, to let them profit by the grace in which he put his trust, telling the people that as a Christian, he was their brother, and urging them and those among them whose children he had killed, for the love of Our Lord's suffering to be willing to pray to God for him and to forgive him freely, in the same way that they themselves intended God to forgive and have mercy on themselves. Recommending himself to holy Monsignor Jacques, whom he had always held in singular affection, and also to holy Monsignor Michel, begging them in his hour of great need to be willing to help him, aid him, and pray to God for him, despite the fact that he had not obeyed them as he should have. He further requested that the instant his soul left his body, it might please holy Monsignor Michel to receive it and present it unto God, whom he begged to take it into His grace, without punishing it according to its offenses. And the said Gilles then made beautiful speeches and prayers to God, recommending his soul to Him. (279)

This climactic moment of the Gilles de Rais trial brings to its point of greatest intensity the synergy between, on the one hand, Gilles's desire to guarantee his salvation through the graphic divulgation of his criminality and, on the other, the efforts of the institutional apparatus of the church to consolidate its political power under the guise of an ideology of faith. As far as Gilles is concerned, his final discourse displays the properly perverse short-circuit through which he effectively performs the crimes as a means of establishing his innocence before God. It is precisely by becoming as guilty as possible before the divine agency, by performing the most taboo actions, that Gilles secures his innocence and therefore his salvation. In other words, Gilles deliberately sins in order to secure the guilt from which he will then be able to beseech God for forgiveness; he violates the law in order to offer himself as the means of its redemption or reparation. Put in more straightforwardly ethical terms, Gilles performs evil as a means of safeguarding the Good, in this instance his favor with respect to God's grace.

It is worthwhile examining more closely the theological logic, if one can put it this way, which supports Gilles's rationalizations. Remarkably, Gilles claims to know with certainty the content of the final judgment: God's desire is to bestow forgiveness on his straying flock, most especially on those among it who stray the most spectacularly. From this premise Gilles proceeds to the far from illogical conclusion that the subject with the greatest sins, and hence the one required to make the most demanding acts of contrition, will best answer to the divine will to grant salvation's grace. It becomes apparent in this way how, rather than pervert the theological position on grace in late-medieval Christianity, Gilles's confession uncovers an authentically perverse kernel within forms of Christian casuistry which safeguard a realm of illicit taboo by granting to the believer the guarantee of divine pardon in advance. Whereas Pascal, as will be explored in the next chapter, insists on qualifying God's will as irremediably indeterminate, as not amenable to predication, Gilles claims to know the secret of his personal Other's desire, which is to bestow innocence on those who acquire guilt. This assumption of knowledge in the Other inaugurates a logic whereby *salvation requires the performance of crime.* If God wishes to forgive the sinner, so the logic goes, then the believer must sin in order to enable God to forgive.

There is a tendency among the available interpretations of the trial of Gilles de Rais—Bataille's being as we have seen the supreme example—to overstate the oddity of the paradox of Gilles's peculiar brand of faith, namely the facility with which his solicitations of his invokers' forbidden powers of black magic, for example, transform into increasingly vociferous promises of moral purgation or atonement. Bataille's claim is that Gilles's unceasing oscillation between transgression and faith, wickedness and saintliness, offers further evidence of his estrangement from normative rationality. Indeed, this very coincidence of high religious piety and murderous criminality constitutes for Bataille Gilles's very foreignness to the human. In my view, however, Gilles's confession makes plain that his mania for the black arts and his conviction in divine redemption manifest the same, properly perverse, subjective structure of abdication and sacrifice. They are both, in other words, desperate efforts to escape the enigma of the Other's desire, to determine, in theological terms, what precisely is required to merit the grace of God. But if we take Gilles at his word when he adamantly denies his monstrosity and stresses the resemblance of the temptations which plagued him to those his auditors might themselves experience, then how precisely must we interpret the strange interimplication of guilt and innocence in Gilles's account of his motivation and intentionality?

When, as mentioned in the previous chapter, he adopted as his formula for perversion a reversal of his formula for fantasy (S ◇ a becomes a ◇ S in perversion), Lacan underscored how the pervert transfers castration's effects from the subjective function properly speaking to the sociosymbolic function embodied by the Other. In order to avoid the anxiety that the neurotic subject experiences regarding what kind of object it is for the Other's desire, the pervert effectively castrates the Other in order then to offer himself through a gesture of pseudosacrifice as the object which will heal the Other's wound, thereby granting it completion. Indeed, as Lacan puts it, the perverse subject obtains its pleasure when it "immobilizes itself [*se fige*] in the rigidity of the object with the aim of returning its subjective division to the Other."[31] Through his criminality Gilles effectively becomes the object-instrument of divine clemency's jouissance by first tarnishing the image of God through crime and profanation and then posturing as the very means of the restoration of innocence. Gilles's perversion consists in taking to its extreme limit what would shortly become, in historical-theological terms, the perverse tendencies of Jesuitical casuistry, which asserted the possibility of earning divine grace in the earthly dimension through acts of contrition and self-justification.[32] In a theological framework which allows for certainty with respect to the content of the final judgment, the believer acquires an ability to "cheat" with respect to its salvation by asserting that the surest means of acquiring God's forgiveness is an active participation in sin. One receives proof of God's love by meriting his forgiveness; in consequence, the most direct way of executing God's will becomes crime.

The attraction of the kind of absolute religious faith that Gilles constructs for himself is that it permits the complicity of an illusory ideal of innocence with a subterranean world of transgression which paradoxically enables this innocent state. One may detect in the trajectory of Gilles's testimony a toleration of contradiction reminiscent of the logic Freud elucidated in his 1927 essay "Fetishism." On a level not too deeply hidden, Gilles knows he is guilty. Otherwise it is impossible to account for his deep-seated need for the moral purgation for which his plan for a holy pilgrimage to Jerusalem, for example, provides evidence. Yet Gilles repeatedly posits during his confession that he is always already pardoned for his sins—that the unceasing act of contrition he performs at the trial serves to preserve him in the condition of beatific grace. Gilles professes to a need for contrition which is strictly speaking unnecessary according to his own moral framework. The believer of Gilles's ilk—the moral[33] fetishist—says to himself, "I know I am guilty of reprehensible injustices, but still, such actions do not tarnish my fundamental, inalienable innocence."[34] Indeed, in this logic crime begins to serve as proof of the subject's worthiness with respect to God's grace: Crime secures the very power of forgiveness through which crime may be expiated.

Here a crucial distinction between the respective logics of neurosis and perversion emerges in regard to their respective relations to law and transgression. Whereas the neurotic inscribed within a religious sociosymbolic framework is perturbed by his inability to conform his actions to a divine will resistant to all attempts at determination, the pervert succeeds in conforming absolutely to his God's desire, effectively attributing to the function of divine forgiveness the quality of obscene enjoyment. The neurotic indulges in crime in consequence of an irrational, pathological motivation beyond his conscious control, and then chastises himself as a means of both intensifying the enjoyment of transgression and reconstituting the contours of his lawful symbolic universe. In this way the neurotic's suffering bears witness to the fact that he psychically experiences the traumatic subjective split between law and transgression; he is condemned to suffer the consequences of his inability to integrate his enjoyment within his sociosymbolic world. The pervert, for his part, transfers this split, along with its painful symptom, onto the Other in order to offer himself as the object which effectively sutures the gap between innocence and crime, grace and sin. In essence, *the pervert commits the crimes God himself cannot allow himself to commit,* thereby offering up to God the guilty substance which he may then elevate through his miraculous gift of grace.

In addition to its moral-theological dimension, Gilles's testimony reveals that an important aesthetic aspect featured within his particular perverse dynamic. Indeed, Gilles was nothing if not an artist of horror: He manipulated the bodies of his victims as if they were works of art in a museum of cruelty. As part of his sadistic ritual, for example, Gilles would suspend the young corpses from poles and hooks in various poses with the aid of ropes and straps, and then proceed to mutilate the bodies with daggers and knives while they were still suspended, most often finally bringing the bloody drama to a close by eviscerating or decapitating them. Gilles's cohort Henriet claimed that these latter torments, generally occurring after the properly sexual forms of abuse, provided his master with the greatest pleasure, greater even than that of ejaculating onto the bellies of his victims (231).

Once the children were dead, the criminal would caress their corpses, "offering for contemplation," in the words of the trial documents, "those who had the most beautiful heads and members" (190, TM). This passage is a truly crucial one, and Richard Robinson's misleading translation provides an inaccurate depiction of the aesthetic dynamic at work in the performance of Gilles's crimes. Klossowski's translation from the Latin clearly indicates that Gilles gave for contemplation the bodies of the dead children (*il les donnait à contempler*), which Robinson fails to render in his phrase "he gave way to contemplating" (190). What the English misses are the elements of passivity and oblation inherent in Gilles's action—the fact that the bodies are, very precisely, *offered up for the aesthetic enjoyment of the Other.* It is not properly speaking Gilles who enjoys the beauty of the corpses; rather, they are given over as objects of sacrifice to an eternal and perfect being, God or Devil, each of whom performs, of course, exactly the same function within Gilles's psychical economy.

The counterintuitive quality of Gilles's perception of beauty in the gruesome spectacle of bloody corpses can be illuminated with reference to this crucial element of the logic of perversion: The object of sacrifice must function to signify both the wounding of the Other which makes reparation necessary, and the results of this reparation. In other words, on one level the corpses function as metaphors for the evil of the fallen human world, for God's failure to incarnate his perfection in the earthly sphere; on the other, however, by almost invariably choosing prepubescent boys as his victims, Gilles is able to capture a moment of seeming corporeal wholeness and beauty after the body is set free from its maternal dependency, but before the traits of sexuality, and hence the psyche's fundamental dependence on the Other, are made manifest. In this way the boys' gruesomely arranged corpses serve to represent for Gilles and his diabolical God a complete cycle of degeneration and redemption seemingly sufficient unto itself, and thereby exempt from the painful consequences of castration, one of which is of course the natural cycle of life and death.

It now remains for us to determine how the Inquisition succeeded in taking advantage of the strange complicity between Gilles's perverse moral self-justification and the trial audience's hysterical identification with his innocence. Clearly, Gilles's eventual execution at the stake for his crimes evinces the danger he posed to the church's moral and political authority. But the apparent facility with which Gilles was reincorporated into the church after his brief excommunication, and later laid to rest on the property of a Nantes church, bears witness to the church's own investment in Gilles's criminality. Indeed, the contextual evidence suggests that the church authorities became aware of how they could benefit from Gilles's seduction of the audience at the earliest stages of the trial, and it is undoubtedly for this reason that Gilles's scandalous confession was allowed to proceed in such an unbridled way. The trial audience's fascination with Gilles discouraged any critical effort to uncover the church's manipulation of the proceedings, to identify how the trial effectively functioned as a distraction from its appropriation of Gilles's enormous wealth. Witnessing the symbiotic interaction of Gilles's perversion with the public's hysterical identification, the church stepped in to secure the spoils derived from its manipulation of the spectacle, confident that the creation of a cult around Gilles would prevent any critical scrutiny of its actions.

Indeed, there is ample evidence to support the claim that the political elites of Brittany and the Vendée, not to mention the authorities of the Inquisition themselves, wanted Gilles dead largely for self-interested economic reasons, and that the church benefited enormously from the manner in which the public's seduction by Gilles helped to occlude the more disturbing political motivations for the trial. During the last five or six years of his life, for example, Gilles's outrageous expenditures had brought him near ruin, and it was with increasing desperation that he turned for assistance to the counsel of alchemists and the liquidation of his property. It appears eminently plausible to think that the ecclesiastical and political authorities delayed their investigation for so long after the emergence of strong incriminating evidence because they were directly profiting from Gilles's self-destruction. In particular, Jean V de Montfort, Duke of Brittany and Jean de Malestroit, Archbishop of Nantes, acquired significant portions of Gilles's property during the years leading up to the trial as they took advantage of his increasingly dire financial situation. Only when the ecclesiastical authorities had fully taken advantage of Gilles's situation did they begin to amass the evidence required for an arrest.

However, during these final years Gilles's profligacy was not entirely out of control for, likely aware that he had no descendants to whom he could bequeath his estate, he made a condition of the sale of his most strategically located castles that his right to reacquisition be recognized for a full six years after the transaction. As a result of this condition, the buyers—effectively Gilles's prosecutors—clearly developed a vested interest in Gilles's demise, since only his death or long-term incapacitation could have safeguarded their ownership of Gilles's property in the short term. In his appraisal of the trial's political stakes, Salomon Reinach suggests that Jean de Malestroit, allied to the English during the Hundred Years' War, had developed a personal vendetta against Gilles, having been arrested in the battle of Saint-Jean de Beuvron by the constable de Richemont under whom Gilles served.[35] As Michel Bataille aptly sums up, "Gilles was not beaten by judges, but by political and financial rivals."[36] Given the somewhat polemical tones of much of the criticism concerning the trial's political aspects, however, it is necessary to point out what should be obvious, namely that the identification of the political and ecclesiastical elites' interest in delaying Gilles's arrest and execution, as well as their facilitation of the strange complicity between Gilles and his confession's auditors, need not lead us to the conclusion that there was a massive conspiracy against Gilles, in other words that his trial was a hoax. Indeed, "villainous judges are perfectly capable of recognizing true crimes," as Jacques Heers correctly concludes.[37]

Viewed against the backdrop of this dark political intrigue, Gilles's gruesome, intensely disturbing articulation of his perversion, so naively and unself-consciously enunciated, acquires an unanticipated ethical dimension when juxtaposed with the manipulations of the church authorities and the astounding complicity of the trial audience. By insisting on including himself within the set of ordinary, failed moral subjects, and by refusing the Inquisition's imputation of an evil, nonhuman intentionality, Gilles disturbingly reminds us that the same subjective impasse which underlies the normal subject's libidinal economy motivated his nonetheless truly horrifying crimes. Gilles challenges us to recognize, in other words, that the line of demarcation between perversion properly speaking and desire's inherent perversity is far from absolute. The ultimate paradox of the case of Gilles de Rais might be that the confession of his perversion—the uncensored transparency of his self-delusion and morbid criminality, as well as the lucidity with which he makes available to us the perverse short-circuiting of sovereign subjectivity to which they bear witness—provides us with the tools we need to decry the disturbing cynicism of the church's and the public's investments in his crimes. Indeed, it is precisely because Gilles made so explicit the perverse logic of his crimes that it is now possible to discern how this perversion extended across the entire hypocritically corrupt social formation which surrounded him at the moment of the trial.

Chapter Three

Cleopatra's Nose

> Cleopatra's nose: Had it been shorter, the whole aspect of the world would have changed.
>
> —Blaise *Pascal, Pensées*

> A virtue absolves no one from sin— which is, as everyone knows, original.
>
> —Jacques Lacan, *Television*

Pascal's Modernity

As I suggested in the last chapter, the interimplication of the moral-theological and the properly sexual denotations of the term "perversion" was already at work in the Latin in use at the trial of Gilles de Rais, even though it seems quite clear that the trial authorities were more interested in cashing in on Gilles's crimes than in measuring the relative severity of their moral and sexual aspects. One of the features of Gilles's confession which proved most interesting for my purposes was its laying bare of a properly perverse theological system which makes of crime the most reliable path toward securing the grace of God, indeed of conforming to his presumed will. Two and a half centuries after the trial of Gilles de Rais, Pascal takes up the theological mobilization of the theme of the perverse, this time in its association with the related terms "sin" and "concupiscence" (though Pascal does indeed use the term "perversion" in *Pensées* as a rough synonym of these terms). But whereas

69

Gilles sought from his Other the guarantee of immunity from his intuitions of guilt, Pascal instead acknowledges the transcendent, inescapable quality of sin in moral life, asserting that the gulf between possible human action and a divine command which remains inscrutable is finally unbridgeable. In psychoanalytic terms, Pascal's systematic attack against an emergent Christian humanism amounts, I will suggest, to an unprecedented hystericization of the theological subject which, though of course circumscribed within a conceptuality limited by a decidedly nonsecular doctrine of belief, nonetheless decisively resists the logic of perversion at work not only in Gilles's confession, but also latently within Christian humanism itself.

Indeed, Pascal's *Pensées*, the fragmentary text which was to become a monumental apology for Christian faith, articulates a particular understanding of perversion which carries tremendous consequences for contemporary theory. Pascal's text is deeply marked by the Judeo-Christian tradition of moral thought which would have tremendous consequences for later mobilizations of perversion in the study of sexuality. Additionally, Pascal wrote at a crucial historical juncture torn apart by the mounting conflict between modern scientific epistemologies and premodern religious and mythological ones. His work voices a strident protest against one response to this crisis, namely to make obsolete matters of a transcendental or metaphysical nature through either an increasingly clamorous emphasis on fact, or a dogmatic insistence on a human rational self-sufficiency grounded on the existence of a knowable God. More specifically, Pascal distinguishes himself from the empiricist current of early-modern philosophy—Hume would be the emblematic figure in this instance—by the especially radical manner in which he posits the "fallen" condition of man, as well as by his consequent unambiguous assertion of the continued importance of the question of belief in the age of science. With respect to Cartesian rationalist dogmatism, Pascal voices his protest by declaring the irreducible opacity of the divine will, which refuses to lay reliable foundations for any claim to a rationally verifiable concept of truth.

But far from simply running against the scientific spirit of modernity, Pascal's work may in fact be viewed to consolidate the scientific revolution through its identification of the limit of the fields of both experience and reason, as well as through its insistence on the continued relevance of the question of the subject's predicament before an unknowable, alien Other. Indeed, for Pascal, the question of faith devolves from the modern subject's commitment to a properly rational interrogation of the natural world; it is only by means of the fullest activation of human rational capacities that one is able to apprehend their ultimate helplessness before the troubling, inescapable problematic of belief. In Pascal's properly religious view, this limitation must be conceived as a consequence of man's deviation from the Good of his first nature—a constitutional perversity, one could say—which he describes with reference to the three related terms of concern in this chapter: sin, concupiscence, and perversion.

Part of this chapter's work will be to qualify as tragic Pascal's simultaneous vindications of the age of science and the practice of faith through his theorization of the inherent limits of human knowledge. It will become apparent, I hope, how Pascal's desire to qualify as tragic the believer's relation to an unknowable God is a welcome corrective to Bataille's effort to link the tragic solely to the effects of a historical-ideological transition from feudalism to capitalism. Indeed, I will suggest that Pascal's idea of tragedy describes the conditions of the subject's relation to its Other in a way which anticipates the paradoxes of the superego in psychoanalysis. Pascal's plea for an acknowledgment of the effects in the human world of a supersensible absolute articulates his particular understanding of the tragedy of the human condition, firmly positioning him, as Lucien Goldmann has correctly argued, in an intellectual tradition which both hearkens back to Sophoclean tragedy and foreshadows the advent of the German idealist philosophical horizon within which Freud's psychoanalytic revolution would take place.[1]

My basic premise will therefore be that Pascalian theology presents a rigorous theory of the human condition which bears witness to the consequences of the intense hystericization of subjectivity inaugurated by Descartes, who nevertheless failed to attest to its full ramifications. By placing the theological subject before an unknowable God, Pascal recognizes that social reality must necessarily be supplemented by a frame of meaning which is beyond the subject's rational or conscious control and which has been theorized, since Marx, under the term "ideology." Through this link to that fundamental concept of Marxian political theory it becomes possible to read Pascal's work as a meditation on both the ethical and political consequences of the human subject's incapacity to reconcile itself fully with the strictures of social existence without the aid of a "distraction" or fantasy which comes to define this subject's very being. As such, Pascal's *Pensées* constitutes one of the most consequential early-modern efforts to come to terms with the inherent perversity of desire without succumbing to the logic of perversion properly speaking.

A glance at modernity's unkind treatment of Pascal's orientation will reveal how it occupies an eccentric position with respect to the dominant relativist and rationalist currents of modern thought; it will additionally serve to pinpoint the fundamental misreading which prevents many readers from appreciating Pascal's significance. Because he unconditionally defended the continued necessity in the age of science of the properly theological question of faith, it is perhaps not surprising that thinkers hostile to any notion of the precedence of a nonhuman agency have been decidedly unsympathetic to Pascal's project. Pascal was famously dismissed first as a misanthropic apologist for Christianity, and later as a philosophical and scientific genius whose brilliant potential was shattered by a conscience tormented by the burden of belief. These two reproaches—the first is Voltaire's, the second Nietzsche's—encapsulate much of the subsequent commentary on Pascal and characterize rather well the general contemporary attitude.[2] In his secular Enlightenment faith in continuous human progress, Voltaire blamed Pascal's investment in Christianity for what he considered the latter's unambiguously dark view of the human condition; Christianity "destroyed" Pascal, in Nietzsche's similar view, as it destroys all those gifted thinkers who recognize the authority of a nonfactual instance in human moral life.

In my view, however, Voltaire's and Nietzsche's familiar secularist concern with the specificity of Pascal's religious faith obfuscates the properly *conceptual* significance of the more important point about the dual and contradictory aspect of human nature as it is described in *Pensées*. For Pascal does indeed qualify man as reprehensible, but also as sublime in his capacity to dedicate himself to God and to the project of reason. From his own point of view, Pascal subscribed to Christianity because he thought it reflected, more accurately than any other religious framework, the duality inherent in the human fabric. His ideas about the nature of the human condition, in other words, determine his choice of faith, and not the other way round. Indeed, Pascal's justification of his religious faith is but one aspect of his thought which lends itself to translation into a nontheological discourse and which gives a taste of the many points in his work, some of which will be explored later in this chapter, which teeter on the edge of an acknowledged atheism. For my purposes, however, it is more germane at this point to underline that both Voltaire and Nietzsche fail to appreciate that for Pascal man is both despicable and sublime, and that it is precisely this ambiguity in his nature which defines his existential situation or, as I will prefer to develop it, the structure of his psychical predicament. Certainly, it would be difficult to deny that large segments of contemporary thought, more specifically those which subscribe in unqualified fashion to the deaths of both God and the subject, would cast Pascal's notion of faith in the shadow of naivety and superstition. In my view, however, the argument Pascal expressed in his *Pensées*, a refutation, prefiguring Kant, of skeptical ("Pyrrhonist") and rationalist-dogmatic responses to the limits of human reason and the ambiguities which ensue therefrom, informs surprisingly well a number of contemporary theoretical aporias, most notably postmodernism's hubristic positing of the end of ideology, and the related relativist and historicist reductions of the ethico-political subject to the particularities of its cultural and historical conditions.

It is in this last sense that one might go so far as to claim that Pascal, at the very dawn of the modern era, performed a theoretical maneuver which closely parallels, at modernity's twilight, that of those who attack the harbingers of ideology's end. Both strategies—that of Pascal and that, for want of a better term, of the antipostmodernists[3]— are at their most basic level characterized by a simultaneous defense and limitation of the scope of reason or science: There does indeed exist an objective, a priori or quasi–a priori network of relations (formulated as language and its structuring of the social relation for psychoanalysis, or commodity markets and systems of value for Marxism) which mediates our relation to nature and which is more or less amenable to knowledge. But this network, however necessary, is neither immutable nor fully determinative, and is therefore, in its essential historicity, subject to properly political mobilization. For his part, Pascal interrogates the human subject's relation to this sociosymbolic Other through a consideration of the Christian themes of sin and faith. Man's fallen condition, in Pascal's view, manifests itself through his fundamentally concupiscent nature: his inability, in other words, to conform his actions to the will of God, which gives rise to stubborn intuitions of guilt. Pascal presents in this fashion a view of the perversity of moral life which may be compared to Freud's evocation of the essential perversity of human desire. In both cases, the subject's grasp on experience is mediated by an impossible absolute (knowledge of God's will, the full genitalization of the drive), which imposes a perspective from which this experience appears fallen, deviant, and lacking. It is precisely this gap between the absolute and the human condition properly speaking that Pascal defines as sin; and faith describes the mode of the subject's necessary relation to that absolute, a relationship of dependence which increases in direct proportion to the vigor with which its necessity is disavowed.

In what might at first glance appear as a surprising or uncharacteristic comment, Lacan endorses in this chapter's epigraph the properly Christian formulation of the original status of human sin. In so doing Lacan implicitly hearkens back to Freud's famous formulation of the lack of adequation between the subject's intuitions of guilt and any action for which it could reasonably be held accountable. In his comment in *Télévision*, Lacan links the cult of virtue to the notion of a "Gay Science" which, from medieval Provençal troubadour poetry to Nietzsche's attack against the alleged melancholy of the tragic ethos, disavows the scandal of the unconscious through its devotion to pleasure and lightheartedness. This gay science "cannot but meet . . . the Fall, the return into sin," warns Lacan. For the subject's happiness is ultimately disturbed by its sense that this happiness exists outside of it, in an imposing Other whose enjoyment makes the subject suffer all the more harshly its lack. In Pascalian terms, our sense of our potential happiness devolves from our lost union with the divine. Indeed, "what is astonishing," concurs Lacan, is that the subject has "an idea of beatitude, an idea which is forceful enough for him to feel himself exiled from it."[4] Unlike the gay scientist, then, whose concern is to enjoy possession of this elusive sense of bliss, Lacan instead insists that such a drive for possession only exacerbates our intuitions of sin, causing happiness to appear in the Other as an obscene jouissance which only reminds us of our distance from our own elusive beatitude.

Thus, in addition to my earlier reference to Goldmann's argument about Pascal's conformity with a certain tradition of tragic thought, it becomes apparent that this conformity also brings him close—somewhat counterintuitively, perhaps—to what I wish to call the spirit of Freudian psychoanalysis. In fact, despite what we might assume would be the allergic reaction of psychoanalytic religious skepticism, articulated most memorably in Freud's *Moses and Monotheism,* to Pascal's adamant espousal of what he presented as a specifically Christian path toward faith, it is possible to show that Pascal's rigorously tragic interpretation of Christianity positions him in an ethical tradition of which psychoanalysis, if we are to subscribe to one of Lacan's central arguments, is perhaps only the most recent articulation. "The ethics of psychoanalysis," argues Lacan, "has nothing to do with speculation about prescriptions for, or the regulation of, what I have called the service of goods. Properly speaking, that ethics [of psychoanalysis] implies the dimension that is expressed in what we call the tragic sense of life."[5] Implicit in my approach to Pascal's *Pensées* will therefore be an insistence that his texts be approached conceptually—as carrying, in other words, notions which may not be reduced without remainder to the context of Christian theology in which they are articulated.[6]

Having (somewhat haphazardly) outlined the assumptions I bring to Pascal, I may now state the general argument I want to develop concerning his *Pensées.* Through his insistence on the actuality of original sin— on the persistence, within the very structure of human subjectivity, of a passionate, irrational force which always and necessarily constitutes the frame of our reality, which in fact determines, as expressed in the fragment on Cleopatra's nose, the very course of human history—Pascal elaborated a profoundly paradoxical theory of the subject. This theory challenges us to recognize without affirming an inherent perversity within ourselves and calls us to appear, divested of our alibis and excuses, before the instance of a final judgment, albeit one which fails to articulate itself in positive, determinate terms. For what, I am finally led to ask, is Pascal's otherwise incomprehensible reference to Cleopatra's nose but a rigorous anticipation of what psychoanalysis would eventually formulate as the "partial object": that object which sustains our desire, causes our very will to live, while at the same time decisively perverting desire's capacity to conform to any Good—sexual, moral or otherwise? Within the terms of our fallen world, Pascal's evocation of a "barred," unknowable deity forces us to recognize desire's constitutive deviation, thereby proffering to us the challenge of a worldly act of faith unsupported by any claim of reason, by any determinate criterion available to knowledge.

The Tragic Absolute

In his classic but neglected study *The Hidden God,* Lucien Goldmann offers a landmark reappraisal of Pascal's thought, situating him in a tragic tradition which attempts heroically to salvage the subject's sovereignty from full rational or empirical determination. Goldmann begins by situating Pascal's work against the background of its seventeenth-century French context, a context dominated by two philosophical traditions: first, a Cartesian rationalist dogmatism which grounds knowledge of the natural world on the basis of positive knowledge of God; and second, an empiricist-skeptical Pyrrhonism—of which Montaigne, for Pascal, was the emblematic figure—which dismisses the legitimacy of any claim to truth not based exclusively on the evidence of experience. Pascal's work represents for Goldmann the turning point in Western thought from "rationalist or empiricist atomism," which he characterizes as the "ideologies" against which Pascal reacted, to what he calls "dialectical thought," a tradition later leading to Kant and Hegel, Marx and Lukàcs (5).[7] We recall that Descartes' initial radical doubt concerning the reliability of sense perception is ultimately assuaged through his notion of a knowable God who renders the natural world accessible to scientific knowledge; the human rational faculty underwritten by God is both unchanging and limitless. Anticipating today's so-called post-epistemology, Montaigne for his part radically distinguishes the category of truth from experience, declaring the underlying perspectivism of knowledge and divesting faith of any association whatsoever with reason; though skeptical empiricism deprives reason of its divine guarantee, it inaugurates a fragmentary, hermetic subjective experience without a formal organization or structure accessible to knowledge. By canceling any perspective from which it could be negated, both the rationalist and the empiricist endorse the natural order of things. The rationalist posits a natural world adequate to God's intention and therefore transparent to human knowledge; the Pyrrhonist renders experience immanent by isolating it from anything outside itself, from anything of the order of a structure or a whole.

In stark contrast to these two contrary but logically similar formulations, the tragic perspective, as Goldmann formulates it, asserts that the human world is separated by an unbridgeable chasm from the divine, a sphere for which the subject has an innate idea but no positive knowledge. This separation makes possible the negation of the natural order—the status quo—on the basis that it fails to reflect divine perfection, that it in fact negates or transgresses the will of God, for tragedy's firm declaration that man cannot know God does not prevent him from gaining the negative knowledge of man's estrangement from the divine. Contrary to rational dogmatism and empiricism, the tragic perspective asserts that man[8] is fundamentally incapable of making his own perspective the only one from which he views the world; he is haunted by his imperfection, by his inability to manifest a will which would reflect a transcendental intentionality fully immune to the inherent ambiguity and relativism of human experience. Though it is from this otherworldly perspective that the subject of tragedy reproaches itself for its shortcomings, it also creates the possibility of conceptualizing change, of negating the world as it exists in the name of a better, though indeterminate, futurity.

Rather than attempt to justify human imperfection with reference to man's mortal condition, tragic thought articulates the incommensurability of the human and the divine through what Goldmann calls a "radical refusal to accept this world as the only possibility and perspective" (33, TM). Whereas both rationalism and empiricist subjectivism take for granted the transparency or self-evidence of reason or experience, the tragic subject apprehends its condition as a violation of the divine principle. The tragic subject thereby qualifies its experience as an insignificant manifestation of our fallen condition, and installs a strict limit on the potential of the rational faculty. Tragic man is thus in acute disharmony with the world and with God, at odds, as it were, with his own conditions of possibility. Severed from its first nature and thrust into the media of time, space, and language which shape and limit its experience, the tragic subject has the strange capacity to reject the validity of its condition from the perspective of an absolute which is absent from all possible experience and also unknowable in its content.

In Goldmann's view, tragic thought upholds that human society cannot embody divine wholeness because within its limitations no authentic value can emerge—no value, in other words, which could be asserted unconditionally, in abstraction from its sociocultural context. But crucially, if we may derive no invariable human value from earthly experience, neither can we posit with certainty a divine one, since for tragedy the divine will remains hidden, veiled, in spite of the certainty with which we can know our distance from it. The God of tragedy offers man "no help from outside," writes Goldmann, "no guarantee of the validity of his own strength and powers of reasoning" (38). Seeking external justification for its earthly engagements, the tragic subject encounters only silence in response to its demand for clarity. Since it cannot conform its actions to the will of an Other who remains opaque, the subject must bear the consequences itself, becoming fundamentally accountable for what it chooses to do.

In stark contrast to the forgiving, humanist God who avails himself of a kind of moral accountancy with his subjects, and to whose emergence Gilles de Rais bore witness in his confession, the tragic deity is demanding and judgmental, solemnly condemning as imperfect all which pertains to the human sphere, yet withholding any promise of redemption. Though it forbids concession and compromise, this Other of tragic thought provides no means of ascertaining which actions would in fact be transgressions of its law. Here we are confronted with the fundamental paradox of a subject placed before an accusatory yet reticent God: It knows it is guilty, but it has no knowledge of the divine precept it has violated. The young Georg Lukács, whose writings constitute the most important intertext of Goldmann's theory, formulates as follows tragedy's uncompromising deity: "There is no relativity, no transition, no nuance" for the tragic God, Lukács writes. "His glance robs every event of all that is temporal and local about it"; as a result, before God "the question of value and reality loses all its meaning."[9] For tragedy the divine judgment is thus indefinite but absolute: resistant to translation into precepts or maxims, yet hostile to every appeal and limitation.

Since its early formulation in Greek culture, authentic tragic discourse has insisted upon the absolute incommensurability between human and divine worlds. From the beautiful cosmos in which man and his gods coexisted in harmony, tragedy brings humanity into a fractured world in which it has been wrested from its source, its coherence. In tragedy "the world become[s] dark and mysterious," Goldmann asserts. "The Gods no longer exist side by side with men in the same cosmic totality, and are no longer subject to the same rule of fate or the same demands of balance and moderation" (44). Notwithstanding this unqualified alienation from the divine, tragic thought postulates that humanity might in fact realize values which transcend relativity and contingency. In light of this apparent contradiction between our ambition of perfectibility and our guilt before divine perfection, tragedy expresses the necessity of a paradoxical view. The tragic subject is enjoined neither to work within the world for the recognition of absolute values, nor to abandon the world in favor of the abstractions of ideas and spirit, but rather to adopt the perspective of what Goldmann terms a "worldly refusal"—a revolt against the world within the limits of the world. Echoing Lacan's assessment of the stance of Sophocles's Antigone (which I will explore in detail in chapter 5), the subject of tragedy chooses to live within the world while negating the legitimacy of life's very terms of intelligibility. Psychoanalytically, one could say that the tragic subject inhabits the position of desire's impossible absolute as a means of acquiring a perspective unlimited by context or (self- or collective) interest. In this sense, the subject who assumes the consequences of tragedy transgresses the very limits of life itself; it refuses to take for granted the world as it is given and adopts as its perspective that which appears as impossible within the historical configuration to which it stands opposed.

Adopting this paradoxical stance as the only possible mode of authenticity or ethical viability available to humanity, the tragic view, according to Goldmann, rejects the legitimacy of the temporal horizon, making an appeal to the agency of an eternal final judgment in order not to abandon the world, but rather to save it. If the only legitimate faculty of judgment for human action is one which is both unworldly and inscrutable, the tragic subject is liberated from any form of ultimate determination, and may therefore reject the natural order of causality in favor of privileged access to a realm of indeterminate freedom. The category of causation applied to human action is set free from the limitations of imaginable possible experience; the human agent, in other words, acquires the capacity quite literally to do the unthinkable. "The unbridgeable distance," writes Goldmann, "that separates from the world the being who lives in the world without taking part in it liberates his conscience from common illusions and everyday concerns, making tragic thought and art one of the most advanced forms of realism" (56, TM).

But here it is crucial to observe that Goldmann's reference to realism is a relatively unfamiliar one, one which bears little relation to the aesthetic concerns of the nineteenth-century novel, for example. Indeed, I would suggest that his characterization of the tragic attitude as realistic benefits from a reference to the Lacanian concept of the real, defined as that which resists representation—reality—in any given historical social formation. Tragedy is a form of realism because it does not take as its term of reference reality as it is presently constituted, but rather aims at the realization of that which is excluded from the realm of possibility in that reality. In order to participate fully in the reality of the world, tragedy teaches, it is ultimately necessary to place oneself outside it, or more precisely at the point of its incoherence with itself. In the tragic paradox the subject rejects the ambiguity and confusion of the world in favor of a demand for definition and clarity. This subject must acquire knowledge of its reality's inconsistency and imperfection in order to reject them, thereby suspending itself in an uneasy state of tension between a call to incarnate absolute values and the recognition of this project's impossibility. In consequence, the subject is required to act in the absence of an objective guarantee of moral legitimacy.

In response to the irreducible ambiguity of the world, of the impossibility of deducing a criterion for right action, the tragic subject defiantly asserts its need for timeless values, absolute truths, and the synthesis of contraries, in utter existential solitude before a silent and inscrutable God. Condemning in advance the Nietzschean historicization of value, tragedy separates the Good from every possible worldly realization by confining it to a divine realm utterly beyond the reach of human knowledge. This means that the Good qua absolute must be salvaged from the wreckage of its concrete historical realizations—from the projects, in other words, of those whose work proceeds under an assumption of knowledge of this Good and what it requires of them on the level of praxis. Tragedy's divinization of the Good must therefore be distinguished from the precepts of the moral agent who would act with reference to a legitimating instance external to itself. Pascal will say, for example, that the Christian's duty is to perform the will of God; but if this will is indeterminate, if it fails to communicate itself to human knowledge, it is the subject itself who must assume sole responsibility for its acts' ethical legitimacy. Any justification which references historically available moral axioms instantaneously condemns the act as unethical.

The tragic position as Goldmann renders it must therefore be rendered with its full, paradoxical implications intact: If the object of tragedy is the realization of a Good which situates itself by definition outside the bounds of the human world's conditions of possibility, then the act which will best conform to this Good tends to make its appearance in the limited world of human experience precisely as evil. Tragedy thus distinguishes itself from a Nietzschean, postmodern ethical relativism through the particular mode of its response to the radical indeterminacy of the divine will, of the Other's desire. Where the relativist proceeds from this observation to the cynical conclusion that this Other is impossible or irrelevant, tragedy enjoins us to devote ourselves to this Other precisely at the point of its inscrutability, at the point where its presence makes itself known as absence, and where this absence grafts itself onto the real. We may now turn to Pascal to discover how his concept of sin and his discourse on faith help to rescue God from his overhastily reported death.

From Sin to Infinity

In conformity with tragic thought as outlined by Goldmann, Pascal never wavered from his notion that man may not be considered outside the frame of his paradoxical and contrary character. If we are fallen beings who are nonetheless defined by the persistence in us of the ideal remnants of a prior perfection, then no undialectical affirmation in our regard—no straightforward philosophical proposition—will accurately describe us. Pascal will say in *Pensées*, for example, that the human subject is at once the most base and sublime creature, an "imbecile worm" who nonetheless is a repository of "truth" and "pride" [*gloire*].[10] Any statement which attempts to shed light on human existence must immediately be followed by one which apparently cancels the truth claim of the first. "It is not enough," Pascal asserts, "to follow a series of harmonious qualities without reconciling contrary ones" (193, TM).

It is possible to deliver abundant evidence of this premise. We are, in Pascal's view, at once "credulous and incredulous" (37), spiritual and material (21), imaginary and real (45), passionate and dutiful (33), rational and intuitive (79). When we closely examine each of Pascal's formulations of our contrariety, however, we notice that the attributes making up each pair are not both located on the same level of determination; our potential for virtue, in other words, does not oppose the evidence of our failings symmetrically. Pascal claims, for example, that we are endowed with "a nature capable of good," yet this nature is nonetheless "empty" of positive content (111, TM). In contrast to the self-evidence of its distance from God, then, humanity's potential for goodness requires a reference beyond experience—a suspension of disbelief or a bracketing of skepticism—before it emerges as a conceivable possibility within the human sphere. Though all we need to do is look around for examples of human sin, we need a faculty other than that of observation, Pascal argues, to apprehend the potential for virtue. In this way Pascal acknowledges that a strictly rational inquiry into the human experience will only lead to cynicism and despair; hope depends, crucially, on an act of faith which is strictly speaking unjustifiable through the claim of reason alone.

Thus, the human field is rife with manifestations of humanity's self-regard, of its desire for glory and distinction, of its drive to rise above the common mass of subjects to a position of exploitative power and material gain. When there only exists evidence of our sensuous self-interest, Pascal argues, it is possible to account for the possibility of human perfectibility only if it is presupposed that we are fallen, more specifically that we fell from a state of felicity and truth to one of sin and falsehood. "If man had always been corrupted," Pascal argues, "he would have no idea of truth nor of beatitude" (121, TM). Our very ability to conceive of truth and beatitude requires us to hypothesize a state of perfection when the path of reason led to certainty of God's existence. For Pascal, then, the persistence within the human species of a horizon which extends beyond known experience bears witness both to our corrupted nature as well as to the desire to at least partially close the distance between the human and the divine. Thus, the idea of a transcendental instance makes us aware of our guilt and instills in us a desire for redemption.

Now what is most suggestive about Pascal's formulation—what constitutes, you might say, the originality of his idea of original sin—is that sin does not remain cloaked in the darkness of a temporally conceived human prehistory, thereby absolving us of responsibility for it because relegated to a distant, historical past. The Jesuitical tradition to which Pascalian theology is polemically opposed advanced interpretations of the Biblical myth which assert precisely such a historical relation between the original crime and our guilt. In this view, Adam's sin is separated from us by time, and thus it is absurd to think that we could be in any way responsible for its occurrence. But from a Pascalian perspective, casuistry is in its essence a frantic, even obsessive attempt at moral rationalization which seeks a futile escape from the ultimately irrational quality of sin. Thus Pascal insists that original sin transcends temporality, that it insinuates itself into consciousness in the present in utter disregard for our moral self-conceptions.[11] Guilt, in other words, cannot be traced to a historical cause, to an empirical event. For Pascal, the primordial sin which causes human guilt is a kind of hypothesis, in itself thoroughly irrational, nevertheless made necessary by the application of man's innate capacity for reason.

In this peculiar fashion Pascal treats Adam and Eve's misdeed as a mythological rather than historical event. Because original sin did not occur in historical time, it is free to become a constitutive condition of every subject's consciousness in a way which exceeds the grasp of the rational faculty. Through this notion of sin's transmissibility, of its irrational reappearance at the limit of subjectivity, Pascal describes what he calls the "mystery" of human guilt. "It is beyond doubt," he explains, "that there is nothing which more shocks our reason than to say that the sin of the first man has rendered guilty those who, being so removed from this source, seem incapable of participation in it" (121). Pascal's notion of sin is therefore tragic in this precise sense: It radically resists rational justification, remains indifferent to all protestations of innocence. In itself inassimilable to reason, guilt—and the original sin which causes it—is nonetheless reason's necessary, unreasonable consequence, its unavoidable, foundational scandal.

Now readers of the psychoanalytic persuasion may detect in Pascal's formulation of original sin a paradoxical echo *avant la lettre* of Freud's *Totem and Taboo*. The ridiculous notion that the primal father's murder occurred in some ambiguous, "primaeval"[12] temporality does not mitigate the fact that it makes me responsible, that I can trace my guilt directly to the perpetration of the original crime. Describing, with reference to civilization's foundational murder, the conceptual status of the subject's guilt, Freud offers in odd but striking terms a version of Pascal's notion of sin's transmissibility. "The sense of guilt for an action," Freud writes, "persist[s] for many thousands of years and remain[s] operative in generations which can have had no knowledge of that action."[13] Guilt acts in us as though it had an empirical cause, as if there were some actual misdeed of which it emerged as an effect. Yet this crime is simply not available to conscious knowledge.

Crucially, Freud offers support for his theory of guilt, along with its properly metaphysical origin, by distinguishing psychical from historical or empirical levels of causality. "What lie behind the sense of guilt of neurotics," he contends, "are always *psychical* realities and never *factual* ones."[14] In Freud's formulation we happen upon an explanation for the mythological placement of sin outside historical time, one which closely parallels Pascal's. The neurotic's irrationalism, according to Freud, causes him or her to assign historical status to a crime which actually took place in unconscious fantasy. For both Freud and Pascal, a sense of guilt for the primordial crime is a condition of possibility of subjectivity as such. As was quite clearly the case in Gilles de Rais' confession, no protestation of innocence, no matter how reasoned, will suffice to eradicate the traces of sin from the subject who remains guilty in spite of its attempts to absolve itself. Indeed, Pascal and Freud each asserts in his own way that the sense of guilt increases in proportion to the zeal with which we actively seek absolution.[15] An axiom describing the counterintuitive agency of the superego emerges: The more we attempt to disavow unconscious guilt, the more we suffer its painful accusations.

Unheeding of the apparent preposterousness of his assertion, Pascal persists in his desire to assert sin's inherent capacity to float above the contingencies of history, violating the mode of causality which regulates events in the natural world. Indeed, Pascal clearly wishes to shock his reader with the scandal of original sin, for he claims that it is not only "impossible," but also radically "unjust" as well (121). Choosing perhaps the most provocative example possible (this is at any rate surely the case today given our characteristic fetishization of childhood innocence), Pascal insists that we must ascribe guilt even to an infant, a subject whose utter dependence would presumably render it innocent of will. Pascal's uncompromising insistence on its transhistorical universality establishes that sin, from the point of view of the subject, is before experience. We are guilty before we act, before our will leads us to intervene in the world. Despite the sharply counterintuitive quality of his premise, Pascal insists that our denial of this "most incomprehensible of all" mysteries makes man more incomprehensible to himself than the mystery is incomprehensible to man (121).

Due to this stubborn insistence of guilt, man may never rejoin his first nature. Yet Pascal asserts that through his awareness of guilt he can presuppose his grace and devote himself to the will of God. But what exactly is God for Pascal? And how does he attempt to explain the paradox of an ethical autonomy achieved through devotion to the will of a divinity he defines precisely through its inscrutability? Further, to voice a concern which is bound to come up given the contemporary ethos, is it not necessary to wonder if Pascal's formulation of the perversity of concupiscence reiterates the guilty Christian association of pleasure with sin, thereby participating surreptitiously in the superegoic logic brought to evidence by my reference to Freud?

Perhaps the most crucial manner in which Pascal explains the inevitability of paradox in the contemplation of the human condition is through his development of the theme of the two infinities. It is also through this theme that Pascal mathematically explores the ambiguous possibility of God's dissimulated being, and that we—Pascal's readers—will be able to shed more light not only on his theory of an ethical agency based on faith, but also on the function of the concept "God" which supports it. According to *Pensées*, nature simply surpasses the capacities of human reason. Writing in the century of the formulation of infinitesimal calculus, the invention of increasingly sophisticated experimental tools for magnification, and the consolidation of astronomical heliocentrism, Pascal was aware that nature is both infinitely large and infinitely small, extending from the far reaches of a galaxy we cannot begin to conceptualize to the microscopic particles of matter which exert a similar pressure on human ideas. When we extend our conceptions "beyond all imaginable space," according to Pascal, we "only produce atoms" which fail to comprehend "the reality of things" (16). Even the deployment of a concept of infinity, Pascal clearly realized, fails to make nature fully knowable to man.

Placed on the scale of these two infinities, humanity appears in all its vulnerability and insignificance as a lost species deprived of any reliable coordinates or verifiable principles with which it could orient itself in space and time. But man is not simply lost in nature; he is also alienated from it. For Pascal, humanity is in essence subtracted from nature and placed in opposition to it, in fact violating its laws. Here we stumble across a fundamental nuance of Pascal's basic claim about humanity's concupiscent kernel. In addition to being cast adrift between two limitless, immeasurable magnitudes, he inhabits a corner of the world "turned away from nature" (17, TM); our very spatiotemporal location is set apart from the natural ways of the world. From this understanding of nature's indifference to humanity's effort to explain its existence to itself, Pascal advances to an ethical invocation. If we cannot derive principles which would produce knowledge adequate to nature, then we must content ourselves with knowledge of our limits. This is the significance of Pascal's central and paradoxical notion of the interdependence of our sublimity and abjection, our *grandeur et misère*: We become closer to God only through the knowledge of our distance from the divine. As a result, humanity must renounce its search for "certainty and stability" (20) in favor of an acceptance of and inquiry into its inherently mediate character. Thus, for Pascal, nature is unified, indivisible, self-sufficient, present to itself, lacking nothing; man, in contrast, is fundamentally dependent on space, time, movement, elements, and energy. Jettisoned from nature, man is inserted into media which separate him from God and from himself.

Consequently, the engagement of man with nature gives rise to a set of relations in which all the elements of nature are interrelated through their common link to "a natural and insensible point," namely the absolute point of the divine reconciliation of contraries. From this standpoint Pascal concludes—foreshadowing in general conceptual terms the dialectical thought of subsequent centuries as well as, more concretely, Marx's concepts of the mode of production and the labor theory of value—that it is possible neither "to know the parts without knowing the whole," nor to know the whole without knowing the parts (20, TM). All the elements of nature, in other words, in addition to their multiple relations with one another, are also linked with an absolute, to an unobservable principle which constitutes their totality. If one were to acquire knowledge of this principle, one might think, one would seize upon the totality of knowledge of nature. In Pascal's view, however, the nature of the whole, in other words the point at which contraries reconcile themselves into unities, is itself unknowable, since it identifies the locus of God, a being whom Pascal famously characterized as *absconditus*, as missing from man's field of vision. Thus, the principle of nature's organization is efficient yet invisible: We know there must be a cause for the order of nature, yet we are unable to qualify this cause, to reconcile it with our understanding; neither are we able to locate it within the realm of human experience.

Pascal offers two mathematical examples to illustrate how reason inevitably falls into contradiction with itself whenever it attempts to provide an adequate understanding of the being of nature. The elements which constitute time, space, and numbers—the elements of Pascal's ontology—place themselves in a series, one after the other, constituting as such an infinite progression, a sequence without a final term. When we represent time to ourselves, for example, we imagine a continuous line extending beyond the horizon, a line devoid of a final point. In spite of time's apparent lack of limit, however, Pascal insists that "there is nothing in all of this that is infinite or eternal" (36, TM). Pascal means that, when considered individually, there are only finite terms in an infinite series. It is clear, for example, that we can only conceive of time as a series of discrete moments; in order to be measured, time must be subdivided into determinate segments. Analytically, however, the concept of time does not feature a final term; time therefore betrays a latent eternity which resists reason's ambition to measure it. Pascal argues that an infinite sequence of finite entities such as the human conception of time necessarily depends on an infinite factor which never appears as such in the sequence. Pascal writes, for example, that only "the number that multiplies" these "finite realities" is truly infinite (37). The factor which constitutes the infinite magnitude does not itself appear within the temporal series of moments; time needs to refer to something outside itself in order to constitute itself as a totality or continuity, in other words to bridge the gap between duration—the natural experience of time—and our capacity to take account of it by means of concepts. For Pascal, the paradox of time is another manifestation of man's distance from God: how man is reliant on mediated representations which denature his existence *in* nature.

Pascal takes up a second, related mathematical example, that of numbers, as a further indication of the "sinful" distance which alienates man from a nature which resists full translation into knowledge. We know, Pascal asserts, that infinity exists because we know that numbers are not finite; it is always possible to add another numeral to a sequence.

If we know that infinity exists, however, we do not know what this infinity is in its "nature" or quantity. Because the addition of a unit to infinity does not increase infinity in its nature, we cannot say that the numerical value of infinity is either even or odd; therefore it appears not to have a determinate quantity (65). At the same time, infinity considered as a quantity must have a definite value if it contains nothing other than a series of integers. Consequently, infinity must be, yet cannot be, a number; must have, yet cannot have, a definite value. Mathematics has of course come a long way since Pascal, and it is now taken for granted that there exists a multiplicity of quantitatively distinct infinities. Yet I would suggest that Pascal's reasoning features a remarkably precocious mathematical intuition which recognizes that even though an infinite multiplicity may become an object of mathematical thought, it remains conceptually vulnerable due to the fact that the procedure of counting is haunted by a contradiction—a conceptual void—which threatens to appear within the realm of presentation of which it is supposed to take account, thereby throwing the count into nondenumerable chaos.

Here it becomes possible to shed more light on the significance of God in Pascal's mathematical conceptuality. Indeed, I would contend that it is not at all preposterous to suggest that Pascal's development of the spiritual or divine infinity features an intuition which anticipates the advent of post-Cantorean set theory. This theory marked a significant revolution in mathematical thought by inaugurating a theory of counting which, by restricting itself to multiples, does not rely upon the latent unicity of the concept of number ("the One"). What Pascal makes clear is that he distinguishes the infinite quality of God from the properly numerical infinity he also evokes. Whereas man can gain knowledge of the existence, but not the nature, of the numerical infinity, he may gain positive knowledge neither of the existence, nor of the nature, of God. More precisely, Pascal states that because God has neither parts nor limits, "we are ... incapable of knowing either what He is or if He is" (66); God is knowable neither in his nature nor in his being.

Pascal's distinction between a divisible, numerical infinity and an indivisible divine one echoes the set-theoretical distinction between inclusion and belonging. Although it is not possible for me to detail this point here, suffice it to say that a structure of presentation, according to set theory, must be redoubled in order to achieve consistency. Because the process of counting the presentation of multiples cannot prevent the emergence of a void which, if presented, would render the presentation incoherent, a second metastructure must be installed in which the process of counting is itself accounted for. At this second level of representation the inconsistent multiples which evaded the count at the level of the presentation may be assembled into subsets, which has the paradoxical consequence that a set's set of subsets exceeds in quantity its terms or elements.[16] In this way, inconsistency becomes the underlying feature, indeed the very condition, of presentation, which is forced to contain, at a second moment of structuration, the emergence of a chaotic void through the assembly of the inconsistent multiples into subsets or parts. The cost of this metastructuring operation, however, is a radical disjunction between the two structures or systems of counting, the second of which is always in excess of the first.

What is significant here is that a continuity may be discerned from Pascal's decision to attribute the name "God" to a kind of indivisible mathematical real at which human rationality encounters a conceptual aporia, and the more sophisticated attempt of contemporary mathematical theories which appear capable of providing consistent accounts of increasingly complex multiplicities only at the cost of producing an excess over themselves in the form of a redoubled counting procedure giving rise to a subset of parts greater than the whole. It becomes apparent in this way that the dialectical contradiction Pascal began to identify within human rationality's ambition to bring nature under a conceptual system still challenges mathematical speculation to this day. In its mathematical mode, "God" names the inherent contradiction of human rational initiative, the point at which human concepts miss the real of nature by producing too few or too many elements or parts. In sum, then, Pascal's figure of the mathematical God further underscores the limitations of human reason and therefore the necessity for a supplement of faith which allows us to resist sinking into despondency before the massive evidence of our impotence. If human reason, fallen into concupiscence from the divine, fails to deliver a model of nature amenable to a knowable, noncontradictory principle of totalization, then the subject is forced to act on faith that such a totality exists in order to act at all. We may now turn to Pascal's evocation of the paradoxical necessity of faith as outlined in his celebrated discussion of the so-called wager.

Ideological State Automatons

In the wager fragment Pascal imagines a theological dialogue with an interlocutor whom he gives himself the task of converting to Christian belief. A long tradition of Pascal scholarship has identified this interlocutor as the seventeenth-century French erudite libertine, the freethinking, atheist Epicurean skeptic of ancien régime culture, nourished by readings of Pierre Gassendi, who disparages the epistemological claims of reason by advancing sense experience as the only legitimate foundation for knowledge, and pleasure as the only admissible motivation for action. When the text is carefully examined, however, it becomes apparent that Pascal's interlocutor does not flatly deny the existence of God. He states, rather, that he truly wants to believe, only his "hands are tied" and his "mouth is mute" (68, TM); the so-called libertine does not believe simply because he cannot bring himself to. Consequently, it becomes necessary to refine the depiction of Pascal's partner in dialogue, who distinguishes himself from the properly atheist libertine—who negates the possibility of a transcendent order, thereby deciding that God does not exist and assuming the consequences—in his ambivalent adoption of agnosticism: "The true course is not to wager at all," he offers (66).

Pascal's interlocutor knows that he should believe but, since he cannot, he disavows the necessity of the forced choice imposed by the question of belief as a means of evading the metaphysical anxiety initially experienced by those who confront it head on. In psychoanalytic terms, Pascal's narrative persona effectively diagnoses his interlocutor's reluctance as a form of hysteria: "You complain," he tells him, "that [the Christians] do not prove [their faith (créance, which can also mean "debt")]" (66). Pascal's response uncovers how the interlocutor's agnosticism features a latent demand for verifiable evidence of God's existence, for a proof upon which he could rationally ground his faith. A God so weak that he is unable to make himself tangible to human reason does not deserve the investment of faith. Thus, the crucial paradox of the libertine's ambivalence devolves from agnosticism's latent belief in a full, potent deity, one who could manifest a determinate will after which the believer could fashion his actions. Revealing the rather fine line between radical Jansenism and outright atheism, elements of Pascal's work suggest that he entertained a certain backhanded respect for the die-hard atheist, who has the merit of recognizing with Pascal that the question of God's existence, which cannot be decided through the exercise of reason, nevertheless requires an answer one way or the other. "Yes," Pascal responds in acknowledgment of his interlocutor's ambivalence, "but you must wager; it is not optional, you are already on board [*embarqué*]" (66, TM). In this way Pascal uncovers how the superficially rational agnostic alternative presupposes a theological certainty which reason strictly disallows.

As the influential modern theorists of ideology have discovered, Pascal's refutation of agnosticism makes the wager fragment something more consequential than a merely irrational apology either for faith in general or for Christian faith in particular. Indeed, Pascal's insights on faith have tremendous ramifications for the theory of ideology. Louis

Althusser, for one, famously identified in Pascal's fragment an articulation in embryo of his critique of idealism in ideological theory. We recall that Althusser disparagingly calls "idealist" all those theories which claim that the subject acts in accordance with his ideas. "The ideology of ideology," for Althusser, upholds that a "'subject' endowed with a 'consciousness' . . . must 'act according to his ideas,' [and] must therefore inscribe his own ideas as a free subject in the actions of his material practice."[17] The scare quotes underscore Althusser's emphatic attack against the voluntarist liberal humanism which supports the notion of a subject capable of translating its own ideas into conscious intentions which may then straightforwardly be realized in concrete action. Althusser credits Pascal with what he calls a "wonderful formula" which allows one "to invert the order" of this "notional schema of ideology."[18] The idea does not produce the action, but vice versa: "Pascal says, more or less: 'Kneel down, move your lips in prayer, and you will believe.'" The reference to Pascal allows Althusser to illustrate his notion that our ideas are aftereffects of the material practices we conduct through the rituals which the ideological state apparatus suggests to us through the mechanism of interpellation. Gone is the premise of a self-conscious agent who freely conjures an ideational framework which then guides its actions; we are left instead with a subject subjected to ideology, a subject whose very actions are caused by its self-recognition as ideology's addressee.

Althusser should clearly be credited with ridding the theory of ideology of its naive, politically problematic individualism by emphasizing the link between socioeconomic structures and the interests expressed through the mechanism of interpellation. I wish to suggest, however, that Pascal's account of the subject of faith is more complex and ambiguous than Althusser's notion of an ideological subject straightforwardly materialized through practice would have us think. For in his desire to jettison the liberal-humanist baggage of ideology's ideology, Althusser loses sight of the distance the subject of ideology tends to maintain with respect to its interpellation which, in order to succeed, must paradoxically partially fail. Indeed, when we read Pascal rigorously, we are obliged to acknowledge that the believer, as he is described in *Pensées*, never actually believes; or rather, more accurately, the believer acts *as if* he believes, and this element of pretension retroactively constitutes belief as such. Acting "as if" one believes, for Pascal, produces the illusion of belief in itself. On account of what Pascal calls the "automaton" (discussed further below), namely its tendency to act unconsciously on the basis of habit or convention, the subject is not inclined to believe in a natural, unmediated or un-self-reflexive fashion. To take up the canonical Pascalian example, after we tell ourselves to kneel down in prayer (or else unthinkingly follow the lead of everyone around us), we note that belief must have caused our course of action. Yet when the next occasion for prayer presents itself, we find ourselves in exactly the same position of having either to perform the appearance or belief, or else to allow an unthinking allegiance to custom to determine our behavior.

When his interlocutor protests that he is unable to make himself believe, Pascal counsels the would-be convert to learn from former agnostics who now assume the wager's risk. In *The Hidden God*, Lucien Goldmann argues that Pascal here insinuates that even he himself must wager; faith is impossible, in other words, in the absence of a prior wager. "The expressions 'to wager' and 'to believe' become synonyms," Goldmann asserts, "and it is no longer a question of separating the wager 'written for the libertine' from the faith of the Christian who does not need to wager."[19] Some of Pascal's readers may wish to object that Goldmann's statement is too strong, that there clearly exist subjects, including perhaps Pascal himself, for whom belief, and the rituals which support it, "come naturally." Yet I agree with Goldmann that the underlying point of Pascal's discussion of faith is that any attempt to distinguish between an organic, unmediated, mystical faith (in a Pascalian "hidden God," that is) and one which emerges as a result of a certain self-discipline is extremely vulnerable. For the majority of subjects who acknowledge the legitimate powers of reason (and Pascal wants us to recognize those powers), the moment of belief in itself is never experienced properly speaking; it may only be posited after the fact, as a cause which in the moment required a suspension of disbelief. In this precise sense belief is not material in the way Althusser wishes to argue. Thus, in contrast to Pascal's subject of faith, Althusser's subject of ideology does not feature the proto-Freudian *Spaltung* which characterizes Pascal's believer, who requires a kind of supplement of self-discipline in order to act consciously, in other words in consequence of something other than mere habit or sensuous inclination. Althusser's subject appears fully and completely through its ideological interpellation, thereby requiring no repression of skepticism in order to believe. Counterintuitively, in today's so-called postideological world of cynicism and despondency, in which genuine belief is precisely what appears most impossible, Pascal's seemingly outdated discourse on Christian faith appears much more persuasive and à propos than Althusser's more contemporary, quasi-Foucauldian evocation of ideology's redoubtable and effective power.

Indeed, in his evocation of the ideological apparatus, Althusser everywhere emphasizes a properly passive and determinate concept of "subject." Through the operation of recognition in response to ideology's address, his subject appears as its realization, as the concrete, material embodiment of ideological control. In spite of its structuralist-antihumanist posturings, then, Althusser posits a decidedly humanist brand of intersubjectivity—of successful, albeit one-way, communication—between the ideological apparatus and the subject it hails. It is thus not surprising that in his discussion of religion Althusser states that the "interpellation of individuals as subjects presupposes the 'existence' of a Unique and central Other Subject, in whose name the religious ideology interpellates all individuals as subjects" (179). Immediately thereafter, he alludes to the Hebrew God's famous declaration to Moses "I am that I am," which serves as an example illustrating the identity of the agency which issues ideology's address.

Through this example Althusser asserts the fundamentally religious (as opposed to spiritual in Pascal's sense) quality of the operation of ideology as such, whose concept depends on the assumption of an "unbarred" Subject—an "Other of the Other" in Lacan's terms—upon whom the subject of ideology relies. For Althusser, the Other from whom ideological hailing issues forth has a name, a determinate identity; the condition of the ideological subject's self-identification within ideology is that it already recognizes its Other as a knowable entity with a determinate message. Althusser here takes for granted the consistency of this Other, its ability to communicate to the subject, who then fully recognizes itself in its message. For Pascal, in contrast, the drama of subjectivity is fundamentally a function of the traumatic opacity of the will of God, whose message refuses to avail itself of communication or interpretation. The Althusserian ideological subject's unproblematic self-recognition in the Other's address is precisely what evades the Pascalian subject, who always fails in its struggle to elicit from its God an ideology to which it could comfortably conform. Only the believer (and the atheist, though Pascal of course does not explicitly admit to this) has the courage to face the consequences of God's distressing silence. From the perspective of psychoanalysis, then, it becomes apparent through Pascal how Althusser's concept of ideology is not rigorously equivalent to what Pascal refers to as belief or faith. Althusser's "ideological interpellation of the subject" is more akin to what Pascal describes as the unthinking, ritualistic behavior which arises not from the Christian believer who subsumes his will under God's, but rather from the agnostic, whose actions are determined by a latent demand that God appear and tell him what to do.

This cynical ambivalence which presents itself at first glance as the easiest and most rational response to subjectivity's metaphysical trauma precisely corresponds in Pascal's thought to the conflict between the spiritual potentialities of faith and the force of what he calls the "automaton" (*l'automate*). This concept also foreshadows in a truly uncanny way Freud's development of the agency of the unconscious. The automaton is yet another concept which allows Pascal to think through the consequences of an imperfect human rationality. More precisely, in the automaton Pascal identifies a force in psychic life outside the bounds of consciousness which is resistant to any form of rational persuasion; it is a kernel of perversity in human desire which rebels against the ambitions of conscious control and sabotages the agnostic's desire to believe. "We are as much automatons as spiritual beings," Pascal asserts (73). Crucially (and surely counterintuitively), Pascal argues that it is only "custom"—by which he means a sincere, unironic conformity to social norms—and not reason, which is capable of reigning in the effects of automatism. Custom "is the source of our strongest . . . proofs," Pascal writes, and it "commands the automaton, which persuades the mind without its thinking about the matter" (73, TM). The work of faith is therefore to eliminate the impasse of agnostic subjectivity, which is split between an automatic, unconscious demand for a fully revealed God, and a rationalist despair occasioned by this revelation's failure. "When we believe only through the force of conviction, and when the automaton is inclined to believe the contrary, it is not enough," insists Pascal. "It is thus necessary to make both of our parts believe: the spirit, through reason, which it suffices to have seen once in one's lifetime; and the automaton, through custom, by refusing to allow it to tend toward its contrary" (73).

Pascal's intimation in this passage of a connection between reason and faith, which he elsewhere flatly denies, is linked to the final portion of the wager fragment, in which Pascal's narrative persona indulges in a kind of metaphysical accountancy which convolutedly bases the wager's rationalism on the incommensurability between the infinite rewards of the afterlife and the finite pleasures of earthly existence. Though it could be argued that even this rationalization depends on a belief in life's infinity which is strictly speaking nonrational, Pascal can be reproached for some inconsistency here. Still, for my purposes the crucial point is that the automaton requires a continual expenditure of psychical energy to bend to the exigencies of faith, and this occurs not through transgression or rebellion, but through conformism. It becomes clear, in other words, that the act of faith depends upon an exercise of will.

This is where the full paradox of Pascal's reference to custom becomes most apparent, I would suggest; it is also where it becomes possible to distinguish categorically between the Pascalian evocation of Christian zeal and the perversion, understood in the strong structural sense I have evoked, of fundamentalist passion. For Pascal ultimately suggests that the automaton, when left to its own devices, fosters a kind of double-mindedness which combines an outward conformity with current customs and practices with the subterranean, unconscious pleasures of the automaton. "When we believe only through the force of conviction, and the automaton is inclined to think the opposite, it is not enough," Pascal writes (74).[20] In other words, the automaton establishes a relation of complicity between an appearance of conformity and obedience of the law, and a hidden, disavowed indulgence in transgression. In contrast, making the effort to believe in law or custom has the paradoxical effect of manifesting the law's injustice. As Pascal's biographical life ably demonstrates, this acceptance does not, as one might expect, lead toward an acquiescent attitude in relation to temporal authority (in Pascal's case, the Jesuitical theological hegemony within the church apparatus).[21] In essence, then, Pascal's imperative of faith implies both a full activation of human rational capacities and a recognition of their tragic imperfection: Reason prevents us from presupposing the consistency of the Other, stops us from positing a God whose knowable will could exempt us from the final judgment, and whose promise could provide a guarantee of otherworldly bliss. But because reason unveils the traumatic possibility of freedom, in other words the truth that the Other does not exist, we require the supplement that the act of faith provides, a regime of willful self-discipline permitting us to muster the courage to act in a world which offers no guarantees.

A Distracted Dialectic

Though the automaton concept allows him to thematize that element of subjectivity which thwarts the hegemony of reason, it is rather through his dialectic of *divertissement*, or distraction, that Pascal evokes most clearly the logical essence of the ethical invocation emerging from his formulation of Christianity's subject of faith. In yet another anticipation of the Freudian ethos, distraction echoes the function of fantasy in psychoanalysis: Severed by the structure of language from its mythical source of primary satisfaction, the speaking subject, under the principle of pleasure, installs an object of fantasy in its place. In general terms distraction is a modality of the general Pascalian concept of sin which, as I have suggested, anticipates the psychoanalytic notion of the essential perversity of desire. For psychoanalysis, then, the subject, by definition, desires something more that what is offered in any sociosymbolic landscape. Pascal, for his part, makes a parallel claim: Though we are weak, vulnerable creatures thrust into an indifferent natural world over which we have little control, we cannot represent the reality of this situation to ourselves without immediately losing the will to live, without succumbing to what psychoanalysis calls *aphanisis*—a "fading" of the subject resulting from the evaporation of the psychical tension which fuels desire.

Pascal argues that the subject must conjure up a distraction for itself in order to veil the trauma of its fundamentally intolerable condition. Anyone who has tarried with the difficulties of meditation, for example, will immediately appreciate this Pascalian observation: "Nothing is so insufferable to man as to be completely at rest, without passions, without occupation, without diversion, without application" (38, TM).[22] The Pascalian subject is thus unable to look upon its actual state as a dependent being destined for death without installing a goal which fleshes out its desire and provides a cause—in both senses of a "mission" and of "that which produces an effect"—for living. For Pascal, humanity is fundamentally incapable of representing to itself the conditions of its existence. A characteristically lucid analogy ensues: Our condition resembles that of a guilty prisoner locked in his cell awaiting a judgment which may condemn him to death. The prisoner will sooner distract himself through a game of piquet (a card game popular during the ancien régime) than consider the true consequences of his situation. What the prisoner simply cannot admit to himself is the fact that, momentarily, he may breathe his last breath (60). Startlingly, it should be noted here that Pascal's example comes perilously close to admitting explicitly the finality of death: The properly irrational act of faith which has the believer qualify life's temporality as infinite becomes allied with a paradoxical (and noncontradictory, from the perspective of Pascal's logic) rational assertion of life's finitude.

Human subjects thrive on conflict and tension, Pascal claims, in particular when they may observe this conflict from a safe distance. The salience of this observation extends to the very essence of the investments of contemporary culture, as everything from sensationalist courtroom television, to no-holds-barred extreme sports and talk shows, and survival-of-the-fittest (or most popular) reality programming plainly attests. Though we enjoy watching what he terms "clashes of opinions" and "struggles" between opposing groups and individuals, Pascal does not want us to assume that what draws our attention—what constitutes, in other words, the principle of suspense—is a desire to see a victor proclaimed, an argument settled. Rather, we watch, enraptured, to revel in the antagonism itself; we become invested in its prolongation, not its resolution. "We never seek things for themselves," Pascal axiomatically claims, "but for the search" (38). Human desire is not for its presumed object, but for desire itself; desire is thus a desire to desire. Indeed, Pascal's subject will go to any length to avoid a confrontation with its underlying, fundamental abjection; strangely, this subject will even jeopardize its existence, propel itself onto the precipice of death, in order to prove that it can defy its mortality.

From the vantage point of the absolute, from the other side of its condition's limits, humanity's petty preoccupations appear superfluous, crazed, lacking a link with reality. To take up again the death sentence analogy, Pascal qualifies the prisoner's inability to think about his destiny as *insensé*—mad. From one perspective, then, humanity is to be reproached for its inability to see things the way they really are. But Pascal finally refuses to chastise us for our weakness, since to do so would be tantamount to expecting the impossible. Our dependence on distraction may indeed render us ridiculous, but not as ridiculous as the Stoic philosopher, for example—or neo-Foucauldian, for that matter— who would want to "raise himself above humanity" in a deluded ambition of ascetic self-mastery or affirmative aesthetic self-stylization (43). Humanity's sinful kernel of perversity—its "insatiable cupidity," as Pascal himself puts it—is properly ineradicable (41, TM). In fact, Pascal reserves his greatest scorn for those who claim that man can master himself, that he may reconcile himself perfectly with the scandal of his destiny. Distraction is thus a properly structural element of Pascalian subjectivity; without it man prefers simply not to live. Even the absolute monarch, whose every whim and fancy is satisfied, remains miserable, Pascal claims, if he does not distract himself through "the conversation of women, war, and grand occupations" (39, TM).

Pascal provides an intriguing example to illustrate a further consequence of distraction: Morally, the human subject is characterized by its constitutive deviation from the path of a purely disinterested will. The example runs as follows: The enthusiast of moralism who would insist on demonstrating that the scholar who secludes himself to solve a problem of arithmetic acts in the name of glory, not of science, erroneously assumes, Pascal argues, that it is possible to act otherwise, that anyone is capable of dedicating his intellectual efforts purely and selflessly to the advancement of knowledge. Though this scholar for Pascal is ridiculous (though no more ridiculous, one would be required to state, than anyone else), Pascal reserves his judgment for his hypocritical denouncer, who acts not from a genuine concern for the advancement of knowledge, but simply to congratulate himself for showing that he knows the secret of the scholar's motivation. Those who exhibit such self-righteousness are "the silliest of the lot," Pascal acerbically avers (42, TM). The fault of men therefore lies not in their search for distraction, but rather in the way they conduct this search "as if the possession of the objects of their quest would make them really happy" (39). Indeed, diagnosing the emergent philosophical hyperrationalism which would come into full bloom in the subsequent century, Pascal chastises those who "think people unreasonable for spending a whole day chasing a hare they would not wish to buy" (40, TM). The lesson of distraction is not that one should attempt to divest oneself of one's object attachments, but rather to abandon the (unconscious) expectation that the object will satisfy one's desire.

We begin to discern at this point the classically dialectical structure of Pascal's argument on the topic of *divertissement*—the formal logic, as it were, supporting his claim that the dialectic of tragedy implies as its telos an undetermined, ex nihilo act of faith. I have just shown how Pascal negates his initial rationalist thesis on humanity's vanity, on its passionate dedication to inessential amusements and diversions, by claiming that it is constitutionally unable to do otherwise. We should not be surprised to discover, then, that Pascal proceeds to negate this negation, to reverse and "sublate," to use the conventional English verb form of the Hegelian term *Aufhebung*, his antithesis. Pascal accomplishes this dialectical move through a reversal of perspective which returns his analysis to its initial premise of man's vanity, only with a difference—with the addition, that is to say, of an element of paradox, a redoubled point of view which outwardly stands in contradiction with itself. Though humanity cannot be blamed for fortifying itself against the scandalous truth of its existence, it is nevertheless not beyond reproach. Or, perhaps more accurately, it cannot *not* reproach itself for its addiction to distraction.

As he does so often in *Pensées*, Pascal has recourse to the motif of two antagonistic natures, or "two contrary instincts" in this case, both of which he qualifies as "secret," to explain our inability to absolve ourselves of our failure to make the absolute perspective—God's, that is— our own. As is everywhere apparent in experience, Pascal advances, human subjects do indeed have a first "secret instinct" which "impels them to seek out distraction and occupation outside themselves" as an escape from their inner turmoil; but they also have another secret instinct which arises, so we recall, from "the grandeur of [their] original nature." So even though we learn from experience that we can only be happy after we have set ourselves a goal whose attainment will instantly dissipate that happiness, we know from our sense of our first nature that "happiness in reality consists only in rest, and not in activity [*tumulte*]." And crucially, Pascal's subject cannot make itself aware of this contradiction between its two natures, which "hides from view" at the "bottom of [its] soul" (41, TM).

In a related fragment, crystalline in its clarity, Pascal brings greater logical precision to the dialectical trajectory of his meditation on distraction by unpacking its paradoxical outcome. Though this fragment highlights the formal features of the Pascalian dialectic, it also serves as an introduction to the tragic doctrine of redemption through grace. In each step of his dialectic, Pascal makes two pronouncements: the first on man's being, the second on his "opinions"—on his ability to think his actions through rationally. At each step Pascal addresses the two natures of man: his nonempirical, divine essence or soul, in other words the absolute remnant of his first nature; and his innate but imperfect rational faculty— his opinions. Pascal's tripartite reasoning develops as follows:

Thesis: Man is vain (his "opinions are destroyed") because he values inessential things. He fails to incarnate the absolute perfection of God, and therefore his opinions are not sound.

Antithesis: Man is not vain (his "opinions are sound") because his imperfect rationality provides him with some reliable knowledge. Since man is jettisoned from the absolute of his first nature, we may not judge him from so merciless a perspective. We must approach man from the perspective of his finitude.

Synthesis: Here Pascal's own formulation is the most concise: "But we must now destroy this last proposition," he writes, "and show that it remains always true that the people are vain though their opinions are sound. For they do not sense truth where it actually lies and, placing it where it is not, they have opinions which are always very false and very unsound." (92, TM)

Each of the first two stages of the dialectic presents a judgment on people's vanity followed by a justification referencing the soundness of their ideas. Notice that Pascal incorporates into his synthetical proposition all the elements of the first two stages with the exception of the antithetical judgment. In other words, Pascal draws his synthesis by subtracting from his combination of thesis and antithesis the claim that man is not vain, a claim made from the relative perspective of the human. The terminus of the dialectic of distraction is a definite judgment (man is vain) coupled with a contradictory justification (man's opinions are both sound and unsound, depending on the adopted point of view). In sum, the only statement which is disallowed is the one which states that man is not vain: Human vanity emerges safe and sound from the operation of Pascal's logic. Pascal's judgment on man's opinions, in contrast, changes from sound to unsound as the vantage point shifts from the limited human perspective to the absolute perspective of God. In the synthesis, then, Pascal retains the ambiguity concerning the value of man's opinions, of his capacity for thought and right, rational action, while advancing a definite judgment on man's being, which remains unambiguously vain, inadequate, guilty, *perverse* before the perfection of God. Here we uncover a rigorous reinforcement of Pascal's central argument about the ineradicable quality of sin, which remains the most *certain*, unambiguous feature of the human predicament.

But what are we to conclude from Pascal's argument? For Pascal, guilt qualifies our very being: No change of perspective, no dedication to a determinate Good, will alter our irreducible culpability before God. But the same cannot be said of humanity's faculty of reason and the projects undertaken in its name. One must look upon human enterprise from two perspectives at once: It has value in that it distracts us from our contemplation of death, a contemplation which deprives existence of any significance or meaning; and its products can also provide us with material comfort and sensuous pleasure. At the same time, however, from the perspective of the absolute, people's projects appear valueless in that they necessarily fail to assert themselves without ambiguity, to provide an adequate justification for themselves before the final judgment of God. Left to its own devices, then, reason proves to be an inadequate motivator of the human subject. If man were not characterized in his essence by the remnant of his divine prehistory, then reason would allow him to undertake projects which could satisfy him, which would not leave him with a residue of guilt accusing him of failure. And Pascal is not at all ambiguous in his belief that the projects of reason, when they do manage to lead to concrete action, tend to miss the point, failing to "sense the truth where it actually is," which for the Christian Pascal is ultimately the mystery of the resurrection. Reason in itself does not indicate to the agent the full range of possibility of human action. Only grace, and the act of faith which is its condition, integrates the subject into the properly miraculous body of Christ, thereby allowing it to see beyond what is merely rationally possible.

Grace, or the Act of Faith

Pascal's decision to place the contradictory or undecidable quality of the human condition at the level of his thought and action rather than at the level of his being serves to indicate how the former bear a relation to a function of freedom—to our capacity, that is, to base our actions not on any quantifiable or qualifiable Good, but rather on the judgment of an indeterminate absolute: the will of the hidden God. As we have repeatedly witnessed, man's grandeur is for Pascal a function of the ideal remnant of his union with the divine. Though we desire to be reunited with our first nature before our fall into concupiscence, we become aware of the unbridgeable distance which separates us from the divine. This distance renders illegitimate any justification for action premised on a criterion of human reason or a notion of individual, worldly intent. In order to conform to the inscrutable will of God, the Pascalian subject is strictly forbidden to act out of any motivation other than grace. So how precisely does an act of faith caused by grace come about? What finally motivates the believer to take the risk of engaging with a dangerous, thoroughly ambiguous world, one which fails to provide the subject with any verifiable indication of what is to be done?

Perhaps the most surprising feature of the late-medieval and early-modern discourses on grace is that they are generally more concerned with the motivation, indeed the causation, of worldly human action than with the otherworldly question of eternal life. In essence, in other words, the doctrines of grace are theories of praxis. To conclude this chapter I wish to examine Pascal's comments on the problematic of grace in order to determine how he draws the consequences of his believer's devotion to an unarticulated divine will. To begin, some context: In the *Provincial Letters* Pascal offers scathing criticisms of the inherent contradictions—resulting from a violation of reason's limits—which ensue from all attempts, both Jesuitical and Thomist, to distinguish *efficient* from *sufficient* grace. The nonaligned first-person voice of the *Letters* presents the controversy as follows:

> The Jesuits maintain that there is a grace given generally to all men, subject in such a way to free-will that the will renders it efficacious or inefficacious at its pleasure, without any additional aid from God, and without wanting anything on his part in order to act effectively; and hence they term this grace *sufficient*, because it suffices of itself for action. The Jansenists, on the other hand, will not allow that any grace is actually sufficient which is not also efficacious; that is, that all those kinds of grace which do not determine the will to act effectively are insufficient for action; for they hold that a man can never act without *efficacious grace*.[23]

The Jesuitical conception assumes that grace is a function of a human will. If earthly human deeds ultimately decide on its efficaciousness, grace becomes a function of a sensuous, individuated will: a will of the ego; of pleasure, as the narrator contends. In contrast, the Jansenist emphasis on efficiency subtends that only the will of God, unknowable to us, determines whether or not our actions result from grace. In consequence, the cause of a proper act of faith informed by grace must be undetermined by anything of the order of human experience or knowledge. Pascal argues that grace must be both sufficient and efficient—must come only from God and remain independent of human will—otherwise it does not qualify as grace at all. The coherence of the concept of grace requires that it be strictly confined to the indeterminate sphere of the divine, radically subtracted from the order of the human properly speaking.

Within the Jesuitical framework, however, the distinction between sufficiency and efficiency allows the casuist to preserve a notion of self-interested human volition, since grace only becomes effective as a function of worldly action separated from, bearing no relation to, the will of God. According to the related Jesuitical doctrine of so-called actual grace, we may be held accountable only for those sins we knowingly commit; further, it is God himself who is accorded the responsibility of implanting that knowledge in us. Crucially, in order to exorcise the specter haunting this argument of a properly diabolical agent, one whose utter ignorance of sin would then justify any action whatsoever, casuistry is forced to posit that "God never permitted a man to sin without giving him previously a view of the evil which he contemplated."[24]

Here we are returned to the logic of Pascal's automaton, through which he denounced the agnostic's "double consciousness," split between an outward knowledge of and conformity with the law, and a disavowed indulgence in self-interested transgression. Similarly, casuistry first puts the onus on God for providing his subject with knowledge of sin, thereby creating a kind of alibi which allows for the possibility of an innocent transgression. At a second moment, however, the casuist casts this transgression under the shadow of guilt by retroactively giving the subject knowledge of its sin. In this way casuistry renders transgression tantalizingly obscene by attributing to the subject the knowledge of its guilt. At the same time, the casuist withholds from this subject any sense of ultimate accountability for its action by qualifying the status of grace as human rather than divine. Notwithstanding the specious rationalizations that the casuist framework permits, the Jesuitical position is finally simply nonsensical for Pascal, for it first posits that grace issues only from God, thereby remaining indifferent to human moral considerations, but then subsumes grace under a properly human volitional efficiency which is then free to determine on its own terms the legitimacy of the act.

From Pascal's perspective, what makes possible this perverse logic of casuistry is finally an unjustifiable certainty with respect to what constitutes sin. Though Pascal's subject of faith experiences intuitions of guilt, these intuitions are radically untranslatable into knowledge: The hidden God refuses to make explicit how we have sinned or how we might achieve innocence. Grace may therefore only ever be postulated, never proven or guaranteed, as the cause of an act of faith. The fundamental call to praxis which underlies Pascal's doctrine emerges as a result of this constitutive lack of knowledge which determines our relation to the Other. The content of the final judgment, paradoxically, is empty. If there is ultimately no way of knowing what God wants, the question of the causation of my act rebounds back to me, forcing me to interrogate the content of my own desire, daring me to purge this desire of any criterion whatever, of any possible reference to an existing ethical norm. In this way Pascal's notion of grace assumes that the world itself is lacking, is devoid of ontological consistency, and therefore creates the possibility of miraculous acts, acts which simply cannot be accounted for by any known measure. But crucially, such possibilities are only visible to the subject who has already acquired faith. This subject has acknowledged the trauma of God's silence *and has acted anyway*—acted in the absence of any framework, signpost or guarantee.

In his *Pensées* Pascal avers that grace properly conceived cures humankind of its two "chief maladies" (116): pride, the source of its alienation from God, which provides the illusion of certainty and which motivates the attitude of moral self-righteousness; and concupiscence, the cult of sensuous pleasure, which limits the ambitions of humankind to purely earthly concerns of self-preservation and advancement. Both afflictions fail to come to terms with the challenge posed by a properly unmotivated act purified of any reference to a supreme Good, including, perhaps especially, that of pleasure. At this point it finally becomes possible to answer my earlier question about the superficially problematic way in which Pascal's concept of sin ties itself to pleasure, inciting in the process the contemporary skepticism about a latent, patently actually existing Christian puritanism. For ultimately, I would suggest, pleasure for Pascal is undecidable: It is as illegitimate to claim that pleasure is in itself always sinful, always alien to any act motivated by grace, as it is to do as the Epicurean libertine, who elevates pleasure into a kind of Urmaxim for action. "If you are united to God," Pascal affirms, "it is by grace, not by nature," drawing our attention to the supersensible attribute of grace. Grace does not present itself to us in experience and in consequence is not amenable to verification or prediction, to explanation with reference to any determinate mode of causality, be it rational, natu-ral-empirical, or otherwise (116).

The Pascalian subject begins its struggle with itself in a state of guilty concupiscence. Incapable of coming to terms with the opacity of God's will, and yet equally incapable of eradicating the stubborn rem-nant of its first nature, this subject seeks to disavow its very conditions through a surreptitious cult of transgression. Such a cult features the unconscious intent of provoking God into showing himself through an active participation in sin. As was the case with Gilles de Rais, sin be-comes the royal road to an assumed personal relationship with a re-vealed, consoling God. Through the apparatus of faith, however, the subject gains an exit from this logic of *perversion*, acquiring the ability to submit itself to the exigencies of *conversion*. Through conversion the subject reorients the causality of its actions with reference to the desire which inhabits them—to their relation, in other words, to the indetermi-nate will of God.

The act of faith, together with the gift of grace which is its cause, therefore performs two crucial functions. First, it prevents us from uncov-ering or revealing the hidden God—from filling out the mystery of his impenetrable will—a God who would otherwise demand our uncondi-tional allegiance and sacrifice, threatening to turn us into instruments of his sinister jouissance. But faith also inserts our act into a larger totality greater than ourselves and invisible to reason. In this way faith gives us a shock which breaks our allegiance to our egoistic self-interest and to the interests of our community of friendly neighbors with whom we identify, thereby integrating the act within the totality of the miraculous body of Christ. "Grace has not destroyed the law," writes Pascal, "but has made it act" (142). To be sure, it will be said that Pascal's theory ultimately fails to spell out the full consequences of the paradox of a fully atheistic faith, one which need not have recourse to a notion of signs communicated through a book of divine revelation. Ultimately, however, the properly theological framework of *Pensées* is in large measure incidental to Pascal's evocation of the act of faith. Indeed, for me, Pascal's final, timely, invalu-able message is that through faith you can become aware that *miracles do happen*. And neither the application of your faculty of reason nor the attachment to your earthly pleasures will enable you to come to terms with their decidedly possible impossibility.

Chapter Four

_____ This Whole World of Perversion

> I was dumbfounded at such sagacity and such baseness, such
> alternately true and false notions, such a general perversion of
> feeling and utter turpitude, and yet such uncommon candour.
>
> —Denis Diderot, _Rameau's Nephew_

> The content of what Spirit says about itself is thus the perversion
> of every Notion and reality, the universal deception of itself
> and others; and the shamelessness which gives utterance
> to this deception is just for that reason the greatest truth.
>
> —G. W. F. Hegel, _Phenomenology of Spirit_

Dialogue and Dialectic

We owe our knowledge of _Rameau's Nephew_, Denis Diderot's celebrated dialogue on the contradictions of Enlightenment culture, to that admirable, intricate web of cosmopolitan intellectual relations known as the "'republic of letters." Fourteen years after Diderot's death, the text was unknown to his literary executor Naigeon when he published his friend's collected works in 1798. It is not known precisely how Catherine the Great of Russia, Diderot's enthusiastic correspondent, obtained the manuscript she deposited in St. Petersburg's Hermitage. But we do know that it was in the form of Goethe's German translation of this version that the dialogue was first made available to the general German reading public. Famously, this public included none other than the young

Hegel, who in the inaugural years of the nineteenth century had begun to compose his magisterial intellectual epic, *Phenomenology of Spirit*. For the Hegel of the *Phenemenology*, *Rameau's Nephew* came to emblematize the inner tensions of the world of culture of the French Enlightenment—including its eventual self-actualization in the bourgeois revolution—whose unprecedented social upheaval was still unsettling European culture as Hegel wrote the influential passages which refer to Diderot.

Intriguingly for my purposes, Hegel chose to qualify the new topsy-turvy world of Enlightenment culture with the term "perversion" (*Verkehrung*). And crucially, he associates the perverse with the Nephew's uncanny ability in Diderot's dialogue to cast suspicion on his interlocutor's every attempt to defend the legitimacy of the ethos of noble virtue from the corruptions of an increasingly hegemonic bourgeois-capitalist world. To be sure, this world had long since begun to penetrate and destabilize the proud terrain of the feudal-cum-monarchical state. Indeed, the Nephew's discourse represents for Hegel the very Spirit of Enlightenment culture itself, which happily runs roughshod over every ethical and political certainty left over from an ancien régime whose desperate efforts to cling to the old ways had long since begun to seem pathetically out of date. Thus, "perversion" in Hegel's analysis refers to the appearance, during the latter eighteenth century, of the effects of an emergent capitalism of private economic self-interest beyond the control of state power; these contradictions turned on its head the worldview of noble privilege and allowed for the vertiginous perception of an absolute relativism of value—the dialectical drama of identities turning into their opposites—to which the Nephew's discourse bears witness.

My suggestion in this chapter will be that Hegel identifies in the character of Rameau's nephew an ambivalent and politically worrisome, but nonetheless potentially subversive, response to the uncertainties of this new unstable world. This response features a latent fetishization of the new economic powers of the bourgeoisie, one which vacillates between a drive toward self-enslavement to the demands of the new economic order, and an embryonic, self-censored critique of its continuing social injustices. But my aim will be not merely to diagnose the Nephew by attributing to his person this or that psychoanalytic clinical category; he remains, after all, a literary character. Rather, I will argue that though the Nephew's discourse as informed by Hegel's interpretation does indeed betray indications of perversion in its strong, structural psychoanalytic sense, it also contains the seeds of an authentically political process of hystericization. Indeed, the Nephew's inkling of the self-deception and ultimate emptiness of a bourgeois ideology which attributes self-consciousness to wealth brings to light the disruptive, at once social and subjective, truth Hegel wants to claim as a valuable legacy of Enlightenment culture.

We may begin by recalling the parameters of Diderot's singular text. *Rameau's Nephew* is effectively a dialogue between two characters, referred to as Moi and Lui, interspersed with occasional first-person narration from Moi's point of view. Moi is an embodiment—but simplified to the point of caricature—of the French Enlightenment philosophe,[1] with his characteristic faith in disinterested virtue, continuous social progress, and innate human rationality. Indeed, Moi provides Diderot with a position from which he can critique the naive assumptions of his own intellectual class, in particular its failure to acknowledge the archaism of a system of noble virtue whose certainties had been crushed by the deterritorializing violence that capital performed on the traditional prerevolutionary social identities. The philosopher's interlocutor Lui is the bohemian, possibly deranged, in any case disreputable nephew of the great Rameau, the noted eighteenth-century French composer. As the reader learns, the Nephew earns his living as a kind of professional clown or court jester who is theoretically hired by rich bourgeois families (with aristocratic pretensions) to work as the children's music tutor, but who in practice provides mindless distraction and amusement for all. Everywhere Diderot emphasizes the Nephew's absolute economic dependence on his nouveau-riche patrons, as well as the virtually unbearable psychical tension to which his position gives rise. Mounting a performance of polite obedience in which on one level he seems desperate to believe, the Nephew is forced to repress his awareness of the brute injustice of his situation in a world increasingly enslaved to the cult of wealth.

Diderot presents his text as a comic pastiche of the Socratic dialogue, albeit one with thoroughly serious philosophical implications. The dialogue pits the philosopher's dogmatic faith in human goodness and the collective good against the Nephew's rather unhinged, yet potentially subversive, discourse which lays bare, often despite itself, the socioeconomic power relations of late ancien régime society. On the surface Diderot's dialogue functions mainly as a vehicle for his discussion of the aesthetic questions—the nature of artistic genius, the relative merits of French versus Italian musical styles—with which he was concerned. But on a deeper level it is to the question of the possibility of an authentic ethics in a brutally unjust world that Diderot devotes his literary and philosophical imagination. And not coincidentally, it is to the suggestive theoretical implications of the dialectical conflict between Moi's moral dogmatism and Lui's relativist nihilism that Hegel, in his compelling interpretation, trains his dialectical eye.

More specifically, the fundamental disagreement between the two interlocutors takes place around the problem of the nature and value of virtue. The philosopher, a sort of journalistic pseudo-Kantian, is convinced of the human agent's capacity to devote itself purely to the public interest, unsupported by the promise of material gain. As I will explore further below, Hegel's analysis implies that in sociological terms the philosopher's ideology arises from the separation of the classical seventeenth-century ideal of *honnêteté* from the structure of noble privilege which was its material condition. The Nephew, better acquainted than the philosopher with life's brute realities, avers that the world, ruled by the law of the jungle, destroys all those who do not presuppose the omnipotence of self-interest in the regulation of human affairs. In Hegel's analysis, the Nephew partially embodies the new bourgeois ethos, which invests its ambitions firmly in the accumulation of private wealth, and which consequently, in proto-Foucauldian fashion, views all normative, altruistic values as impositions of an alien power. But because the Nephew is only a parasite of the bourgeoisie, and therefore not in any objective sense a member of it, he is capable of recognizing the fundamental illusion on which its thought is based. Such, then, is the context of the controversy that the dialogue enacts. For the Nephew, everything is permitted in a transformed, untrustworthy world in which all values tend toward their ignoble opposites; the philosopher, in pathetic contrast, valiantly advances his faith in the imminent transcendence of human interest, all the while being forced to grant the scandalous truth of the Nephew's counterarguments, and failing to match in examples of virtue his opponent's seemingly endless stream of evidence of the baseness of human motivations.

The placement of the commentary of *Rameau's Nephew* within the general architectonics of Hegel's text provides a number of clues about the significance of his interpretation of Diderot. The section containing the rather discreet references to the dialogue is situated within the subchapter "Self-alienated Spirit. Culture." This section outlines the dialectic of Enlightenment's "pure intellectual insight," which attempts to recuperate faith's placement of the essence of consciousness in an otherworldly beyond within a form of being-for-self located inside the limits of a worldly, secular culture.[2] For Hegel, the moment of culture (*Bildung*) to which *Rameau's Nephew* belongs refers historically to the apogee of French court society which, he suggests, already contained the seeds of its own destruction. With its characteristically intricate battles for distinction and recognition through the performance of conversational brilliance, as well as its embodiment of political authority in the sole personage of the absolute monarch, culture represents within Hegel's larger dialectical framework an unprecedented extraneation of the self from its natural immediacy into a universal form. Hegel considers this modern self-alienation to be much more radical and universal than that suffered by the atomized consciousness articulated through Spirit's previous incarnation in Roman legal right. On a more abstract or conceptual level, culture's significance consists for Hegel in the unprecedented manner in which it attempts to resolve the contradiction between the in-itself and the for-itself by means of a forced externalization of consciousness in the universal substance, one in which the self could then presumably recuperate its being in a unified self-apprehension, alienated by no objectification from a form of self-consciousness external to itself.

As the rest of Hegel's analysis makes clear, the emergence of this ever-changing field of culture is made possible by the destabilization of the old feudal social identities put in place by the differentiating, abstracting, and relativizing forces of monetary relations which begin to act in modernity as the new magnets for self-consciousness. Referring to the emergent class of financiers already socially visible in the late seventeenth century, La Bruyère claimed that such people "are neither parents nor friends, citizens nor Christians, nor perhaps are they even men—they have money."[3] Thus, the early-modern, prerevolutionary period inaugurates for Hegel a world in which the subject's essence is no longer identified with its objective positioning within the social hierarchy, as was the case in the feudal social formation. Rather, this positioning becomes a function of the subject's ability to alienate its natural essence through a skillful manipulation of the codes and conventions by which it is circumscribed, a cultural mobility made possible by the new mobility of capital. Indeed, in the world of culture which produced Diderot's dialogue, these externalizations of consciousness acquire an ambition of absolute totality, giving rise in the process to what Hegel calls "pure intellectual insight," a form of self-consciousness which recognizes no alien "outside," no stubborn in-itself which resists such an imperative of extraneation. Recognizing "everything as self," pure intellectual insight negates the possibility of both the transcendental self-presence posited by the heavenly beyond of faith, as well as any immanent, intrinsic objectivity which would place a limit on either the secular absolute Being of Deism—that peculiar, nominally atheist religion of Enlightenment—or the hegemony of the principle of utility, which would finally come to dominate the development of Enlightenment ethical ideology (486).

Intellectual insight's unlimited mediation of consciousness comes to define the very essence of Enlightenment culture for Hegel. "This insight, as the self that apprehends itself," he contends, "completes [the stage of] culture. It apprehends nothing but self, and everything as self. It comprehends everything, wipes out the objectivity of things and converts all intrinsic being into a being for itself" (486). In this way Enlightenment Spirit in its most developed form attempts to transform the field of culture into an independent, hermetic, full totality severed from any form of suture to the real of sociopolitical antagonism. In psychoanalytic terms, Hegel's world of culture puts into practice a kind of proto-postmodern ego psychology in which, though allowance is made for continual flux and dialectical reversal, consciousness is nonetheless formed through a gesture of disavowal. What is disavowed is the ego's subjection to a painful exclusion from consciousness which disallows the full translation of the cultural universality into the terms of symbolic or linguistic exchange. By denying that culture (or discourse in the contemporary Foucauldian sense) might prove inadequate to the historical or psychical real, Enlightenment's pure intellectual insight declares its opposition to faith and the supremacy of the principle of utility: No reference to a transcendental or unknowable realm of divinity is required to legitimate the field of cultural forms; nor is there any longer a conceptual impediment to the full extension of a rational criterion representing the collective Good.[4]

Through its proclamation of the absolute Self, radical Enlightenment for Hegel effectively collapses the distinction between subject and object, thereby equating consciousness with the objective forms through which it is made manifest, and subsuming judgments pertaining to cultural and political value under an unlimited and omniscient sensuous ego. This unlimited, perverse extraneation of self-consciousness disallows all reference to anything outside itself, thereby inaugurating a radical epistemological relativism and linguistic nominalism, the distressing consequences of which, I will suggest, are figured in the person of Diderot's Nephew. But before turning to a closer examination of how the Nephew embodies the symptoms of Enlightenment's cultural ambition, let us first interrogate in greater detail this ambition's kinship with the project of a contemporary postmodernity.

The Cynical Other

In his *Critique of Cynical Reason*, first published in German in 1983, Peter Sloterdijk takes the occasion of the bicentennial of Kant's *Critique of Pure Reason* to decry the resigned attitude of intellectual despair which arose in the wake of the dissemination of those discourses of the

1960s and 1970s which have come to be called "postmodern." While quite clearly this tendency features a number of disparate subtraditions which are not in full agreement with one another, we might take the risk of advancing that they tend to hold in common a view of discourse or culture which is "realtight," to use Joan Copjec's word. The Hegelian "pure intellectual insight" anticipates the underlying claim of post-modernism through its unlimited extension of the terrain of culture which, however marked by instability and flux, remains unencumbered by any obstacle or impediment—any negativity—either within itself or without. Through its particular response to the ultimate undecidability of meaning and the impossibility of grounding or justifying any specific brand of political engagement, postmodernism, Sloterdijk suggests, is characterized by a fundamental melancholic reticence, a "reflexively buff-ered" consciousness which dissuades the subject from performing a true political act.[5] And crucially for my purposes, both Diderot's dialogue and Sloterdijk's argument suggest that this reticence carries within itself a worrisome potential to resolve itself through perversion: that is, not through an authentic engagement with social conflict, but rather through an acute but hypocritical conformism, a powerful drive to refuse the consequences of genuine social involvement. As I will try to show, this refusal presupposes a very particular kind of onlooker of the political field that I will wish to compare to the pervert's Other as posited by psychoanalysis.

Sloterdijk's prescient book was among the first to question the va-lidity of postmodernism's proclamation of the end of ideology. As is well known, this proclamation's logic tends toward the argument that power's saturation of the forms of knowledge and discourse problematizes, often to the point of delegitimating, all forms of political resistance on the basis that they are already irremediably complicit in power. In sharp contrast Sloterdijk seeks polemically to renew the engagement of the philosophical tradition in the development of a kind of social knowledge which produces not a guilty, obsessional self-reflexivity which continu-ally postpones the moment of intervention, but rather a renewed inquiry into the nature of social antagonisms and the political interests which shape them. In contrast to its figuration in postmodern doctrine, then, the term "critique" as Sloterdijk appropriates it from the Kantian tradi-tion implies both the possibility of formulating social knowledge which is not perfectly reducible to the exercise of normative power, as well as the citizen's capacity to intervene concretely in the world in the interests of progressive, authentically democratic political change. Sloterdijk defines the "cynical reason" he considers characteristic of the postmodern moment as an "enlightened false consciousness": enlightened because it has acquired knowledge of specific political interests disguised under self-proclaimed universal or disinterested judgments; but false because it characterizes action based on that knowledge as naive, retro, unsophisticated, and apt to make the agent appear ridiculous in the eyes of an authoritative Other.[6] In this way cynical reason effectively dissociates the acquisition of social and political knowledge from any possible application to the historical here and now.

The connection between Sloterdijk's evocation of cynicism and the discourse of Diderot's Nephew immediately becomes apparent.[7] In his conversation with the philosopher, the Nephew betrays a curious admixture of, on the one hand, an acute awareness of the dynamics of the ancien régime patronage system responsible for his dependent state and, on the other, an equally acute fear that any attempt to articulate openly the dynamics of this system will provoke a humiliating social isolation even more intolerable than extreme material hardship. Fundamentally, what binds the Nephew to his exploitative patron-masters is his desire to avoid looking "ridiculous," that nefarious eighteenth-century adjective which exerted tremendous normative power in the decadent monarchical salons, as Stephen Frears's filmic adaptation of Laclos' *Les Liaisons Dangeureuses* or Patrice Leconte's *Ridicule* bear witness. What is most important to note on this question, however, is that the fear of ridicule animating the Nephew's discourse is motivated not by the prospect of being discovered indulging in secret transgressions, but rather of being caught missing out on a jouissance newly revealed by the Other, a jouissance which the Nephew comes to perceive as the very dictate of its law. As Leconte's well-intentioned provincial noble discovers at the court of Louis XVI, what renders him ridiculous in the eyes of the Versailles sophisticates is the notion that he would sacrifice the tantalizing pleasures promised by social success at court in favor of the prosaic, boring sincerity of an environmental engineering project which promises to save his peasants from disease.

The discourse of Rameau's Nephew exhibits the same assumption of an Other whose law imposes, rather than forbids, enjoyment. While recommending to his interlocutor the edifying lessons of classical French comedy, for example, the philosopher claims that Molière's theatre imparts "knowledge of one's duties, love of virtue, hatred of vice." The Nephew responds in agreement, but then asserts that such knowledge is useful not because it allows one to avoid vicious actions, but rather because it prevents one from appearing vicious before others. "When I read *L'Avare*," the Nephew states, "I say to myself: Be a miser if you want to, but make sure you don't sound like one. When I read *Tartuffe* I tell myself: Be a hypocrite, by all means, but don't talk like a hypocrite."[8]

The Nephew's attitude appears at first glance to conform to the well-known bourgeois maxim which informs us to "keep up appearances": You can do whatever you want as long as you are seen to obey the precepts of *honnêteté*. But Diderot's version of the world of culture puts forth a crucial, precociously postmodern nuance when the Nephew reveals that in his perception such hypocrisy is the rule rather than the exception: "My only merit," he claims, "is that I have done systematically, with a spirit of accuracy and a true and reasonable view, what most others have done by instinct" (662, TM). Using Molière to criticize vice betrays a faith in virtue which makes one appear ridiculous—duped—before an anonymous observer whose thoroughgoing cynical enjoyment is automatically presupposed. From the properly bourgeois world of surreptitious transgressions which must be concealed from a virtuous Other, we advance onto a decidedly different terrain on which the Other's normativity no longer holds. This Other unveils, displays its no longer secret transgressive enjoyment and *commands* its subject to indulge. The judgment of ridiculousness comes to target the very sincere conformity with virtue to which the philosopher steadfastly adheres.

It is interesting to note that Sloterdijk's insight about the devolution in postmodernity of a progressive, authentically critical ancient cynicism finds a curious echo in a detail of Diderot's text. This detail also allows us to discern more clearly the social anxiety forestalled by the modern cynic-pervert: the ominous threat of subjective destitution which his conformity is designed to stave off. Tellingly, the cynic Diogenes figures in Diderot's dialogue as Moi's intellectual ideal. For Sloterdijk, Diogenes is "the earliest example" of what he calls a "declassed plebeian intelligence." Diogenes made use of scathing irony and bitter social satire to attack the hypocrisies and injustices of the polis, leaving no citizen to escape, Sloterdijk contends, "his crude unmasking gaze uninjured."[9] But whereas the Greek cynic paid the price for his subversive outspokenness by cutting his ties with respectable society and being forced into the position of an abject, marginal outcast, the modern cynic, for Sloterdijk, is rather an "average social character" whose strong sense of resentment at social inequalities neither interferes with his complicit economic productivity nor inspires a desire for political engagement and social change. The contemporary cynic, in other words, is the consummate professional whose definition of happiness, Sloterdijk writes, citing Gottfried Benn, is "to be dumb and have a job."[10] Association with such déclassé categories as the plebeian constitutes for the modern cynic an unnecessary sacrifice of distinction and enjoyment which jeopardizes the prospect of assuming the lifestyle of the hegemonic class.

The distinguishing feature of the cynical-perverse stance is therefore its positing of an idealized, potent Other whose enjoyment, rather than shaming or traumatizing the subject, instead places this subject under its command. Whereas the Greek *kynicism* condemned a hypocritical discrepancy in the political Other between the moral ideals it gave itself and the corruption of its citizens, the postmodern cynic bears witness to the collapse of the law into enjoyment, such that transgression begins to constitute the social world's very principle of consistency, thereby becoming the essence of the law itself. In this way the Other of radical cynicism is no longer fraught by the contradiction between the law it purports to uphold and the violation it seeks to dissimulate. In Lacanian terms, the Greek cynic's capacity to perceive this contradiction in the Other and assume its consequences causes it to appear as subject in the form of *objet petit a*, as the putrid social detritus banished from social intelligibility—Diogenes in his famous tub. In contrast, the very function of the perverse, postmodern cynicism is to dissimulate, indeed to disavow, this inconsistency in the Other, thereby installing a full narcissistic reciprocity which produces no alien residue, no unsightly, stigmatized stain. This "postliberal"[11] Other issues a commandment to enjoy; and the cynic eagerly subsumes his will under that of his obscene master, happy to avoid the risk of social marginalization presented by a more doubtful, inquisitive—indeed neurotic—stance with respect to the Other's desire.

No doubt the psychic suffering to which the Nephew's symptoms attest—his hysterical absences and quasi-psychotic fits of musical pantomime—show that the complexities of his discourse cannot satisfyingly be reduced to either the despairing conformism of Sloterdijk's yuppie, Reaganite cynic, or the clinical formulation of the perverse structure in psychoanalysis. Still, I would suggest that the Nephew's discourse does indeed feature what we might wish to call an "ambition of perversion." Indeed, in his disavowal of the legitimacy of the pointed criticisms he himself directs against the bourgeois world which thwarts him, and in his desire for a unified audience whose demand his performance could straightforwardly fulfill, the Nephew does indeed express that fundamental desire for strict conformity with a certain and perfectly knowable law which is so characteristic of the perverse structure. And to be sure, one of the most striking manifestations of this desire is the Nephew's veritable revolt against a function of negativity embedded in the very structure of language, a function which renders all utterable judgments endemically controvertible, and which grants to language its disquieting, fundamentally artificial and unreliable quality.

A Revolt against the Negative

As the frustrated philosopher of Diderot's dialogue quickly discovers, it is impossible to argue with the Nephew because he refuses to stand behind any particular statement he makes; in analytic terms, he refuses to offer a proposition which he would not immediately contradict. Each of Moi's attempts to take issue with the Nephew on any given point inevitably fails, since the Nephew immediately grants his interlocutor's point in response. Insofar as the Nephew articulates anything in his discourse, he articulates the full set of all possible judgments. He has already said everything; or, perhaps more accurately, he is always trying to say everything, to adequate his discourse to the real.

In the course of a quintessentially Enlightenment discussion of pedagogical priorities, for example, the philosopher congratulates the Nephew for his belief in the importance of systematic study with acknowledged masters. As the Nephew specifies, "It was only after thirty or forty years of practice that my uncle got his first glimpses of musical theory." The Nephew then spells out the terms of his all-or-nothing approach to the pursuit of knowledge: "When you don't know everything, you don't know anything at all" (58, TM). Two fundamental assumptions underlying the Nephew's discourse emerge: First, there exists a total, perfect knowledge embodied in a number of idealized masters such as his celebrated uncle; and second, as is the case with Hegel's "pure intellectual insight," the true knowledge assimilates "everything to itself," tolerating no murky region of uncertainty or negation. Going so far as to dismiss the legitimacy of modern physics on the grounds of the incompleteness of its findings, the Nephew explains how in his view any epistemological project must be undertaken with the assumption that knowledge constitutes an untarnished totality. Any knowledge which fails to conform to this ideal is fundamentally useless, even shameful.

The Nephew's effort to acquire such a seamless brand of knowledge causes his speech to feature a peculiar resistance to negation. Indeed, as the philosopher-narrator remarks at the outset of the dialogue, the Nephew incarnates in his very physical person the coincidence of opposites which results from this phobia. The Nephew is "a compound of the highest and the lowest, good sense and folly," the philosopher states, and he variously appears "thin and gaunt" or "sleek and plump," "in dirty clothing" or "well dressed," "gloomy or gay" (33–34, TM).[12] In both his corporeal and discursive manifestations, then, the Nephew proffers a challenge to all forms of thought which distinguish between contraries and set a limit to the qualities which may legitimately be attributed to objects. A precise way to characterize formally the Nephew's discourse is to describe it as an absolute, positive assertion which erases all possibility of negation and absorbs all difference into itself.

In its inability to represent negation and its deranged affirmation of contradictory statements the Nephew's discourse resembles that of the Freudian unconscious. "In analysis we never discover a 'no' in the unconscious," Freud writes, "and that recognition of the unconscious on the part of the ego is expressed in a negative formula."[13] In an obscure 1910 essay called "The Antithetical Sense of Primal Words," Freud makes a similar statement concerning the dreamwork: "The attitude of dreams towards the category of antithesis and contradiction is most striking. This category is simply ignored; the word 'No' does not seem to exist for a dream. Dreams show a special tendency to reduce two opposites to a unity or to represent them as one thing."[14] Insofar as the Nephew negates nothing, his discourse may be said to express unconscious material more directly than that of the normal subject. But Freud's association of the function of negation with the ego indexes a splitting of consciousness which the Nephew's discourse is designed to avoid. What is lacking in the Nephew's discourse is therefore this gesture of exclusion from the terms of consciousness, a gesture which paradoxically grounds the subject's capacity to individuate, to establish a precarious identity by distancing itself from what it does not want to be. Here we encounter the ambiguity of the Nephew's relation to language. Though it allows him to articulate what in a neurotic subject's speech would be repressed, he loses through his unconscious automatism a certain command over his utterances which would otherwise allow him to say something definite, to formulate a coherent, logically controvertible proposition. What is truly unthinkable for the Nephew is that he might let slip a judgment which his Other could then refute; indeed, he associates this prospect of being proven wrong with a humiliation to be avoided at all costs.

One of the advantages of such a position is that it provides the Nephew with an alibi by means of which he can deny any form of responsibility for his utterances. When, for example, the philosophe suggests that his interlocutor, in spite of his hardened, cynical shell, still harbors a "delicate soul" wounded by the world's injustice (79, TM), the Nephew responds defensively, denying that he has any knowledge of himself at all, and asserting that he only says whatever is most propitious or appropriate given the demands of the immediate context. The Nephew allows himself to be guided by what he considers his most spontaneous sensuous interests, which suspiciously appear to coincide with the requirements he perceives in the communicative situation in which he finds himself. From his own perspective, in other words, the Nephew's speech is solicited, commanded by his Other. Whereas the neurotic is continually haunted by a minimal gap between what he effectively says and what he intends to say, the Nephew eliminates this position of reflexivity with respect to his own statements by allowing them to emerge, so to speak, of their own volition. "I have never reflected in my life," the Nephew claims, "either before speaking, during speech or after. And so I give no offence" (79).

This fear of giving offense is especially instructive in this regard, since it highlights not only the tremendous power which the Nephew's discourse abandons to his Other, but also the underlying ambition of conformity which motivates its attribution of authority. In effect, the Nephew does not regard himself as an agent with respect to signification; or, perhaps more accurately, he desperately attempts to disavow this agency or responsibility which lies in the gap between his intention or meaning and its linguistic articulation. Far from producing an unconscious spontaneity which would expose what is most hidden from the terms of the social contract, the Nephew's position with respect to language makes clear that his fundamental conscious intention is one of strict conformity: to satisfy through his discourse a demand he perceives as emerging from his privileged Other—*les grands*. Indeed, the Nephew is perfectly up front about the link he sees between his strategy of self-instrumentalization and the rewards of social success. Giving voice to his idea that the virtuous life produces nothing in the way of enjoyment, the Nephew instructs the philosopher that the secret to life is to "serve the court, observe the powerful, study their tastes, and lend oneself to their fantasies, pander to their vices, condone their injustices" (65, TM).

In the Nephew's characteristic refusal of the risk of controvertible assertion we may begin to discern what appears at first glance to be the paradoxical coincidence of his extreme, artistic or bohemian individualism with his desire for absolute social conformity. As the philosophe explains in the dialogue, the aim of human consciousness to preserve within itself a glint of particularity results in an obsessive phobia of self-externalization which has a paradoxically difference-eradicating effect. Similarly, in Hegel's analysis of the workings of the world of culture, the self may only achieve actuality—become "individuated," in the familiar and problematic terms of liberal psychologism—through its alienation in external, nonorganic, universal cultural forms. Yet Hegel implies that this alienation is never achieved without producing a remainder which calls into question the very terms of culture itself. Significantly, Hegel relates this remainder to the very figure of the Nephew, whose resistance to Moi's conviction in the noble values of *honnêteté* has him appear as a mere *espèce*—"that most horrid of all nicknames" expressing "the highest degree of contempt" (489)—within the terms of culture. Hegel's use of the term *espèce* suggests an instance of particularity which contradicts the universalizing ambitions of Enlightenment culture. The theological meaning of the term refers to the concrete appearance of the body and blood of Christ in the form of bread and wine after transubstantiation. More concretely, the term implies a sense of social abjection, a field of cultural unintelligibility which unsettles the coherence of culture's terms and disrupts the very functioning of the process of cultural normalization. The *espèce* is what is left behind after the process of cultural transubstantiation is complete; it is that which thwarts the Enlightenment self's ambition fully to reconstitute itself within the universal sphere of culture.

I have suggested that the perverse, logically unspecifiable attribute of the Nephew's discourse is intimately related in the dialogue to his fear of appearing ridiculous before the Other, to his disavowal of the consequences of a law which requires an alienation in form. In other words, the Nephew simply refuses the imperative of cultural alienation which Moi upholds. The latter's naive, precritical faith in virtue surely corresponds within Hegel's framework to precisely this Enlightenment ambition of a pure, normative extraneation in substance which would resolve the tension between egoic self-interest and the unifying impetus of a collective culture. This ambition presupposes a process of cultural normalization which would produce no Nephew—no *espèce*—to contradict it; its premise is a "power of the individual" which could "establish itself as substance that has objective existence" (490). What Hegel's analysis brings to light is therefore the unanticipated dialectical identity of two apparently contradictory stances: on the one hand the radical imperative of normative, universalizing self-extraneation in the world of culture and, on the other, the perverse disavowal of alienation embodied in the Nephew's discourse. Both stances result in the same fetishizing gesture which refuses to recognize the failure of culture's attempts at perfect normalization, which disavows, in other words, the law's inability to legislate effectively against its violation. Both the philosophe's desperate clinging to a belief in human altruism and the Nephew's self-subjection to the command of his bourgeois masters feature the same reluctance to recognize a fundamental function of negation in the Other, one which renders it traumatically opaque and unreliable, and which prevents the subject from attributing to it any definite, incontrovertible content.

Wealth and Power

Hegel's development of the consequences of this vacillation in the content of the judgments of late ancien régime society presents an opportunity to gain a more detailed understanding of the social and political dynamics at work in both Diderot's dialogue and Hegel's interpretation. It is in relation to the notion of the perverse interimplication of subject and object, in other words the desedimentation and relativization of value which capital introduced into the social fabric of early-modern France, that Hegel develops his dialectic of state power and wealth.[15] Though most commentators of Hegel's extremely complex analysis have underlined how the Nephew's discourse enacts the destabilization of the noble and ignoble judgments which, according to Hegel, originally structured ancien régime society, my sense is that Diderot's interlocutors may be placed in a more direct relationship with the terms of Hegel's interpretation.

This interpretation formulates the various ways in which the abstract judgments of pure consciousness, what Hegel calls "the good" and "the bad," can be linked to the objective forms available to self-consciousness in ancien régime society, namely state power and wealth. In the specific sociopolitical context of prerevolutionary France, these essences constitute what Hegel calls "objective moments," in other words concrete manifestations of substance in a particular sociohistorical configuration (494). Hegel acknowledges that the social tension between city and family which, as will be discussed in the next chapter, characterized the ancient polis had been transformed by the institutions of legal right and private property into an antagonism between the general interests of the state and the private interests of capital. As a result, early-modern social life is fractured by the opposing values of two distinct projects: A philosophical universalizing operation which seeks to unify disparate wills into a collective cultural or national project is pitted against a liberal atomistic desire for the generation of private wealth intended to facilitate individual enjoyment.

On the first level of Hegel's analysis self-consciousness relates to the two available objective essences through simple relations of likeness and unlikeness. He calls "noble" the judgment which identifies with both state power and wealth: this judgment "sees in public authority what is in accord with itself" and in wealth an "awareness of its other essential side, the consciousness of being *for itself*" (500). The ignoble judgment, for its part, distances itself from both state power and capital, finding in the former only "a suppression of its own *being-for-self*," and in the latter only the awareness of itself "as an isolated individual, conscious only of a transitory enjoyment" (501). In the noble and ignoble judgments Hegel has in mind the older, feudal, more stable incarnation of the ancien régime before the mobility of capital and social identities had begun to transform its cultural landscape. In this system there was no contradiction between selfless devotion to the state and the possession of material wealth, which was still largely tethered to a system of feudal ownership and familial lineage. Noble titles were not yet sold on the open market, and subjection to the codes of *honnêteté* went hand in hand with the social privileges which sustained them. The nascent liberalizing sentiments were still largely taboo: It was a source of shame to consider state power an unduly normative agency which should foster a desire for revolt, and suspicion concerning the value of wealth was tantamount to questioning the very legitimacy of the entire feudal system.

In the Enlightenment world of culture, however, these certainties sink into chaos. With the emergence of an urban merchant bourgeoisie, in other words of an accumulation of private capital separate from the system of noble privilege, honest service to the state is no longer automatically accompanied by material compensation. Conversely, the private interests of capital are no longer necessarily in agreement with the political whims of the monarch and his court of powerful noble bureaucrats. As a result, the noble and ignoble judgments are subjected to an unprecedented flux, and we find evidence in Diderot's dialogue of an attempt to reanchor the moments of self-consciousness onto new, reconfigured essences.

Whereas in the previous state of affairs the relation between self-consciousness and substance was one of straightforward likeness and unlikeness, in the new one each way of judging "finds a likeness and a disparity," as Hegel puts it. In the first case, which we might attribute to the Nephew, "consciousness judges the state power to be essentially different from it, and the enjoyment of wealth to accord with its own nature." In other words, this new consciousness projects itself into the promise of enjoyment represented by money, and the traditional authority of the state comes to appear as an obstacle to the exercise of the new individual freedoms. In the second case, which corresponds to the views of the philosopher Moi, "consciousness judges the state power to accord with its nature and the enjoyment of wealth to be essentially different from it" (all 499). That is to say, social value is placed exclusively on the traditional imperative of state service, and the emergence of private wealth takes on the cast of a shameful perversion of the universal cultural project.

In the social world indexed by Diderot's dialogue, then, the ideology of *honnêteté* is severed from its connection to economic privilege, which now appears in a corrupted private form isolated from the moral prestige of the noble, universal state. Diderot's philosophe's position might be compared to the tenets of the classical French moralist tradition as emblematized by La Rochefoucauld: While preserving the latter's antiegoism and dutiful allegiance to a higher interest, it sheds the pessimistic *ressentiment* of a nobility in its death throes, finally accepting the *déclassement* which is the consequence of a rejection of the new bourgeois values. The Nephew's discourse, in contrast, gives voice to the investments of a crude economic hyperliberalism, for which the normative claims of the state may only appear as unnecessary fetters to the free expansion of capital motivated by private self-interest, but at least in principle of benefit to all. Not coincidentally, Hegel had read the German translation of Adam Smith's *Wealth of Nations* before composing these aspects of his consideration of the Enlightenment world of culture.

The point, however, should not merely be to plot Diderot's characters onto the Hegelian conceptuality, for the argument of the dialogue attempts neither to adjudicate between the two types of judgment, nor to declare the political or ethical superiority of one over the other. As Hegel demonstrates in his interpretation, what is required is rather an analysis of the dialectical conflict between the two mentalities in view of determining what occurs as a result of their dynamic interaction.[16] For the point of Hegel's analysis is to show that the apparent accommodation to the new social realities effected by this rearrangement of the noble and ignoble judgments ultimately fails to fix their contents, which promiscuously insist on turning into their opposites, thereby throwing the entire system into chaos and giving rise to the disorienting moral vertigo from which the Nephew's discourse seeks relief.

The arguments of Diderot's interlocutors dramatize Hegel's point about this instability of the noble and ignoble judgments. On several occasions the philosophe stresses his devotion to virtue: He tries at all moments, more concretely, to take as his maxim for action his duty to the state before his desire for private enrichment or sensual pleasure. As the Nephew repeatedly points out, however, in the new bourgeois world service to the state has a tendency to link up with the production of private profit, and it is never possible to ascertain that such an impure motivation has not contaminated the intentions of the virtuous philosopher. It is never entirely clear, in other words, that the prospect of wealth produced by the attitude of conformity has not actually formed the true ground for the philosopher's obedience to the state system. While the noble consciousness "behaves as if it were conforming to the universal power," Hegel concludes, "the truth about it is rather that in its service it retains its own being-for-self, and that in the genuine renunciation of its personality, it actually sets aside and rends in pieces the universal Substance" (513). The paradoxical outcome of a continued devotion to the state in the new social circumstances is thus the sundering of the very universality of Enlightenment's cultural project.

The same variety of dialectical metamorphosis may be detected in the trajectory of the Nephew's discourse. Not only does the enjoyment he receives for his devotion to the cult of wealth embodied in his bourgeois masters prove to be transitory and ineffable, it also brings to light his utter dependence on their benevolence. The ignoble consciousness of the earlier stage had already recognized that the alienation of self-consciousness in the substance of wealth has the effect of isolating the individual, of rendering its pleasures empty and ephemeral. Now, in the context of the world of culture's bourgeois ideology, the self "sees its self-certainty to be completely devoid of essence," thereby coming to see its dedication to the accumulation of abstract wealth as an inauthentic, contingent state of dependency (517). No doubt with Diderot's Nephew in mind, Hegel describes as follows what becomes of the initial thankfulness with which this form of self-consciousness initially greeted its monetary reward: "The spirit of [the self's] gratitude is . . . the feeling of the most profound dejection as well as of extreme rebellion" (517). Whereas at first the Nephew is able to rationalize his dependency with reference to the material support his patrons provide, the entire system of bourgeois values crumbles to dust when this support proves hostile to the claims of self-consciousness. In other words, wealth is transformed from a promise of liberated enjoyment to a humiliating enslavement. This transformation gives rise to a spirit of rebellion in which all existing values appear baseless and contingent. The final result of the flirtation of self-consciousness with the cult of wealth is thus that "all identity dissolves away" (517).

It is here that Hegel chooses to locate the very essence of the world of culture which his analysis conveys. It is also at this point that we may begin to discern the subtle hinge on which the Nephew's discourse swings between a properly perverse self-instrumentalization to the perceived dictates of the new bourgeois ideology, and the emergence of a hysterical knowledge of this ideology's inconsistency and ultimate emptiness. I have suggested that the Nephew's discourse may be qualified within the terms of Hegel's analysis through its identification with material wealth and the enjoyments it purportedly allows, coupled with its disidentification with normative state power. The absolute relativization of value—the impossibility of attributing judgments to the contents of self-consciousness—is what results from the eventual disillusionment experienced by what Hegel calls "this disrupted consciousness" (520). Hegel then identifies a possible outcome of this chaotic state of affairs which corresponds to what I have identified as the "ambition of perversion" in the Nephew's discourse. The subject of pure culture—the cynical, perverse subject embodied in the Nephew—responds to the groundlessness of its new situation by means of a peculiar resistance to its alienation in the structures of language and state power. The pure Spirit of culture, as Hegel puts it, "rebels against the rejection of itself" (520) in an attempt to enjoy a form of self-consciousness which would be unmediated by the universal forms of language embodied in the state and its various apparatuses. But far from liberating the subject of culture from the injunction of externalization, however, such a resistance imprisons this subject all the more radically in the formal structures of language, and in such a way that reference, denotation, and meaning become acutely problematic.

Hegel uncovers the objective social correlative of this phenomenon in the profusion of the language of "base flattery" in the new bourgeois patronage system of the late ancien régime, a language of flattery to be distinguished from an earlier form of sycophancy inscribed within the monarchical state system (520). In other words, this flattery bespeaks a subjection not to the state form, but to capital. It is in relation to this notion of bourgeois flattery that Hegel details his view of the political consequences of the subject's necessary articulation through language and the multiple institutional discourses in which it is embedded. According to Hegel, flattery comprises a form of self-consciousness which attempts to negate the imperative of externalization by positing a self-identity in "absolute disruption" with a substance whose legitimacy it denies. The culture of flattery is thus "the pure mediation of pure self-consciousness with itself": a substitution, in other words, of a pure, solipsistic self-reflexivity, of the empty point of the subject's self-identity, for a relation which would effectively link the subject to its sociosymbolic environment (520). Because this feature of the world of culture absorbs all objects into itself, the contents of culture become purely contingent. Immune to the requirement of describing anything in reality, to associating in any way with the objective mediations of substance, the world of culture is thus characterized by an "infinite judgment" in which "subject and predicate are utterly indifferent" (520). We recognize in Hegel's infinite judgment that aspect of the Nephew's discourse which makes it impossible for the philosophe to argue with him, since he fails to enunciate a coherent point of view from which the terms of a discussion might ensue.

In his discussion of the infinite judgment Hegel provides his reader with a hint as to what prevents the discourse of culture from reconciling itself with Spirit, thereby establishing some means of communication between the aspirations of its members and those of society in general. Hegel's suggestion is that Enlightenment culture performs an extreme overvaluation of the empty, self-relating essence of self-consciousness above its rendering or articulation in the forms of the social world. Because these forms have been deprived of their capacity to contain any stable content, the subject of culture takes as its essence the "unity of absolutely separate moments," in other words the very point of contradiction which has each of the contents of consciousness turn into its opposite. Hegel's description of this aspect of Spirit as pure culture recalls not only the underlying orientation of the Nephew's discourse, but also the radical linguistic nominalism characteristic of certain familiar strands of postmodern discourse which reduce the contingency of meaning in language to idiosyncratic characterological differences between self-interested liberal individuals: "What is learnt in the world of pure culture is that neither the actuality of power and wealth, nor their specific Notions, 'good' and 'bad,' or the consciousness of 'good' and 'bad' (the noble and the ignoble consciousness), possess truth; on the contrary, all these moments become inverted, one changing into the other, and each is the opposite of itself" (521).

The outcome of the world of culture therefore begins to pivot around the response one brings to this absolute perversion, and the ambiguity of the Nephew's discourse on this point is everywhere highlighted in the dialogue by Diderot. As Moi remarks on a number of occasions, it is impossible to qualify morally or intellectually what the Nephew advances; it might just as well be good or evil, reasoned or absurd, guided by noble or ignoble motives. Though, as the philosopher admits at the outset, the Nephew "brings out the truth" and "unmasks the scoundrels" of ancien régime society (35, TM), he is nevertheless so "vacillating in [his] principles" (93) that the philosophe remains "unable to sort out" if the Nephew "speaks in good faith or bad" (78, TM). Indeed, the question of the mode of enunciation of the Nephew's discourse acquires tremendous significance here. An interrogation of the suffering to which the Nephew's symptoms attest will allow us to discern that the superegoic, properly perverse Other under which his discourse is subsumed may in fact be, at crucial points of the dialogue, on the verge of collapse.

Hysterical Pantomime

I have suggested that the cultural project of Enlightenment as Hegel sees it is to institute a set of universal cultural forms in which all subjects may recognize themselves and one another within a single, positive and coherent totality. Hegel consistently emphasizes the impossibility of conceptualizing the universal culture without taking into consideration the role of language. Indeed, prefiguring Lacan's development of the consequences of the speaking subject's subjection to a symbolic order, Hegel underlines that the radical and deathlike "renunciation of existence" (507) the Enlightenment subject suffers in order to accede to culture parallels the drama of this subject's externalization in properly linguistic forms. Through this externalization the existential self—the self in its immanent, in-itself mode—is lost only to be recovered in a different form. Crucially, this form into which the self is alienated features a *split* between what Hegel refers to as a general and a specific component:

> This alienation [of the subject] takes place solely in language, which here appears in its characteristic significance.... [Language] is the power of speech, as that which performs what has to be performed. For it is the *real existence* of the pure self as self; in speech, self-consciousness, *qua independent separate individuality*, comes as such into existence, so that it exists for others.... Language ... contains [the self] in its purity, it alone expresses the "I," the "I" itself. This real existence of the "I" is, *qua* real existence, an objectivity which has in it the true nature of the "I." The "I" is this particular "I"—but equally the *universal* "I"; its manifesting is also at once the externalization and vanishing of *this* particular "I," and as a result the "I" remains in its universality.... [I]ts real existence is just this: that as a self-conscious Now, as a real existence, it is *not* a real existence, and through this vanishing it *is* a real existence. (508)

No doubt on the more concrete, historical level of his analysis Hegel has in mind in this section of the *Phenomenology* the passage from a feudal, properly military form of self-consciousness, which required the risk of literal death on the battlefield to accede to the substance of nobility, to a more cultural monarchical one, in which battles for distinction took the form of displays of sophistication and wit, of linguistic dexterity, in the salon milieu. Still, language acquires in these passages a more conceptual function, becoming a moment of the dialectic of Spirit in general, and the notion of the "I" comes to summarize the effects of the mediating function that language performs. Émile Benveniste offers a view of the role of this personal pronoun—a so-called "shifter"—which is strikingly similar to Hegel's. Just as, for Hegel, the "I" denotes the paradoxical coincidence within a single signifier of an objective, general form of self-consciousness and the traces of an independent, but vanishing, particularity, for Benveniste it "refer[s] indifferently to any individual whatsoever and ... at the same time identif[ies] him in his individuality."[17]

For his part, Hegel chooses to express this duality in terms of a distinction between the particular I and the universal I: The subject makes use of this pronoun to differentiate its desires from other subjects, but it quickly discovers that the same function, denoted by the same signifier, is available to everyone else. Hegel identifies in the pronoun "I" a function we might qualify as *generically particular*. It provides the subject with a form of self-consciousness which makes it visible to other subjects, yet it pays the price by witnessing the vanishing of its particularity. Thus, though the subject has no choice but to suffer the death of its immediate, natural self-presence in order to gain a self-consciousness recognizable to others, it never fully recuperates itself within the forms of language in which self-consciousness becomes real. This vanishing of the subject of the I bears witness to a self-splitting between an objectively recognizable or communicable form and a mysterious absence—a "real existence"—which for Hegel at once exists and does not, which *per*sists precisely through its disappearance. The subject's vanishing "is thus itself at once its abiding," Hegel says; by passing away into the universal form it retains an empty, generic excess over itself left over as a paradoxical negative remainder of the process of externalization (508).

Now Lacan made of the vanishing to which Hegel points a key feature of his own formulation of the subject of desire. For Lacan, the subject's alienation in the structures of language is punctuated by the "moment of a 'fading' or eclipse ... that is closely bound up with the *Spaltung* or splitting that [the subject] suffers from its subordination to the signifier."[18] The innovation of Lacan's thesis with respect to the semiological tradition in which it intervened was to locate the subject not in the "signifying chain" where it finds what Hegel would call its "substance," but rather in the very moment of this fading itself, in other words at the place in the chain where a signifier lacks. The subject must then compensate for this lack through the development of a properly unconscious fantasy, that is to say one which may be neither signified nor subjectivized and which therefore refuses to appear within the signifying chain. The Lacanian concept of a subject of the unconscious and Hegel's notion of the I's vanishing specificity therefore share the same generically particular status: generic because necessarily at play in any speech act, because a necessary effect of speech as such; yet particular because indicative of an essential but indeterminate subjective nucleus which remains inaccessible to language's forms.

Hegel appears to have anticipated Lacan's decision to define the subject as this unknowable but necessary, indeed *objective*, absence when he qualifies this vanishing of the subject in and from language as the I's "true nature" (508). The paradoxical location of the subject at the point where its content disappears is thus what ultimately defines self-consciousness for Hegel; the vanishing of the particular I, in other words, is self-consciousness as such. To return to Hegel's analysis of Diderot, then, it becomes apparent that it is precisely this empty, disappearing form representing the self-identity of self-consciousness—this mediating "middle term," as he calls it (509)—which makes apparent the mutual interimplication of the competing noble and ignoble judgments in Hegel's dialectic. This essence of the I functions as the medium for the dialectical transformation of subjective content into its opposite, and this continual transformation is the *Verkehrung* or perversion which constitutes for Hegel the underlying radical negativity of Enlightenment culture. Indeed, in a passage which clearly seeks to evoke the Nephew's discourse, Hegel claims that the negativity of what he calls "true Spirit" "exists in the universal talk and destructive judgement which strips of their significance all those moments which are supposed to count as the true being." The truth of Spirit, Hegel continues, "is equally this nihilistic game which it plays with itself" (521). By mercilessly destroying each of the moral certainties and grounded views to which the philosopher clings, the Nephew's discourse articulates the very essence of the Enlightenment world of culture.

As I have intimated, however, this nihilistic game the Nephew plays features a worrisome ambivalence, for his steadfast negation of the philosopher's faith in virtue assumes the form of Hegel's "infinite judgment"—an unlimited affirmation, that is to say, of all judgments which could possibly be uttered, an affirmation whose ambition is to leave nothing unsaid. We have already acquainted ourselves with the properly perverse, absolute Other to which the infinite judgment is enslaved: The subject is free to react to the relativist-nominalist vertigo which Enlightenment culture finally produces through the restoration of a certainty bestowed by this Other whose enjoyment corresponds with its law. I have shown how the Nephew's discourse contains indications of this logic. Hegel, however, clearly sees redeeming qualities in the radical

negativity of Enlightenment culture, a negativity which unsettlingly brings
to the fore the splitting of the I. We are now in a position to explore how
the Nephew's symptoms contain within themselves the seeds of a different, nonperverse outcome, one which refuses the strategy of disavowal of
the Other's self-difference the pervert enthusiastically puts into effect.

These symptoms appear most memorably in the dialogue in association with the Nephew's talent for what the philosopher calls "pantomime." The term refers to the moments in the dialogue when the Nephew,
transported by his musical passions, mimics in a fit of unconscious
spontaneity an entire repertoire of performances from comic operas of
the day. From a psychoanalytic perspective these performances may be
read as manifestations of the absences, or losses of consciousness, which
confronted Freud at the early stages of his work with his hysterical
analysands. As such, they bear witness to a traumatic vacillation in the
Other, a vacillation which reveals a gap or absence in response to which
the Nephew produces his symptom. In other words, the symptom
emerges as a result of the impending failure of the full, "unbarred"
Other whose command the Nephew's perversion would have him obey
and whose imperfection must be covered up by the performance itself.

As the Nephew himself describes it, the art of the bohemian enter-
tainer in the prerevolutionary bourgeois salons of Paris consists in anticipating what is desired of him, of doing whatever is required to satisfy
the audience's perceived demand. But because this demand is in actuality never coherent or unambiguous, the Nephew is forced to engage
in a frantic attempt to conform in advance to all demands; to act out,
more specifically, the full repertoire of all possible musical performances
in a doomed effort to satisfy all parties present. The Nephew expresses
as follows his thoughts on how the salon jester-musician should handle
the difficulty of trying to satisfy an audience's multiple musical tastes:

You must know how to prepare and where to bring in these
peremptory tones in the major key, how to seize the occasion
and the moment, for example when opinion is divided and the
argument has worked itself up to the highest pitch of violence,
when everybody is talking at once and you can't hear what they
are saying. Then you must take up your position some way off
in the corner of the room farthest removed from the battlefield,
having prepared your explosion by a long silence, and you suddenly drop like a bomb in the middle of the contestants. No-
body has ever touched me in this art. . . . I have some soft notes
which I accompany with a smile and an infinite variety of approving faces, with nose, mouth, eyes and brow all brought into

play. I have a certain agility with my hips, a way of twisting my spine, raising or lowering my shoulders, stretching my fingers, bowing my head, shutting my eyes and being struck dumb as though I had heard an angelic, divine voice come down from heaven. (73-4)

We discern in the Nephew's "infinite variety of approving faces" a perverse reflection of the Hegelian infinite judgment which, in its limitless expansion of subjectivity, admits of no negation or lack. In effect, the Nephew's corporeal contortions and nonsignifying noises allow him to offer himself as the object which reconciles the audience with itself. His aim, in other words, is to reduce the audience's multiple and contradictory expectations into a single, uniform taste, which then manifests itself to the Nephew in the form of the otherworldly voice he imagines he hears (and which he acknowledges does not objectively exist). At work in the pantomime is once again the Nephew's desire to incarnate an expressive totality which leaves nothing unarticulated. It becomes apparent as well how his effort, were it to succeed, would place the Nephew in a position of utter dependency with respect to his performance's addressee.

Yet Diderot makes clear that the pantomime does not properly come off, for the Nephew begins to suffer anxiety at the prospect of the impossibility of conforming to a multitude of aesthetic opinions. Indeed, it is this dimension of anxiety which most distinguishes the Nephew's discourse from the clinical picture of perversion psychoanalysis offers. At a very early stage of the dialogue, the narrator is struck by this emergence of suffering in a performance designed to entertain both performer and audience. "Is it not a painful thing," he asks, "to see torment in somebody who is supposed to be giving a representation of pleasure?" (53). It becomes clear that the Nephew advances his pantomime as a response to the enigma of the Other's desire, to its frustrating inability to tell us clearly what it wants. While theoretically his performance constitutes for the Nephew an ideal compromise formation which makes use of sound and gesture as a way of attempting to circumvent the strictures and limitations imposed by language, its underlying impotence becomes plainly apparent to Diderot's philosopher, who looks upon his interlocutor's strange performances as a fascinating but ultimately pathetic form of acting-out.

The musician clearly suffers in a worryingly immediate way from the lack of certainty he begins to discover in his Other. Indeed, it becomes apparent that the prospect of failing to satisfy his audience is so traumatic for the Nephew that he effectively loses consciousness during his performance, retaining no memory of it when he comes to. Though it is clearly quite tempting to qualify his pantomime as an instance of the putatively subversive deterritorialization of language Gilles Deleuze and Félix Guattari attribute to the "minor" literature of Kafka, it becomes clear that whatever liberation the Nephew achieves during his performances not only comes at a formidable psychical cost, but also, in its properly unconscious manifestation, fails to meet the criteria for even the most modest conception of agency. The narrator describes as follows the aftermath of the most intense of the Nephew's strange performances: "By now he was quite beside himself. Knocked up with fatigue, like a man coming out of a deep sleep or long trance, he stood there motionless, dazed, astonished, looking about him and trying to recognize his surroundings. Waiting for his strength and memory to come back, he mechanically wiped his face. Like a person waking up to see a large number of people gathered round his bed and totally oblivious or profoundly ignorant of what he had been doing, his first impulse was to cry out "Well, gentlemen, what's up? What are you laughing at? Why are you so surprised?" ' (104).

It is indeed not at all surprising that the Nephew's rebellion against the formal strictures of language has lent itself to comparison with Deleuze and Guattari's thesis on so-called minor literature: The Nephew's praise of what he calls the "animal cry of passion" evokes precisely the unimpeded, fully embodied, affect-laden expressionism through which the French critics mount their rebellion against the logic of the signifier (105). During his pantomimic absence the Nephew no doubt experiences the temporary fusion of the "subject of the enunciation" and the "subject of the statement"—what Hegel referred to as the "universal" and the "particular" I—which Deleuze and Guattari want to valorize in the nonsemiotic expressivity they claim to find in Kafka's story "The Investigations of a Dog," for example. In this story they identify "language tonalities lacking in signification" extremely similar in their manifestation to the products of the Nephew's own protest against a properly symbolic castration.[19] But the very lack of continuity between the Nephew's performance and the moment of coming to indexes the presence of the traumatic negativity in the Other which the more properly perverse tendency of his discourse seeks to disavow. The fact that the Nephew cannot subjectivize his performance, cannot integrate it into his sociosymbolic universe, points toward the conclusion that the utopian expressive unity Deleuze and Guattari think they find in Kafka is impossible. The properly unconscious quality of the Nephew's pantomime reveals that the splitting of the subject between its statement and its enunciation, the very splitting the schizoanalyst seeks to overcome, is constitutive: The Nephew will never successfully remember his performance; it will remain, like the navel of the Freudian dream-text, untranslatable into the terms of conscious speech.

It is interesting to note that Diderot provides a precociously psychoanalytic clue concerning the aetiology of the Nephew's performances. Diderot in fact directly associates the Nephew's reluctance to submit to the subjective self-estrangement that language imposes to his massive investment in the cultural prestige and authority of his celebrated uncle. The Nephew reveals that it is his fear of failing to measure up to the stature of the great Rameau which causes him to refuse the risk of a perceived sacrifice of enjoyment which a serious engagement with the music world would entail. Indeed, the patronym "Rameau" begins to function as a veritable Lacanian Name-of-the-father in the dialogue, such that the entire economy of the Nephew's reluctance to submit to symbolic castration revolves around this proper name. Lacan used the term "Name-of-the-father" in association with the separation the subject undergoes upon entry into the order of signifiers; it is "the support of the symbolic function,"[20] the signifier which holds the place of the lack in the socio-symbolic network, simultaneously constituting it as a closed totality and designating the limit or absence which haunts it.

Diderot explicitly indicates that one of the sources of the Nephew's hysterico-perverse symptoms lies is his inability to assume the name of which he is the involuntary inheritor. It is indeed difficult not to notice while reading the dialogue that the Nephew demonstrates through its entirety a tortured relation to the uncle who, it should not take a Freudian to discern, figures paternally within his psychical economy. Though at the text's conclusion we are not at all certain what will become of the Nephew, there is little doubt that he will fail to attain the renown of the great Rameau. When the philosopher, in a moment of facile optimism, suggests to the Nephew that a retired life of reflective introspection, combined with the sublimation of his cynical ideas in the writing of a book, might help alleviate his torment, the Nephew responds defensively: "[B]ut I haven't the courage—and then having to sacrifice one's happiness for a success that might not come off! And look at the name I bear—Rameau. Being called Rameau makes things awkward. It's not the same thing with talents as with noble blood, which can be passed on and becomes more illustrious as it descends from grandfather to father, father to son, son to grandson, without the ancestor's obliging the descendant to have any merit. . . . In order merely to be as famous as your father you must be cleverer than he was. You must have inherited the aptitude. I didn't" (116). In order to measure himself against the family name, the Nephew would be forced to "sacrifice his happiness," as he puts it, and thus risk looking ridiculous before his patrons, failing thereby to live up to the stature, thoroughly inflated through fantasy, of his celebrated uncle.

One begins to see that the Nephew's refusal to submit to the sacrifice necessary to assume the name Rameau is intimately related to his ambivalence about submitting to the formal imperatives of signification in general. The Nephew's error consists in his conflation of the properly symbolic status of the paternal function with the imaginary representation of his uncle; he fails to do what Lacan counsels the analyst, namely to "distinguish clearly . . . the unconscious effects of [the paternal] function from the narcissistic relations . . . that the subject sustains with the image and the action of the person who embodies it."[21] In other words, the Nephew suffers not because he fails to take seriously the significance of the inherited proper name, but rather because, on the contrary, he takes it too seriously. The Nephew interprets the paternal function as an imaginary ideal to which he feels obligated to measure up and which never ceases to pronounce critically on his comparative musical merit. In unconscious fantasy the Nephew has mistakenly concluded that the assumption of symbolic castration requires him to perform at the level of his uncle-father. The Nephew's inability to disentangle his narcissistic investment in his uncle's celebrity from the properly symbolic function Rameau serves to represent jeopardizes his capacity to take command of the symbolic function, causing him to resort to the pantomimic performances which leave him physically exhausted and mentally confused.

The Beyond of Perversion

Up to this point we have seen that Hegel advances two fundamental arguments about Diderot's *Rameau's Nephew*. First, the Nephew's discourse, insofar as it stands in for the Enlightenment world of culture, articulates the content of Spirit at one specific historical moment. And second, this discourse of culture effects a distortion of reality—an "absolute and universal perversion[22] and alienation of the actual world and of thought" (521, TM)—characteristic of the social milieu of the late French ancien régime, as well as, more generally, the constellation of Enlightenment thought in its characteristically French, though thoroughly Anglophilic, incarnation. For my purposes the most significant consequence of Hegel's depiction of this helter-skelter world of culture is that in spite of its systematic inversion of acknowledged assumptions it manages to articulate what Hegel calls a hidden "truth." The truth of *Bildung* consists for Hegel in the recognition that in the new world the nobility of state power is contaminated by private capital, and the logic of capital features an underlying synergy with the normative power of the state. In such a state of affairs the notions of wealth and state power— the means by which the noble and ignoble forms of self-consciousness attribute the judgments "good" and "bad" to their objects—lose their stability, their capacity to signify a stable signified. "All these moments become perverted," Hegel concludes, "one changing into the other, and each is the opposite of itself" (521, TM).

Hegel's argument here identifies a fundamental dialectical paradox we can articulate both in particular historical terms as well as in general theoretical ones. In the context of the ancien régime just prior to the revolution, the nobility found itself in the situation of witnessing a new bourgeois class increase its private wealth and usurp noble privilege while paying lip service to the state. Conversely, the private, liberal pursuit of economic self-interest produced dividends which accrued to the state and the general public it in principle represents. Of course, the outcome of this state of affairs was the destabilization, and eventual overthrow, of the monarchy, as well as a further blurring of the boundary between the state form and capital. But Hegel's discussion also allows us to advance to the formulation of a general, nonhistorical law of subjectivity: The subject may only return to itself—constitute itself as an authentic subject—by means of an initial radical alienation it experiences as a traumatic expropriation. During this process what is most revered and idealized is shown to harbour a disgusting and base truth. It should come as no surprise, then, that in spite of Hegel's obvious discomfort with what he terms the "nihilism" of the Nephew's discourse, he shows nothing but disdain for the "uneducated thoughtlessness" (521) of the philosophe. If we compare the movement of Hegel's dialectical interpretation to the progression of a proper psychoanalysis, we are forced to state that the Nephew, in Hegel's view, is at a very late stage of the process, lacking only a final shift in perspective; the philosopher, in stark contrast, has not yet really begun.

Hegel will in fact suggest that the form of Spirit which Diderot's dialogue finally uncovers—that is to say, not the naively virtuous Spirit of the philosophe, but rather the truly dialectical Spirit—gestures toward a conclusion which differs from both the Nephew's relativist nihilism and the philosopher's precritical faith. Reason, indeed, has its limits: The forms of knowledge and culture through which human civilizations intercourse with the world attempt in vain to fill a central void of nonknowledge, of nonsense—the pure, empty self-relating agency of self-consciousness itself. Nonetheless, precisely because of this inherent limitation to what it is possible to know, it is necessary to underline that the ideas of difference and contingency toward which

cultural knowledge leads are also—in themselves—limited. It is therefore of paramount importance for Hegel to refuse the absolute isolation
of the self from reality and thereby to resist the temptation of the enjoyment I have been calling "cynical."

Instead of asserting with certainty the impossibility of certain or
nonrelative knowledge, Hegel's reading of Diderot gestures toward an
alternative conclusion: The subject must neither arrest its search for
knowledge at a kind of affirmative, nonpropositional declaration of absolute contingency and difference (which at any rate, as the figure of the
Nephew ably demonstrates, becomes in its most interesting form the
hysterical protest that there should be a limit to the proliferation of
differences), nor fall back onto the "nearly animal consciousness" which
subsumes the world's objects under the command of the erotic ego's
quest for pleasure. Rather, the subject must truly tarry with the scandalous void of nonsense which the limits of language and knowledge impose in order to identify the necessarily political zone of fracture which
separates the sociosymbolic world of culture from the historical real.
Hegel elucidates as follows the misleading implications of the sham
ultimatum Diderot's dialogue would seem, if only on the level of form,
to impose: "If the demand for [the] removal [of this "whole world of
perversion"] is directed to the universal individuality, it cannot mean
that Reason should give up again the spiritually developed consciousness it has acquired, should submerge the widespread wealth of its
moments again in the simplicity of the natural heart, and relapse into
the wilderness of the nearly animal consciousness, which is also called
Nature or innocence. On the contrary, the demand for this dissolution
can only be directed to the Spirit of culture itself, in order that it return
out of its confusion to itself as Spirit, and win for itself a still higher
consciousness" (524).

Though, in other words, it would be a mistake to retreat from the
disquieting instabilities of developed Spirit to firmer precritical ground,
the cynical reason the Nephew's discourse articulates cannot represent
the terminal point of the dialectic as articulated through the world of
culture. The musician's absolute, nihilistic relativism must be traversed
in order to accede to the "still higher" form of consciousness to which
Hegel here—rather cryptically, to be sure—alludes. So what exactly is
this higher form of consciousness for Hegel? And does he provide any
indication of how the Nephew's consciousness might move on toward a
more desirable outcome?

Most readers of the *Phenomenology* would surely agree that the
distinction Hegel draws between pure nihilistic relativism and the ambiguous still higher consciousness is rather sketchily developed in the

passages which relate to Diderot. Nonetheless, Hegel's argument appears to be that the Nephew has in a sense already attained it, but that its perspective on this consciousness requires a subtle but crucial final adjustment. More specifically, Hegel avers that the Nephew's consciousness, however developed, still lacks the double character of authentically dialectical reflection. It is not merely a question of coming to terms with the vanity of every judgment featuring pretensions to certainty; one must additionally arrive at an analogous, negative and reflexive, perspective with respect to the nominalist-relativist consciousness itself. Hegel thereby suggests in truly paradoxical fashion that the problem with the Nephew's discourse is not that it is cynical, but rather that, if one may put it this way, it is not cynical enough. The world of culture's cynicism lacks the gesture of negation proper to the relativist moment with respect to relativist consciousness itself.

In effect, it is not merely that any judgment pertaining to reality is necessarily contingent, context specific. Additionally, the consciousness of the contingent judgment is itself also limited: Contingency is in itself also contingent. Ultimately, for Hegel, reason does not allow thought to move from the observation that any particular truth claim one might come up with has limited validity to the conclusion that the category of truth as such is conceptually irrelevant, that it pertains to precisely nothing within Spirit's dialectic. Enlightenment culture encounters a resistance within itself where it wants to transform its negative, critical work into a kind of program—a set of positive cultural values. In essence, Hegel thought that only brutish, absurdly solipsistic and antisocial forms of hedonistic utilitarianism can result from the systematization of Enlightenment-brand rationalisms and empiricisms. By resisting this final gesture of radical alienation—this alienation with respect to one's own consciousness of the world of objects—the Enlightenment subject is condemned to the suffering demonstrated by the Nephew and to the slavish emulation of valued personages and ideas to which he dedicates his life. He is destined to pay the devastating price, in the form of his stubborn, dysfunctional nominalism, of his ambivalent subjection to the sociosymbolic order.

One particular detail of Hegel's cryptic intimations of perversion's beyond appears to refer to an anecdote recounted in *Rameau's Nephew*; it also provides a more concrete depiction of what the Nephew's discourse lacks. The philosophe tells the story of the second son of the Calas family who goes off to Cartagena when his elder brother is handed the family fortune. Later, after the story's protagonist learns that his brother spoiled the fortune, stripped the parents of their assets and abandoned them to their own devices, the second son immediately returns home, whereupon he restores his family to its accustomed level of material comfort through dedication and hard work. "That man looked upon this period as the happiest in his life," concludes the philosopher (67), his voice trailing off in a paroxysm of edified moral satisfaction. From the philosopher's perspective this single example suffices to establish both that the performance of virtuous deeds secures happiness and that humanity can rise above its natural, self-involved psychology. Like the Nephew, however, Hegel clearly remains unconvinced. "To represent the existence of the good and noble as an isolated anecdote," he maintains, "is the most disparaging thing that can be said about it." The singularity of the virtuous action stands as an "espèce, a mere 'sort' of thing" before "the universal actuality of the perverted action."[23] And if the philosopher were to address himself merely to the concrete sensuous individual, Hegel continues, beseeching him to exit what he memorably calls "this whole world of perversion," he would simply contradict himself, since this individual extraction remains impotent in the face of the corruption of the "real world," and the individual, despite his best efforts, remains "conditioned" by it as is "even Diogenes in his tub" (all 524).

Hegel's answer is therefore that it is not to the individual in the particularity of its interests, but rather to what he calls the "universal individuality," that the demand for a decisive exit from the world of perversion is to be addressed. This change of address, according to Hegel, prevents the descent into the "animal consciousness" which is the admittedly counterintuitive endpoint of *Bildung*'s hegemony, but still allows for the preservation of the "spiritually developed consciousness" which reason acquires through acculturation. But the distinction drawn between the world of perversion and the still higher consciousness proves to be rather tricky, for Hegel asserts unequivocally that the Nephew is essentially already there.

By no means does Hegel wish to suggest, in other words, that the consciousness of the equivocal quality of the contents of the noble and ignoble judgments must be abandoned in favor of the outdated certainties of the virtuous moral philosopher. On the contrary, consciousness of the "vanity of all reality and every definite Notion" (525) constitutes, in a manner of speaking, the base from which the superstructure of the higher, supraindividual spiritual consciousness is achieved. Insofar as the subject remains imprisoned in its empirical specificity, Hegel implies, the ambivalence of value—its contingency, one might say—can only appear absurd and meaningless. The only available rational response to such an individualistic world is the combination of cynicism and base utilitarian pragmatism that the Nephew wants to embrace. If the world is made up of species which devour one another, so the logic goes, you might as well go ahead and devour all you can before you become someone else's supper. From this perspective, the phenomenal world is constituted by objects which are, so to speak, structurally hypocritical. The spirit of pure culture has refined into an art of the highest order the ability to pass judgment on a world which perverts all unequivocal judgments of value.

But what this self has not yet learned to do, Hegel continues, is to "comprehend" (526) this deeply unreliable world. The narcissistic, self-interested self which passes judgment on the world's incoherence derives its own vanity precisely from the vanity that it has itself already attributed to the objects which comprise it. In the manner of a self-fulfilling prophecy, the cynical hopelessness and isolation of the subject of culture ensue directly from the despairing gesture through which it first characterizes its surrounding world as vain. To render his point more concrete, Hegel returns one final time to his historical example of the nouveau-riche bourgeoisie of the late French ancien régime who purchase their feudal titles—buy their way, in other words, into a social position which, through that very action, ceases to exist. "Through renunciation and sacrifice (526)," Hegel explains, this emergent class played the game of courtly deference to state power—flattery, in other words—as a means of acquiring not only wealth, but recognition and distinction, within the state structure; it disguised its particular interests under the cloak of its obedience to the universal form.

But Hegel argues that once the real goals of power and riches are achieved, they are shown to be not the form of mastery over state and subjects in which they originally appeared, but rather a means of subjection to what Hegel, I wish to argue, characterizes as capital's abstract, superhuman forces—forces which ultimately thwart the individual's ambition to represent its particularity to itself and to the world. The subjective essence of the historical moment of pure culture proves to be not the wealth and power for which the sacrifice of flattery was originally undertaken, but the form of this flattery itself—this pure, perverse, duplicitous discourse in which appearance and truth are combined into a unique, self-subverting and self-contradictory whole. Accordingly, the endpoint of the dialectic of culture reveals itself to be not some normalized, reconciled version of the scandalous Nephew, but rather the Nephew on the very level of the awareness of his own self-antagonism, as the hysterical "consciousness in revolt" which best approximates, according to Hegel, the pure, empty point of Spirit's—and every subject's—self-relation; the point from which the contradictory contents of subjectivity are sublated into a fractured, imperfect whole.

Jean Hyppolite's analysis of this aspect of Hegel's dialectic under-scores how the Spirit of the world of culture "returns to self" in both Rousseau's evocation of the "new positivity" of a "return to nature" and the conflict between faith and "pure intellection," which will of course make up the contents of the subsequent stage of the dialectic of Spirit.[24] But Hyppolite's accurate observations nonetheless underestimate the significance of the more *formal* quality of Hegel's figuration of Spirit's return to self in the form of the Nephew's "self-consciousness in revolt." The continuation of the dialectic under the guise of the new contents of faith and Enlightenment reason is a regression of Spirit, though an entirely necessary one, into a new manifestation of its alienation. In other words, because of the purely formal character of Spirit's self-reconciliation, its occurrence is always on one level the same regardless of the nature of the specific historical contents whose conflict paves the way for this reconciliation. Insofar as it uncovers the roots of the second-degree or redoubled alienation of self-consciousness in revolt, the Nephew's discourse may be said to convey the endpoint of every phase of the Hegelian dialectic, an endpoint which is nonetheless destined to attempt a new, imperfect realization in the substantial forms of the world.

It is not the least merit of Diderot's dialogue that it reveals how the Nephew is himself conscious of the manner in which power makes use of his madness as a temporary distraction which serves to domesticate the forces working against the political status quo. The function of the Nephew's discourse from the perspective of power is to provide a sem-blance of resistance, to provide the general public with false evidence of the social immanence of subversion. In effect, the new bourgeoisie uses such figures as the Nephew to hide from itself its own self-enslavement to the cult of wealth. What it purposefully fails to recognize is thus the merely performative character of the Nephew's speeches, in other words their playful, ludic, carnivalesque enunciation designed to subordinate its potential political effectiveness to the power relation in which it is inscribed. From a psychoanalytic perspective, the Nephew's discourse becomes problematic by virtue of the fact that the ostensibly critical, subversive character of his indictments ally themselves, on the level of their enunciation, with either an implicit, hysterical call to a master ar-ticulating between the lines a demand for recognition, or a rather more insidious, and properly perverse, renunciation which posits an absolute Other whose cynical enjoyment comes to constitute a law whose very letter can be obeyed. Though it is possible for us—Diderot's readers—to uncover in what the Nephew says to his patrons a critique of the entire sociopolitical system which grants them their newfound status, the Nephew's professed concern to conform to the complex demands of his audience betrays the true nature of his desire: To gain through the pantomime his audience's love; to be recognized for the entertainment value, rather than the actual contents, of its articulations.

Power requires its clownish other to indicate to those subject to it that they need not take the law at its word because it contains within itself its own transgression. In the meantime, of course, power appeals to the law in its effort to undertake and enforce concrete social transformation. The Nephew's performances lack authentic political significance because they articulate their social criticisms in a feigned, ironical mode which masks a conformist demand for recognition under the ostensibly subversive surface of critique. Far from constituting a deterritorializing strategy which subverts the signifying apparatus of language and the sociosymbolic efficacy of the law, the Nephew's discourse is a symptom of a profound and unacknowledged ideological misrecognition, one which is clearly still disturbingly ambient today.

For the Nephew's discourse surely all too clearly anticipates the contemporary theories of radical difference and contingency, with their cult of idiosyncratic self-fashioning and their a priori distrust of the normalizing function of public discourses and institutions. Indeed, the more I consider Diderot's uncannily compelling dialogue, the more parallels I see between the disorienting world of perversion it puts on display and our own, only superficially contradictory, early twenty-first century world of rigid fundamentalist certainties and cynical, solipsistic nihilism. If we take, as we must, Hegel's interpretation of *Rameau's Nephew* at its word, we are led to the conclusion that what the Nephew—and perhaps the whole of late- or postmodern culture—needs to do is not normalize his perversion (revert, in other words, to the philosopher's untested, precritical faith), but rather allow the scandalous truth of his insights to lead him toward a conscious political *act,* one which openly acknowledges the consequences of the law's disjunction from itself and assumes the risk of socio-subjective abjection which any authentic political act must entail. In the end, Hegel's analysis teaches us that we tend toward the execution of such an act when we accept the paradox that the apparent sacrifice of enjoyment required for integration within a normative sociosymbolic framework effectively functions as a precondition for its thoroughgoing political renegotiation. And perhaps such a difficult but necessary acceptance will finally unleash the long overdue revolution of our time.

Chapter Five

The Guardian of Criminal Being

Let us now attempt to wash our brains clean of all we have heard
about Antigone and look in detail at what goes on there.

—Jacques Lacan, *The Ethics of Psychoanalysis*

The tragic is the expression of the absolute position.

—G. W. F. Hegel, "Über die Wissenschaftliche
Behandlungsarten des Naturrechts"

Woe for sin of minds perverse,
Deadly fraught with mortal curse.
Behold us slain and slayers, all akin.
Woe for my counsel dire, conceived in sin.

—Creon, in Sophocles' *Antigone*

Lacan contra Hegel

Because tragedy, and more specifically Sophoclean tragedy, is the genre
privileged above all others by both speculative philosophy and psychoanalytic theory, it should come as no surprise that the tragic ethos per-
meates the dialectical structures of both discourses, particularly in their
ethical modes. Famously, Hegel's *Phenomenology of Spirit* bases its analysis of the dialectic of ethical substance in the ancient world on Sophocles'

Antigone. Somewhat less famously outside French analytic circles, Lacan's 1959–1960 seminar on the ethics of psychoanalysis culminates in a difficult but spellbinding reading of that exemplary tragedy. As Suzanne Gearhart has argued, speculative philosophy and Freudian psychoanalysis "are modeled after and elaborated to an important extent in terms of a particular view of tragedy."[1] However, one of Lacan's main intentions in revisiting Sophocles was to draw a line of demarcation between Hegel's interpretation and his own.

In this chapter I wish to perform a close reading of Lacan's interpretation of *Antigone* by specifying what is at stake in the Lacanian articulation of psychoanalytic ethics and by exploring the understanding of tragedy through which Lacan's argument takes shape. Though I will suggest that his interpretation is not as inimical to Hegel's as he appears to have thought, Lacan brings to bear a structural understanding of ethics which contrasts sharply with his predecessor's historical method. Lacan's reading of *Antigone* features the additional and singular merit of defining the paradoxical relation between the two understandings of perversion in psychoanalysis I have pointed out: The motive of the pervert, embodied by Creon in the tragedy, is characterized by a paradoxical attempt to depervert desire—to have desire conform, in other words, to a determinate, unlimited, and universal construct of the Good. Lacan's formulation is unique in the history of psychoanalytic theory (not to mention the history of ethics) in the radical negativity of its insistence that ethics must by definition be disruptive, antinormative, hostile to all attempts at systematization and rationalization. Whereas the pervert's psychical economy depends on the positing of an unlimited norm which allows for no deviation (and therefore enforces the strictest obedience), the ethical act makes visible the law's inability to conform to itself; it makes manifest the law's perverse deviation from its own precept. The ethical act is thus inimical to the conformism of what Lacan calls the "service of goods."[2] It emerges as an *event*—unforeseen, unjustifiable, unintelligible—with respect to the sociopolitical context in which it occurs.

The *Phenomenology* contains Hegel's first major interpretation of the tragedy. In it Hegel advances the position that each of the two protagonists, Creon and Antigone, personifies one aspect of an ethical substance split between the human law of the polis and the unwritten, divine law of the family.[3] In Hegel's view, the unwavering single-mindedness with which Creon and Antigone cling to their respective laws causes the action each performs in its name to manifest itself as a contradiction of its content. Antigone defends the familial law of the underworld when she spreads ashes over her brother Polynices' body. For his part, Creon defends the law of the political order by forbidding the ceremonial recognition of an enemy of the polis. Hegel faults the two protagonists equally for the tragic outcome of the drama, suggesting that the organic, unmediated relation of the Greek subject to law and custom was destined to self-destruct to pave the way for the modern mediated forms of legality which for Hegel made their first appearance during the Roman Empire. Hegel's "ethical substance" therefore corresponds to a historically specific set of social customs with which subjects immediately identified; a set of duties and responsibilities not yet embodied in an external legal apparatus presupposing individual freedoms which might contradict it.

The intransigence with which Creon and Antigone adhere to their ethical precepts precipitates the collapse of the beautiful ethical world which defines the tragic for Hegel. Tragedy thus functions on two different levels in Hegel's analysis: First, sociopolitically and historically, it describes the transformation of Spirit which destroys the ancient ethical world and clears the way for the emergence of the forms of modern legality; and second, psychologically or subjectively, it designates the lack of balance which characterizes the protagonists' ethical positions. Creon and Antigone are equally guilty, in Hegel's eyes, for their failure to recognize that the human and divine laws partake of the same substance and in consequence are to be attributed with the same degree of ethical legitimacy. There is properly speaking no hero in *Antigone* for Hegel. Sophocles' drama does not depict the resistance of a heroic subject against an unjust political authority; rather, the tragedy provides evidence for the cause of the disappearance of an outmoded form of society.

In contrast to Hegel's, Lacan's understanding of Sophocles' tragedy is decidedly more partisan. It is Antigone who personifies the heroic, tragic position, and Creon who adopts the erroneous, perverse, antitragic one. The spectacle of ancient tragedy for Lacan reproduces on the Athenian stage the purification of desire which, he wishes to argue, is the primary ethical goal of psychoanalysis. During this process the subject abandons the imaginary fixations which defer its confrontation with desire and impede its apprehension of the available opportunities for the execution of a properly ethical act. In Lacan's view, such an act is by definition beyond the Good—beyond, in other words, the attribution of its motivation to a sanctioned, socially intelligible end. Creon's commitment to the good of the polis features an inherent repudiation of this seemingly destructive, radically nonutilitarian aspect of desire, and it is this repudiation which motivates his stance vis-à-vis Polynices. No subject who fails to recognize that which is accepted as the collective good—as determined by Creon, of course—merits the ceremonial recognition of being which the funeral rights accord.

Though both Hegel and Lacan present *Antigone* as a privileged locus of ethical conceptuality, Lacan's stance toward the Hegelian analysis
was decidedly unkind at the moment of the ethics seminar. Lacan offers
his reading as a corrective to a long tradition of obfuscating misreadings
which emerged, in his view, in the wake of Hegel's influential commentary. The rhetorical weight of Lacan's analysis is directly targeted at
Hegel's ethical dialectic, presenting in its stead a radical reformulation
of the ethics of tragedy. Indeed, Lacan presents his reading of Sophocles
as a return to a true tragic essence which the critical tradition has long
since rendered banal and ideological. Contrary to Hegel's position, Lacan
underlines the significance of Creon's error, signified by the Sophoclean
term *hamartia*, which Lacan renders in his ethics seminar as a "mistake
or blunder" (277). Lacan's interpretation underscores how Creon's actions betray a perversion of his desire—a perversion arising paradoxically from his failure to respect a certain irreducible, excessive perversion
in the subject which subverts the homogenizing and normalizing pretensions of notions of the collective Good. Bearing in mind Lacan's crucial
point, it becomes possible to appreciate the significance of Antigone's
act as a paradoxical purification of desire from perversion—paradoxical
because it depends on the recognition of an inherent perversity in desire. This purification finds its dramatic correlative in the Chorus's progression from its sympathy with Creon's edict to its wonder at the
heroine's tragic beauty, which appears, Lacan suggests, in consequence
of her martyrdom for desire.

Lacan's structural interpretation of *Antigone* clears the ground for a
properly negative formalization of psychoanalytic ethics. In contrast,
Hegel's concern for the ethical substance and the fall of the polis features a sociohistorical emphasis which contrasts sharply with Lacan's
desire to describe formally the ethical importance of Antigone's subjective structure. For Hegel, *Antigone* bears witness to a dialectical transformation of Spirit; the tragedy stages the end of ethical custom and the
birth of a historically unprecedented tension between a discrete, self-
interested citizen and the norms embodied in the state's legal forms.
For Lacan, in contrast, *Antigone* identifies a particular orientation with
respect to desire potentially available to all subjects regardless of both
their circumscription in a concrete historical reality, and their particular
situation—of class, sex, race, ethnicity, and so on—within that reality.
The "and so on" is particularly apt here because the realm of the ethical,
in Lacan's view, is located precisely where the subject's positive differences from other subjects—what are sometimes referred to as the
subject's "positions"—are not. Indeed, this explains why Lacan's view of
ethics must be distinguished from the historicist limitations of Hegel's

perspective on *Antigone*: An ethical act will always feature the same structure regardless of its historical circumscription precisely because such an act challenges the very terms of this circumscription, occurs at the point of its antagonism with itself. I suggest we begin our discussion, then, with a closer look at the Hegelian interpretation of *Antigone* in view of setting the stage for Lacan's intervention.

Ethical Beauty

Greek antiquity incarnates for Hegel the ethical substance at the earliest stage of the dialectic of Spirit; it functions within the whole of the *Phenomenology* as an idealized, antediluvian direct democracy against which all future manifestations of Spirit within European culture are to be compared. Hegel's references to *Antigone* appear at the beginning of the large section on Spirit, prior to the discussion of the world of culture in which figures Hegel's other literary reference, to Diderot's *Rameau's Nephew*. If the Nephew's nihilism serves as the emblem of the chaotically unstable culture Hegel saw figured in the ancien régime, the forgotten beauty of the ethical polis negatively reveals the extent of European culture's loss of its unmediated moral certainties. For Hegel, *Antigone* articulates a tragic conflict between political and extrapolitical ethical norms which created conditions under which the instance of public authority was to be experienced as an imposition of an alien will. In this way Greek tragedy inaugurates the introduction of an underlying disharmony within the ethical substance which would go on to present, as I have suggested, a dimension of individuated interest at odds with the normative framework of the modern state.

In Hegel's view, this process begins at the historical moment of the Athenian city-state when the ethical substance breaks off into two component parts: the public, general, masculine, human law of the collective civic will; and the private, familial, feminine, divine law of the dead. Human law is the law which is conscious of itself; it subsists explicitly in a universal form as the "known law" and "prevailing custom" providing a normative framework for the everyday functioning of public life.[4] Human law is a function of the conscious relation of each subject to the collective of citizens; it represents the spontaneous, unmediated identification of the (male) citizen with the will of the polis as a whole. In conflict with this generic feature of human law is the immediate substance of divine law which, in its universal incarnation, substantiates itself in the form of the "natural ethical community" represented by the family (450). Embodied in the Penates, the household gods of the Athenians, the family represents in Hegel's analysis an unconscious or noncognitive mode of being which works to connect the individual citizen to an ancestral community reaching beyond the earthly, pragmatic limitations of political discourse. In contrast to the immediate, but abstract, universality of the political community, within which the citizen recognizes himself as an entity formally equal to all others, the family embodies the citizen's belonging to a concrete particularity which eludes the collective interest, deforming and indeed perverting it. "As the immediate being of the ethical order," writes Hegel, "[the Family] stands over against that order which shapes and maintains itself by working for the universal; the Penates stand opposed to the universal Spirit" (450).

Each of Hegel's two opposing laws works on its own behalf to realize its formative principle. The human law ensures that citizens will immediately identify with the collective interest of the polis, ensuring that they will receive not even an inkling of an interest which threatens to conflict with the general will. The divine law maintains the relation of each citizen to a family matrix within which he appears not simply as a function of the collective's recognition of his public work, but as an essence worthy of respect merely by virtue of his intrinsic being. From the unified perspective of the ethical substance the two laws appear as a harmonious, mutually complementary whole. "Each of the opposites in which the ethical substance exists," writes Hegel, "contains the entire substance, and all the moments of its content" (450). But the discontinuity between what the ethical laws are for themselves and what they are at the level of their mutual participation in the ethical substance leads to the disintegration of the Greek political ethos; and it is precisely as the narrative of this disintegration that Hegel considered the action of *Antigone*. Through the act the ethical agent attempts to realize concretely in the world what its law upholds. But because the agent in the Greek polis adheres, according to Hegel, only to the law with which it identifies, it remains ignorant of the mutual implication of the laws in the ethical substance. In consequence, the act results in the agent's confrontation with what Hegel calls "destiny" (*Schicksal*)—a certain irreducible negativity in the ethical substance which brings to an end the harmonious interimplication of its human and divine aspects.

Plainly, there is no ambiguity as to which law each of the protagonists of Sophocles' tragedy obeys. Creon defends what he considers the public interest in denying burial rights to Polynices, who waged war on the city in the name of the familial order of succession. From Creon's perspective, the threat Polynices poses to the public order supersedes any right he might have, as Oedipus's first-born son, to rule over Thebes. In Antigone's case, however, the precise motivation for her adherence to the divine law is less clear in Hegel's interpretation. On one level, insofar as the divine law embodies the recognition of "the blood relation" (451), Hegel suggests that Antigone's defiance is in part a defense of the purely contingent natural fact of Polynices' precedence in birth. As a representative of the family, Antigone defends the concrete ordering of subjects as they appear in the familial realm as opposed to the abstract equality of citizens—all male, of course—as they appear in the political sphere. On a deeper level of Hegel's analysis, however, Antigone's action acquires a more consequential ethical meaning. Rather than defend the rights of her brother as he appears from the perspective of life—as, in other words, a concrete individual inserted by the contingencies of birth into a particular sociosymbolic situation—Antigone draws her motivation from the "nether world" (455), where each subject is granted a supplementary, metaphysical completion, thereby acquiring membership in a whole which extends beyond its existence as a mere biological individual subject to the vagaries of fate.

Because Hegel's assessment of the import of Antigone's motivation is the aspect of his interpretation which most resembles Lacan's, it will be profitable to add further detail to Hegel's presentation of the divine law's significance. Hegel states that what is most properly ethical about the family "is not the *natural* relationship of its members," including, more specifically, any cultural significance attributed to sibling birth order, but rather the manner in which the family functions as the guardian of a certain nonconcrete specificity among its members, whom it insists on considering abstractly, in other words as universals (451). An act performed in the name of the divine law, Hegel explains, must be "related to the *whole* individual or to the individual *qua* universal" (451); what appears from the perspective of human law as an illegal particularity is abstracted into universality by the function of divine law. With Antigone's burial of her brother firmly in mind, Hegel adds that the act performed according to this law acquires an attribute of necessity: It may not be determined by any contingent element derived either from its subject or its object. The end of the act, Hegel specifies, cannot be the "education" (*Erziehung*) of the subject on behalf of whom it is undertaken. Nor is it acceptable to act in such a way that the service provides help to the patient, assists him or her in the reaching of a particular goal (451). Least of all may the act make reference to the merit of the patient, to the extent to which the person in question deserves the service performed. We may not intervene, Hegel implies, in such a way that our motivation refers to the Good—be it our own good, or the good of the party on behalf of whom we act. The act performed in accordance with divine law must be purely unconditioned by anything of the order of life and what Kant would call its pathological interests. Hegel expresses as follows how the ethical act presupposes in the subject who motivates it a serene, holistic, non-phenomenal supplement he associates with death: "The deed no longer concerns the living but the dead, the individual who, after a long succession of separate disconnected experiences, concentrates himself into a single completed shape, and has raised himself out of the unrest of the accidents of life into the calm of simple universality" (451).

Hegel's evocation of the consequences of adherence to Antigone's divine law emphasizes both the properly morbid quality of the heroine's position—she acts on behalf of, personifies, death—and the fraternity of the purified, disinterested character of her law with the Kantian categorical imperative, according to which, as is well known, the moral subject may act ethically only if it can first universalize its maxim. Very much anticipating, as we will see later on, Lacan's appraisal of the motivation of Antigone's act, Hegel argues that the subject who inspires the divine ethical act transcends its concrete, sensuous existence, and is attributed a supplement of ontological completion which is inconceivable within the limited perspective of its biographical life. Divine law confers an act which is therefore performed in the name of death, for the sake of that aspect of the collective ethos, in other words, which remains socially inadmissible, unintelligible. In the Greek polis the divine law may not be explicitly acknowledged; it remains, as Hegel puts it, "unconscious" (450). Consequently, the act which attempts to obey this law takes on a transgressive, otherworldly quality which radically questions the public order, uncovering in the process a world of painful abjection jettisoned from public visibility.

An example from the tragedy illustrates the effects of this eminently political violence. When the guard describes to Creon the sight of the heroine attempting to bury her brother for the second time, he refers to the spectacle as a "godsent affliction" and compares Antigone's anguished cry to "the piercing note of a bird when she sees her empty nest robbed of her young."[5] Hegel's conception of the divine law picks up on that aspect of the messenger's description which qualifies Antigone's action as one which challenges the limits of what qualifies for representation within the terms of the eminently civic order Creon upholds. Because life in the polis is circumscribed by the communitarian ethical imperative of the male citizen, Antigone's transgression necessarily appears within the public realm as performed on behalf of the dead. The interest on behalf of which Antigone acts is simply inconceivable from Creon's perspective of public order. As Lacan emphasizes in his seminar, Antigone's law is unwritten: It cannot be formulated in the objective, recognizable terms through which the human law is articulated, and the ritual acknowledgment of Polynices' demise must remain, in consequence, hidden from public view.

It is with respect to this idea of an unrecognized death left to the contingent cruelties of nature that Antigone's action acquires for Hegel its ethical significance. Antigone breaks Creon's interdiction in an effort to transform the randomness of his destiny into a consciously assumed choice. For Hegel, the formal quality of the burial ceremony keeps away the "unconscious appetites" and "abstract entities" (452) which cast a disturbing, absurdist shadow over Polynices' destiny. One has the sense while reading Hegel's analysis that, had Antigone not performed her sisterly duty, the spirit of Polynices would have remained in a state of unrest, tormenting his survivors with the guilt of their unforgivable oversight. The nature of the ethical act consists therefore in adding to the merely natural phenomenon of death a human, cultural, properly symbolic feature whose function is to designate that aspect of each subject which remains immune to any moral qualification one might wish to bring to the events making up its life story. In Lacanian terms, the symbolism of the funeral rite aims at demarcating the limit of the symbolic order itself; the empty place which defines the subject as a subject, where it remains unexpressed, undetermined by its every representation.

As I will further explore below, Hegel and Lacan share this perspective on the ethical significance of death in *Antigone*. Each interpreter brings to our attention both the absolute, noncognitive, unconditioned nature of Antigone's defiance of Creon's edict, and the destructive force this defiance exerts on Creon's concern for the public good. In contrast to the ponderous rationalizations which characterize Creon's defense of his actions, Antigone's decision to defy Creon's edict distinguishes itself through its exciting spontaneity. Antigone's speeches are marked by their utter lack of psychological depth. She acts unconditionally, without thinking; without deliberating whether or not her deed will conform to this or that standard of moral action.

Now the difficulty with Hegel's analysis is surely that the ethical substance he needs to presuppose as a kind of prehistory of the dialectic proper is intimately connected to his problematic sexual differentiation of the two laws. From a psychoanalytic perspective, Hegel's association of the beautiful ethical world of Antiquity with a presumptive notion of the sexes' complementarity indexes the thoroughly idealized construction of the Greek polis which characterized Hegel's generation of German intellectuals. But insofar as the trajectory of the dialectic deems the destruction of the Greek polis a question of a properly historical necessity, it becomes possible to attribute the following, admittedly generous, reading to Hegel's ethical narrative: The sociopolitical structure of the polis—its tidy separation of men and women, citizen and noncitizen, public and private, universal and particular—depends on an ideological fantasy veiling a fundamental, traumatic reality intrinsic to the very motion of Spirit. And in the context of the *Phenomenology* this underlying reality—this element, more exactly, which returns to disrupt both the illusory, pseudonatural complementarity of the sexes and the substance of the beautiful ethical life—is, I wish to suggest, what Hegel in the *Antigone* passages refers to as *destiny*, what Sophocles in the tragedy calls *fate*, and what, in the vocabulary of Lacanian psychoanalysis, is known as the *real*.

The Real of Destiny

Destiny is undoubtedly one of the most suggestive and overlooked elements of Hegel's discussion of *Antigone*. When we read his account retrospectively from the moment of destiny's intrusion into the dialectic of ethical substance, it becomes possible not only to discern the more problematic aspects of Hegel's idealization of the Greek polis, but also to specify, more concretely, both the affinity and difference of Hegel's view of *Antigone* with respect to the Lacanian reading. To be sure, things fall apart in Thebes, according to Hegel, when Antigone and Creon decide to act. As the protagonists put their respective laws into practice, a negative movement is introduced into ethical life which, Hegel avers, "engulfs in the abyss of its single nature divine and human law alike, as well as the two self-consciousnesses in which these powers have their existence" (464). The result of this introduction of negativity into the ancient ethical substance is a kind of subjectivization of Spirit; the transfer of the forms of consciousness, in other words, from the stuff of ethical custom to the individual ethical agent. In this fashion self-consciousness represses its knowledge of the opposing law and forgets the laws' mutual dependence. From the perspective of the intervention of destiny, then, Hegel's account of the end of Antiquity begins to take on the cast of a kind of allegorical representation of the birth of subjectivity as such, for which the beautiful ethical world functions as a mythological trope representing the prehistory of the dialectic proper.

After *Antigone* it becomes impossible to imagine in the Hegelian ethical framework an unmediated relation between subject and law; henceforth the law of proper action splits itself from the ethical substance and discovers a new realm of negative universality associated with the family's implication in a deathlike realm of being at odds with the utilitarian interests of the public law. Though Hegel clearly believed not only that the citizen of the polis enjoyed an immediate identification with social customs, but also that the possibility of such an identification would emblematize a just and harmonious political order in modernity, today we are justifiably more concerned with the social exclusions which made citizenship possible. To the extent, however, that Hegel's account of *Antigone* may be read to allegorize the birth of this new, properly modern, subject of desire—a subject divided between its adherence to a known law and its unacknowledged implication in the law's subterranean negation—it becomes possible to qualify Hegel's nostalgic view of the beautiful ethical world as both properly mythological and conceptually necessary in precisely the same way that, in *Totem and Taboo,* Freud's appropriation of the Darwinian notion of the "primal horde" was required to explain the paradox of masculine sexuation.

Freud remarked apropos the primal horde that it "has never been an object of observation."[6] And, though he himself clearly does not, we should not be deterred from making the same claim about Hegel's construction of the ancient polis. Neither has been observed, I wish to suggest, because each exists only on the level of unconscious fantasy. Athens (or Thebes) and its ethical substance were surely neither beautiful nor harmonious. Indeed, as I will go on to argue, the supreme virtue of Lacan's reading of *Antigone* over Hegel's is that it insists on training our eye to the structural necessity of violent exclusion to the establishment of any social order featuring pretensions to the reconciliation of antagonism. With this in mind, Hegel's balanced attitude with respect to Creon's and Antigone's ethical positions becomes significantly less convincing. For insofar as it allies itself with both a divine law which cannot be written and the forces of a nether world jettisoned from public visibility, it is Antigone's act, not Creon's, which best corresponds to the destructive and rejuvenating effects of Hegelian destiny. I would in fact suggest that Hegel latently privileges Antigone's transgressive deed insofar as it functions in a more directly subversive way in the undermining of the illusory harmony Hegel considered characteristic of Greek ethical life.

To be sure, Hegel's discussion of destiny's agency in *Antigone* bears an uncanny resemblance to Lacan's extended gloss on the Sophoclean term *atè,* which serves as a crucial point of reference in his own interpretation of the tragedy. In this light, it will be helpful to explore further what Hegel means by destiny in his discussion of *Antigone* as well as in the broader parameters of the *Phenomenology* as a whole. Hegel uses the term *Schicksal*—which A. V. Miller renders as both "fate" and "destiny"—to designate the contradiction which necessarily arises when the agent of human or divine law attempts to realize the law's content in the world through what Hegel calls "the deed." Destiny introduces an element of negativity which disrupts the translation of law into action, thus rendering the law impossible to put into practice in a way which does not distort or pervert its ideational content. Destiny thus describes the necessity with which the ancient ethical world collapses; it signifies that neither the human nor the divine law succeeds in conveying in absolute terms the substance of ethics and, in consequence, they must both be sacrificed in order to create the possibility of a new manifestation of Spirit aspiring to a higher form of justice. "Only in the downfall of both sides alike," Hegel dramatically concludes, "is absolute right accomplished, and the ethical substance as the negative power which engulfs both sides, that is, omnipotent and righteous Destiny, steps on the scene" (472).

Hegel supplements his reference to the signification of destiny for the political structure of the city-state with a consideration of its intrusion on the level of the individual agent's relation to its law and to its act. It is here that the psychoanalytic resonance of Hegel's discussion becomes most clear. Both Antigone and Creon, in Hegel's view, set the stage for their eventual demise by refusing to acknowledge the legitimacy of the law to which their acts stand opposed. Each of Sophocles' protagonists is thus "split into a conscious and an unconscious part" (472), Hegel avers, for the properly structural reason that it is impossible to act, within the terms of the world in which they are situated, in accordance with both laws simultaneously. From the perspective of a particular agent in the world of ethical custom, the dissolution of that world through the act is lived as the experience of destiny, or "fate" as Miller prefers to translate Hegel's *Schicksal* in its subjective manifestation. Moreover, the act's execution gives rise to a residue of guilt and crime as the agent becomes aware of its transgression of the other, opposing law. In Hegel's view, the subject's application of the law with which it identifies runs up against a kind of structural resistance which impedes the accomplishment or realization of the full ethical substance. On this level, then, destiny names the impossibility of incarnating the complete ethical substance in a realized action, and fate is the subject's encounter with this impossibility, experienced as a malignant necessity imposed from without or, more precisely, from a divine or quasi-divine realm of causality beyond the reach of human knowledge.

Though for Hegel this structural impossibility is first and foremost a nonsubjective consequence of a contradiction located within the ethical substance itself, it is possible for us to reinterpret what Hegel considers the ethical act's failure as a consequence of the necessary incommensurability between the act and its means of representation within the sociosymbolic order. Hegel himself, in fact, provides a glimpse

at this modified understanding when he claims that the agent acting
under the law necessarily remains ignorant of certain forms of knowledge inscribed within the ethical substance; it is for this reason that
Hegel insists that one cannot act (within the context of ancient ethical
substance) in a manner which does not give rise to guilt. In other words,
the ethical act is by definition criminal. To sum up: Hegelian destiny
denotes at a first moment the agent's unwitting affirmation through the
deed of the law which opposes it; in *Antigone,* for example, Creon's
decree against the recognition of Polynices' death ultimately brings forth
the public scandal of Antigone's defiance. At a second moment, however, destiny refers to the accomplishment of what Hegel calls "absolute
right" (472): Only by bringing out the latent contradiction lying beneath
the harmonious surface of ethical substance can Spirit finally reincar-
nate itself in a more formal, symbolic universality—one which acknowledges a modern conception of right embodied not in a spontaneous,
unmediated, organic set of customs perfectly sutured to its citizenry, but
rather in a discrete subject who is subject to a law to which its rebellious
desire refuses to conform.

To the extent that Hegel stresses the inevitability of the intrusion of
destiny's destructive negativity on the occasion of the law's materializa-
tion in the act, it is possible to attribute to his analysis a latent critique
of the rigidly hierarchical and sexist democratic mode of Athenian ethical custom. Hegel's notorious comment regarding womankind as "the
everlasting irony of the community" (476) is therefore both a nostalgic,
misogynistic yearning for a smoothly functioning patriarchal democracy
which never existed and a conceptually necessary identification of the
symptom which thwarts Creon's ambition with respect to his version of
the public good. Though this latter aspect of his analysis is crucial—
Antigone's feminine protest ultimately constitutes, in the terms of Hegel's
own argument, the condition of possibility for the advancement of Spirit
to more developed forms—it is nonetheless necessary to point out how
Hegel fails to identify the true significance of Antigone's deed, the one
that Lacan manages to extract from Sophocles' tragedy.

More precisely, when he distinguishes between a criminality stem-
ming from knowledge of the single substance of ethical custom from
one, less blameworthy, proceeding from ignorance of this interdependence, Hegel points not to Creon but to Antigone. "The ethical consciousness is more complete, its guilt more inexcusable," he writes, "if
it knows *beforehand* the law and the power which it opposes . . . and, like
Antigone, knowingly commits the crime" (470). It is this aspect of Hegel's
analysis that feminists have rightly considered problematic. Indeed, one
should not fail to note the self-contradictory quality of Hegel's attribution

of such a complete form of ethical knowledge to an agent whose divine law is explicitly related to the unconscious depths of a nether world alien to knowledge's forms. This attribution of guilt to Antigone is Hegel's *hamartia*, his own tragic error: the place, more precisely, where his analysis deviates from what Lacan calls the "essence" of tragedy.

Hegel's attribution of ultimate blame to Antigone for the beautiful ethical world's disintegration betrays how he takes the particular sociopolitical order of the Athenian polis as the measure for his ethical judgment. He fails, in other words, to meet the challenge presented by his own concept of destiny, which would suggest, I wish to argue, the assignment of ethical correctness not to the positive, publicly recognized legality Creon desires to defend, but rather to the properly negative agency and consequences of Antigone's collusion with the forces of the nether world. Though Hegel comes close to accepting guilt, crime, and perversion as necessary consequences of any authentic mode of worldly intervention, he stops short of the much more radical conclusion that the negativity and destructiveness of Antigone's transgression might formally characterize the ethical act as such. In this latter view, the ultimate function of the ethical is precisely to bring to public visibility the violent exclusions which function to constitute the very notion of the public good upheld by any specific sociosymbolic order.

It is in this sense that Hegel ultimately misses the broad significance of Sophocles' understanding of tragedy, which is to be qualified not as a nostalgic idealization of an illusory and harmonious world of ethical custom, but as an affirmation of the cathartic violence with which the disavowed violence of this world is finally brought to light. In Lacanian terms, Hegel has taken the acknowledged political symbolic, rather than the scandalous real of destiny, as his ethical point of reference. Given that Creon's human law has a monopoly on public representational legitimacy, it only makes sense that Antigone's guilt would appear more monstrous than her opponent's, and that the responsibility for the perversion of the ethical order would come down on her shoulders. In short, Hegel has no notion of causality with respect to the action of Sophocles' drama. As Lacan crucially points out, it is only because Creon utters his "insane orders" (277) that Antigone is led by her desire to perform Polynices' burial rights herself. By the time Creon realizes that he has transgressed, in defense of the polis, a certain limit no mortal has the right to transgress, the action has advanced to such a degree that the prevention of the mass carnage with which the tragedy culminates has become impossible. Creon's edict *forces* the performance of Antigone's transgressive act: He, therefore, is the guilty one. Antigone remains, in contrast, not precisely innocent, but certainly pure on the level of her desire. We may now take a closer look at Lacan's consideration of the tragedy in view of determining precisely what he means when he talks about the purity of Antigone's desire.

Pleasure Unbound

Lacan's formulation of psychoanalytic ethics proceeds from the claim that its mode is tragic; his understanding of tragedy thus becomes crucially important to an appreciation of his reading of *Antigone*. Lacan's idea of tragedy hinges on the motif of a limit he discusses in relation to a number of concepts derived from Aristotelian poetics and Kantian ethics and aesthetics. This limit identifies a fundamental "economic," to use the Freudian term, imbalance in the subject resulting from its problematic being in language. The ethical for Lacan thus becomes a function of the subject's self-antagonism, in other words the incommensurability between the two principles which regulate its psychic life, principles whose aims are at odds with one another.

By way of specifying the consequences of this imbalance, Lacan comments on the well-known association of tragedy with catharsis, which Aristotle famously defines in the *Poetics* as a purgation or purification of the *pathemata*: "pity and fear."[7] In the eighth book of the *Politics* Aristotle revisits his notion of catharsis, this time in relation to the music which accompanied tragic performance in Antiquity. Lacan suggests that this type of music finds its modern equivalent in the Parisian spring of 1960 in the genres of rock and roll or hot jazz, adding that these musical forms produce an excitation in the subject—what he terms a "Dionysian frenzy" (245)—which is followed by an impermanent return to equilibrium and calm. Similarly, in his discussion of the pedagogical and cathartic functions of music, Aristotle states that while listening to certain musical performances "some persons fall into a religious frenzy," adding that they are "restored as a result of the sacred melodies ... as though they had found healing and purgation, ... their souls lightened and delighted."[8] The purgation effected through the practices of ancient tragedy consists in a discharge of excess excitation, a process which converts the unpleasure of the *pathemata* into a pleasurable release. Lacan's gloss on Aristotelian catharsis attributes to the human subject an underlying disequilibrium which makes the organism's energetic balance depend on periodic releases of surplus excitation. In this way Lacan identifies a point of commonality between Aristotle's poetics of tragedy and Freud's understanding of the psychical economy: Just as Freud was forced to posit that the sexual instinct thwarts the pleasure principle's design to keep constant the quantity of mental excitation, Aristotle acknowledges in his notion of tragic catharsis an unpleasurable emotional tension which demands periodic therapeutic release.

Lacan spends a great deal of time in his ethics seminar working through the implications of this dual economy which characterizes the psychical apparatus, repeatedly underlining the disjunction—the lack of logical relation—between the elements of each of the two fundamental antinomies in Freudian thought: first, the primary and secondary processes, and second, the pleasure principle and its excessive "beyond." Freud's own efforts to come to terms with these antinomies led to the well-known paradoxes of *Beyond the Pleasure Principle*, whose analytic rigor leads toward the apparently counterintuitive conclusion that "the pleasure principle seems actually to serve the death instincts."[9] Freud's insight in this text was to associate the (potentially) life-creating sexual instincts not with the organism's tendency toward balance and self-preservation, but rather with the disruptive, excessive stimulation which emerges from within the organism and which the ego experiences as unpleasure. It is for this reason that Freud found Weismann's biological distinction between "soma" and "germ-plasm" so attractive: The "potentially immortal" cells involved in reproduction, and therefore in the perpetuation of the species, expose the organism to dangerous, life-threatening stimuli in the environment, thereby subjugating its narcissistic interest in prolonging its individual life to a higher, transpersonal, properly biological one. The difficulty with Freud's terminology of life and death instincts, and hence the surprise of his concluding proposition, is therefore that it is species life, and not the life of the individual organism, which is finally at issue in his argument. Sexual life is at variance with the organism's instinct for self-preservation; it is for this reason that Freud ultimately associates the ego's mechanisms of defense with the entropy of death. Freud's basic argument is therefore that an excessive and traumatic internal excitation works against the ego's ambition of energetic homeostasis, periodically interrupting the normal functioning of consciousness, and introducing a compulsive, conservative impulse into psychic life which undermines the subject's conscious intentionality. Crucially, Freud is led to insist that it is not within the capacities of the psyche to accommodate these disruptions—to "bind" their energy, as he puts it—into fixed representations in consciousness: signifiers. "No substitutive or reactive formations and no sublimations," he writes, "will suffice to remove the repressed instinct's persisting tension."[10] The unconscious sexual instinct—the drive, to call it by its proper name—cannot be subjectivized; its pressure resists being tamed through integration into the subject's socio-symbolic world.

Lacan's reference to Aristotle's notion of catharsis serves not only to underline the radical incommensurability between the two systems which characterize the human organism in its tragic dimension, but also to show how this incommensurability identifies an agency in psychic life which cannot be mastered, cannot be recognized by any symbolic system available to conscious knowledge. Lacan's recollection of early developments in the theory of hysteria further underscores the ethical import of this disjunction between the order of signifiers and the drive. In their preliminary communication to *Studies on Hysteria*, Freud and Breuer define what they term "abreaction" as an affective discharge through which the subject releases surplus excitation produced by the memory of a traumatic event. A "reaction," the authors claim in their neurological idiom, is a physical action performed in response to an excitation, advancing the provocation of revenge as their example; abreaction, in contrast, is an alternative response which substitutes for such a physical action the representation of the traumatic stimulus in speech. At the moment of its inception the psychoanalytic method hypothesized that hysterical symptoms result from "traumas that have not been sufficiently abreacted."[11] According to this view, the therapeutic dividend of analysis accrues from the catharsis the patient achieves through the translation of traumatic fantasies into language. The hysterical symptom emerges when the abreaction insufficiently discharges the excitation produced by the trauma. By extension, then, Freud and Breuer posited the clinical possibility of a sufficient abreaction leading to a perfect dissolution of the symptom. Through speech, in other words, the patient may reconcile her internal excitations with the parameters of her conscious universe.

Now it is precisely to this notion of sufficiency in the early etiology of hysteria that Lacan voices his objection. Though it is clear that the psychoanalytic method would be of no benefit to the hysterical analysand if the abreaction of trauma in speech did not to some extent alleviate suffering, the more fundamental theoretical point is that the trauma stubbornly remains in excess of its representation and, in consequence, the subject forever retains a symptomatic nucleus which cannot be rendered in the forms of consciousness. By the time of *Beyond the Pleasure Principle,* Freud himself had come to the same conclusion, linking the necessary failure of abreaction to the manifestation of the transference. Because "the patient cannot remember the whole of what is repressed in him," Freud admits, "he is obliged to repeat the repressed material as a contemporary experience instead of . . . remembering it as belonging to the past."[12] The elusive material Freud here evokes causes the insistence of the repetition compulsion, and it is precisely this element—the nonsubjectivizable trauma which is the condition of possibility for a consciousness from which it is necessarily excluded—which Lacan identifies in his commentary on abreaction. Thus, Lacan's reprise of the theory of hysteria underlines that the libidinal cathexis of the trauma and the energetic discharge enabled in the clinic by the patient's associations are fundamentally irreconcilable. A renegade quantity of psychical energy forever remains "unbound"; consequently, the kernel of the subject's fantasy is to be situated outside the limits of possible representation in language.

The stuff of this nonrelation—this unrepresentable, paradoxically immaterial substance—is of course what Lacan calls the real, and he goes on to make of it the only legitimate criterion of his ethical theory. What becomes clear is that Lacan bases his view of psychoanalytic ethics on the subject's antagonism with itself. The subject's status is ethical because its satisfaction is disjoined from all possible objects of experience. If nothing, no Kleinian good object, can be presented to the subject either to satisfy its desire or to dissolve its symptom, then it follows that the realm of the ethical is antithetical to any determinate norm. There is no Good which would qualify as satisfactory to all subjects, including in particular the utilitarian good which purports to uphold the principle of the greatest satisfaction of all. If the only legitimate ethical criterion is of the order of the real, then ethics by definition cannot be systematized, bureaucratized; ethics cannot be rendered as a knowledge which could then be applied to specific sets of circumstances.

It now becomes possible to ask how this ethical beyond of the pleasure principle—this field of surplus excitation which challenges the limits of representation—figures in Lacan's reading of *Antigone*. Lacan links the purging of excess affect through the cathartic method to the vicissitudes of the image of Antigone in Sophocles' tragedy. Lacan's suggestion here is sure to strike some readers of Sophocles as odd, since there is very little commentary in the tragedy on the topic of Antigone's appearance. And yet the beautiful image of Antigone, according to Lacan, is the key to a proper understanding of the Sophoclean message. Lacan's seemingly contradictory statements about the function of Antigone's image are best understood, I would suggest, when it is acknowledged that his analysis operates simultaneously on two levels: On one level, Lacan describes the nature of Antigone's heroic subjective structure— how she places herself, in other words, at the point of the beyond of an atè whose meaning we have yet to discern; on another level, however, Lacan describes the tragedy as the enactment of desire's *purification*, in which the chorus functions as an externalization of the audience's experience of catharsis. For this reason, the question of perspective becomes crucial to our understanding of Lacan's interpretation: To whom does Antigone appear intimidatingly beautiful? When does this fascination occur? And also, to link up with our main theme, what is the link between the phenomenon of beauty and the properly perverse fantasy Lacan uncovers in Sade?

Suffering for Beauty

The sole reference to beauty in *Antigone* occurs in what the Sophocles scholars have baptized the "Ode to Love." This is the part of the play during which the chorus begins to vacillate from its unconditional solidarity with Creon's interdiction against the performance of burial rights on Polynices' body, revealing an inkling of sympathy for Antigone's transgression. Immediately after Creon announces that he will bury Antigone "still living, in a rocky cavern," the chorus breaks into a discourse about a violent love which wrenches "just men's minds aside from justice."[13] The ode is eminently ambiguous: It is unclear whether the chorus addresses its warning to Antigone, Creon, or both, and this ambiguity indexes the chorus's ambivalence at this point in the play. To be sure, though the chorus admits to its fascination with, indeed to its seduction by, this beautiful image of Antigone, it is not until a much later point in the action, when the authoritative seer Tiresias prophesies the tragedy's bitter conclusion, that the chorus sees the injustice of Creon's edict and decisively sides with Antigone. Even at this relatively early stage, however, the chorus concludes the ode with an unambiguous pronouncement on the identity of the eventual winner of Antigone's and Creon's tragic conflict: Victory will go, says the chorus, to the "beautiful bride" whose eyes emit a "visible desire."[14]

Now Lacan makes much of this central Sophoclean image of the appearance of desire in the visible world in the form of an image of beauty: this radiant *imeros enarges* which, Lacan seems to suggest, arises as an effect of the heroine's placement in that zone of the tragic absolute he designates by the term *atè*. At the moment of its absorption by Antigone's beautiful image, the chorus utters its most deeply felt words, assuming its function as an external body with which the audience identifies and through which it experiences its vicarious catharsis. Expressing extreme emotion at the sight of the headstrong virgin as she listens to Creon's cruel sentence that she be buried alive, the chorus bears witness to Antigone's beauty and to the "visible desire" which is its phenomenal manifestation.

It is at this point in his interpretation that Lacan turns to his well-known "Kant with Sade" motif, advancing the scandalous thesis that aesthetic contemplation is latently perverse, indeed that it reveals a disturbing limit in the experience of pleasure which, if disavowed, can lead to the psychodynamic fixation of sadism. Lacan observes that in analytic practice the patient's references to aesthetic categories are consistently associated with unconscious aggressive impulses, with what he calls in the ethics seminar a "destructive drive" (239). And in Sade, Lacan claims to discover a properly perverse fundamental fantasy in which the tormentor's violent abuse of his victim is entirely dissimulated by a perception of the victim's grace and beauty. "The function of the beautiful," Lacan asserts, is to introduce a "barrier" which "forbids access to a fundamental horror."[15] On the basis of this claim Lacan advances that Sade and Kant are interested, the former through his notion of crime and the latter through his idea of the beautiful, in describing the same region of absolute, unconditioned freedom. Just as Sade's concept of crime claims to liberate the cycle of life and death from its own law, thereby inaugurating a dimension of immortality utterly immune to natural causality, Kant argues that the aesthetic judgment must be perfectly free of any form of interest which would be determined by the object on which the phenomenon of the beautiful is nonetheless based. In both cases the object ceases to have causal power over the subject, who is then emancipated from any form of dependence or need; and in both cases this freedom is associated, Lacan suggests, with a radically destructive drive which tends toward the elimination of any trace of the object. Thus, Sade's texts have the virtue of plainly revealing a truth which remains dissimulated by the serene tone of Kant's analytic. The aesthetic experience of the beautiful marks the limit of a scandalous, traumatic psychical reality so intolerable, so resistant to subjectivization, that it must be veiled by an image which entraps—lures—desire.

According to Lacan, then, Kant's judgment of taste and Sade's perverse fantasy have in common the manner in which in both relations the object as such disappears. As Lacan puts it, "the forms that are at work in knowledge . . . are interested in the phenomenon of beauty, though the object itself is not involved. I take it you see the analogy with the Sadeian fantasm, since the object there is no more than the power to support a form of suffering" (261). But a more detailed consideration of key passages of Kant's *Critique of Judgment* will be necessary to show just how closely Lacan appears to want to link aesthetic contemplation to perversion properly speaking. My own suggestion will be that Lacan does indeed want to equate what Kant qualifies as a pure judgment of taste with his own concept of perversion's fundamental fantasy, though Kant himself goes on to question the preponderance, and indeed ultimately the very possibility, of a judgment which would qualify as purely aesthetic.

We recall that in his analytic Kant evokes the beautiful by distinguishing it from the good and the agreeable. The beautiful, Kant argues, is radically disinterested and nonutilitarian, determined neither by any concept of the object which would attribute it with a determinate purpose, nor by any feeling of the subject for the object, a feeling which would betray a pathological sensuous interest. Thus the agreeable and the good both partake of interest, of desire. In the former case this interest is of an empirical variety; in the latter it is rational or intellectual. Kant specifies that the agreeable object elicits in the subject an earthy, properly sensuous, pleasure: "It gratifies us," he straightforwardly avers.[16] As for the good object, it presents to the subject a concept featuring a rational purpose. Interest, in this latter case, predicates itself on a pragmatic goal and functions to determine the will.

In contrast, the definition of the beautiful features neither of these attributes.[17] Strikingly, Kant insists that aesthetic contemplation has nothing whatsoever to do with its object; nor does it partake in any way of the pleasure we experience in our relation to the agreeable and the good. Indeed, Kant qualifies the subject's relation to the beautiful nonobject not in terms of sensuous pleasure or a determinate purpose, but rather with respect to what he calls the "free play" of the subject's "cognitive faculties" (62). The starkly counterintuitive quality of Kant's association of aesthetic contemplation with the experience of what he calls "pleasure and displeasure" here becomes glaringly apparent, for Kant's insistence that the pleasure offered by the beautiful is devoid of interest and desire implies that the aesthetic must be purified of all pleasure as pleasure is commonly understood. In strict Kantian terms, in other words, as soon as a presentation provides us with either an agreeable feeling or the concept of a purpose, our experience ceases to be an aesthetic one. This is indeed the sense in which the Kantian discourse of aesthetic pleasure approximates the Freudian "beyond" of the pleasure principle, and points towards the kind of excessive, unbound libidinal energy which cannot be domesticated by the forces of the ego, cannot be contained by the signifying function. That is to say, the ego experiences this pleasure as, precisely, unpleasure. Lacan's point, in other words, is that Kant's own argument implies against itself that *pure aesthetic experience may only be an experience of (the infliction of) pain.* The truth of the subjective experience of absolute aesthetic disinterest, which substitutes for an object relation properly speaking the "free play" of the "cognitive powers" (62) and the apprehension of a "purposiveness without a purpose" (65), depends on an economy of pain

which the subject inflicts on an object whose damage is then dissimulated behind the curtain of beauty. Indeed, Kant's qualification of the
coercive aspect of the aesthetic judgment even intuits the manner in
which the pervert subjectively experiences the pain he inflicts as a response to an unconditional demand. As Kant himself insists, the requirement of universal communicability forces the aesthetic judgment to
"permit no one to hold a different opinion" (89), positing in this way a
common sensate receptivity which allows for no deviation, no exception
to its aesthetic law.

To be sure, though he betrays the same disquieting, superegoic
reverence for what he calls "free beauty" as he does for his sublime
moral law, Kant stops short of a full implicit endorsement of a latently
sadistic aestheticism when he restricts his notion of a properly human
beauty to an "accessory" status (76), and when he finally questions
whether the "common sense" which in his view underlies contemplation
of the beautiful might be only "the idea of an ability yet to be acquired"
(90). In other words, human subjects may not function as objects of
perfect indifference for one another (without adopting the perverse structure, Lacan would add); nor does the universal consent demanded by
the aesthetic judgment manage to realize itself in a demonstrable general sensibility. In this way Kant reintroduces a limit in the aesthetic
subject. This limit not only attributes to the judgment of taste an element
of uncertainty which prevents one from establishing in experience what
remains a merely theoretical universality, but it also implies that aesthetic contemplation is usually, if not always, contaminated by what Kant
calls "charm": a pathological element which makes manifest in the subject a sensuous interest, an element which indeed offers itself for comparison with the causal faculty of Lacan's *objet petit a*. Ultimately, Kant
does not appear to believe too strongly in the purely aesthetic contemplation he evokes.

Nonetheless, in my view Lacan is entirely correct to detect in Kant's
analytic a latently perverse fantasy. Indeed, this fantasy is nowhere more
evident than in Kant's evocation of the constancy or *stasis* of aesthetic
contemplation in its energetic dimension, a stasis which persuasively
echoes both the tiresome monotony of Sade's thoroughly unerotic stream
of torture scenarios, and Freud's evocation of the "regressive" aim of his
death instinct, which is to achieve, once and for all, what he calls "an
abolition of [the] chemical tensions"—to finally eliminate the traumatic
excitations which are the motor of sexual life itself.[18] To be sure, the
serene impartiality of Kant's aesthetic subject echoes the dreary rationalization, indeed the bureaucratization, of sexual experience in Sade,
whose ultimate desire is clearly to deprive sexuality of its passion, of its

mastery over the subject who experiences it. Similarly, for Kant the "pure judgment of taste" cannot be influenced "by charm or emotion"; it must reflect an experience of perfect, detached indifference based not on the object, but rather on the "purposiveness of the form" (68).

In one of many passages of Kant's analytic with tremendous Freudian resonance, Kant explains that the aim of the beautiful is "to keep us in the state of having the presentation itself, and to keep the cognitive powers engaged in their occupation without any further aim" (68). Not coincidentally, the phrase Kant uses to describe the psychical condition of the aesthetic subject recalls the fetishist's relation to his construction of the maternal phallus, which causes not a desire in the subject, in other words the experience of the interruption of satisfaction, but rather the restful libidinal equilibrium of a drive which has reached, and therefore mastered, its target. In sum, the ambition of the subject of both perversion and pure aesthetic contemplation is to eliminate its dependence on the object, to conjure a dependable, concretely available pseudoobject which does not, like the object of desire, insist on remaining stubbornly veiled or threaten to fail or disappear if encountered too directly. Remarkably, it becomes apparent that the pervert and the pure Kantian aesthete are the only normal subjects, the only ones who succeed in remaining immune to the object's determinative power, indeed to what I have been calling the inherent perversity of desire. If Lacan insists that the object disappears in both the aesthetic and perverse scenarios, it is because in them the subject effectively objectifies itself, becomes the support, indeed the instrument, of a beautiful suffering's jouissance.

Turning back to *Antigone,* then, we can now ask the question how the complicity of sadism in the phenomenon of the beautiful relates to the action of the tragedy. Lacan links his notion of the limit made manifest by the beautiful to the theme of the second death, which refers to an excessive supplementary death conferring an eternal suffering on the subject who suffers it, casting life's termination not as a release from this mortal coil, but as an exacerbation, a prolongation, of its torture into eternity. In this sense the second death is what Creon inflicts on Polynices when he proclaims his interdiction against the performance of burial rights on his body, which remains gorily exposed to animals and birds of prey throughout most of the action of the tragedy. Lacan also associates this second death to Antigone herself when, in the concluding sections of the play, she is enclosed alone in the rocky cavern in which she finally hangs herself. Creon's infliction of this second death on Polynices has the effect of displacing Antigone from the terms of life, from the sociosymbolic coordinates within which takes place the day-to-day life of the polis. Lacan suggests that it is precisely Antigone's ambiguous position between life and death which allows her to act in a perfectly unconditioned way, unmoved by the concerns of ordinary living existence.[19] It is also what renders her act unintelligible, and therefore criminal, within the framework of Creon's commitment to the political good. Clearly, Lacan wishes to highlight the kinship between the unconditioned freedom Antigone is able to derive from her status between two deaths and the absolute, undetermined disinterest evoked in the "Kant with Sade" argument. In other words, Antigone's act of resistance against Creon's infliction of the second death on Polynices takes the paradoxical form of an affirmation of the inherent perversity of desire—precisely the perversity the pervert conspires to eradicate from his libidinal economy.

The primary consequence of Antigone's affirmation is that it jettisons her from any position within the sociosymbolic order. Referring approvingly to the work of German classicist Karl Reinhardt, Lacan highlights what he calls this "special solitude of Sophoclean heroes," who are "always isolated . . . always beyond established limits, always in an exposed position and, as a result, separated in one way or another from the structure" (271). As Reinhardt himself observes, "[A]ll Sophocles' tragic characters are outsiders. What is valid for them is not to be measured by the usual standards; their central interest is not the centre of the events in which they are involved."[20] Erwin Rohde, to whom Lacan also favorably refers in the ethics seminar, similarly underlines the monumental solitude of the Sophoclean hero. It is precisely this solitude, Rohde suggests, which distinguishes the Sophoclean tragedies from those of Aeschylus and which attributes to them their uncannily precocious modernity. "The individual man, stamped with the unique impression of his particular being, [in Sophocles] becomes more fully detached from the background of omnipotent might and universal law. The individual finds within himself the rules of his behaviour, the causes of his success, or his tragic failure."[21]

Lacan's enlistment of the work of Reinhardt and Rohde provides crucial clues as to what motivates him to distance himself from Hegel's thesis that *Antigone* stages a struggle between two conflicting ethical laws. For Reinhardt as for Lacan, there is only one ethical position in Sophocles' tragedy, and that is Antigone's. With reference to the conflict between Antigone and Creon, Reinhardt writes, "This is not right against right, idea against idea, but the divine, the all-embracing with which the young girl knows she is in harmony, against the human, which appears as limited, blind, self-pursuing, self-deceiving and distorted."[22] Antigone places herself, in other words, in a place where social recognition is impossible; her very existence at this position calls into question the terms of social intelligibility. Creon's interdiction against Polynices' burial rites is tantamount, from Antigone's perspective, to an ethical violation which places her brother in the same liminal space she is forced to occupy to defend him. Without the symbolic recognition that the rites' performance would accord, Polynices is relegated to the realm of the living dead: biologically no longer alive, yet still lacking the act of consecration that would put his spirit to rest. Creon's *kerygma* effects the exclusion of Polynices' being from the immortal symbolic chain. This exclusion creates a disruption in the symbolic fabric of the community which Antigone experiences as an unconditional, supracognitive demand to act: Her brother's undead spirit simply requires the recognition denied him.

The relation of the central motif of Antigone's beautiful image to Lacan's pairing of Kant with Sade consists, therefore, in this coincidence of, on the one hand, the inhuman cruelty of Creon's punishments of Antigone and Polynices and, on the other, the full deployment of the heroine's aesthetic splendor in the eyes of the chorus. Antigone becomes beautiful in the eyes of the chorus (and therefore for the audience) at the moment when she fully assumes her loss and suffering, uttering her celebrated lament at having to die without the "bridal"(89) that was her due—before having, from a certain conventional perspective, even begun to live. Antigone's beauty is made manifest in consequence of her status "between two deaths," having renounced life from within the bounds of life itself. From Antigone's tragic perspective, life, considered as promise or possibility—as hope—acquires the cast of something irrevocably lost. It is in this sense that Antigone merits the charge of inhumanity for which the chorus reproaches her and through which she approaches the Kantian ethical ideal of a purely nonpathological and disinterested act. Crucially, however, the possibility of such an act is opened up, indeed precipitated, by Creon's prior transgression, more precisely his unjustifiable and unlimited extension of the political good and his refusal to tolerate any exception.

The authentic ethical act, according to Lacan, may only be performed by that subject who has rejected the very conditions of possibility of life as it is hegemonically constituted, and for whom, in consequence, life's promise may only be represented as having already been sacrificed not in response to an injunction coming from elsewhere, but rather in an act of lucid, self-knowing, absolute freedom. The Lacanian ethical hero must experience the internalization of a sacrifice which makes life appear beyond a limit as forsaken and unattainable. But what alters somewhat the superficially harrowing cast of this injunction is the notion that the sacrifice here in question is a purely formal gesture in the precise sense that what is sacrificed was in fact never an object of experience. Indeed, this notion of the nonempirical content of the object of sacrifice can be located within the play: At the moment of her lament, Antigone had never experienced the pleasures of the conjugal bed. For this reason, the object of sacrifice may only be described negatively, as a sense of promise or hope, as a horizon of impossible happiness unfurling in a future which never arrives. We now arrive at the paradox of Antigone's sacrifice, of the heroic, full assumption of her castration: What is required is *the sacrifice of the fantasy that there is something to be sacrificed*; that something was in fact lost by the subject as a condition of its access to desire.

Creon's commitment to the good of the polis is intimately, indeed structurally, tied to his refusal to accept the challenge of this empty sacrifice. It is precisely his hope for a serene, harmonious polis fully subsumed under the ruler's command that causes Creon to view Polynices' aggression as an external force which acts as an obstacle to the realization of a beautiful polity bereft of social antagonism he imagines in the form of a generalized civic good. Polynices thus figures in Creon's fantasy as a hindrance, on the level of social actuality, to a realizable or attainable possibility, rather than, as actually accords with the laws of psychic life, as a properly fantasmatic representation of an internal or inherent impossibility. For Creon, Polynices is the cause of his ruin; Antigone, in contrast, tells everyone who will listen that she has brought her atè upon herself.

Artfully Screwed

As the sources advance, the term *atè* was used throughout Greek antiquity, first in Homeric epic, then in archaic lyric poetry, and finally in the tragedies of Aeschylus, Sophocles, and Euripides. Generally, atè featured in each of these genres two different, but not unrelated, meanings. The first, objective sense suggests a "ruin, calamity, or disaster" the Greeks often, but not always, viewed as sent by the gods as punishment for human error. The second, subjective meaning conveys a notion of "blindness, infatuation, or folly" often associated, as in the case of Oedipus, with an erotic context.[23] This second sense concerns, in other words, a lack of knowledge, particularly of a sexual kind. The interimplication of the objective and subjective modes is highlighted when atè is further defined as "a temporary clouding or bewildering of the normal consciousness," often resulting in "unwise or unaccountable behavior."[24] Two points will be helpful to retain. First, atè describes a calamity which befalls us in consequence of a lack of knowledge; and second, the concept features an inherent moral ambiguity: Whether or not human guilt causes the disaster of atè is open to question. To be sure, the Greeks were certain that the gods lay at the origin of atè; what was less clear, however, was why, with such apparent cruelty, they make mortals suffer.

Lacan's comments on the most celebrated passage of *Antigone*—the ode or hymn to man,[25] which has been subject to massive amounts of often painfully detailed exegesis in Sophocles criticism, brings into relief the function of this atè in the heroine's drama. As is well known to readers of the tragedy, the ode to man designates an ambiguously ironic, anthropological statement of the chorus which, according to the critical tradition against which Lacan acerbically argues, has justified the elaboration of a doctrine of Sophoclean humanism. The passage occurs at a crucial juncture of the tragedy following the messenger's first report of the illegal burial of Polynices' body, and immediately prior to the poignant appearance of Antigone before Creon subsequent to her arrest at the burial sight. The first part of the hymn extols humankind for the technological achievements through which it harnesses the hostile forces of nature: Seafaring, agriculture, and hunting all bear witness to humankind's prowess and ingenuity. This admirable being has even devised language and thought, the ode continues, and goes some way toward creating a rational political order. But here the chorus's tone abruptly shifts, and Lacan underlines how Sophocles identifies the inviolable limit of our resourcefulness and control over our own destiny: unsurprisingly, death. Humanity shows tremendous ingenuity in adapting to the natural world but, the chorus claims, before the spectre of death we find ourselves without recourse.

It is at this point in his close reading of the Greek text that Lacan offers a radical reinterpretation of the ode, one which is pitched against the heavily ideological elaboration of Sophoclean humanism, and which additionally attributes to the Greek tragedian the invention of a concept whose originality and rigor would remain unparalleled until Freud's elaboration, more than two millennia later, of his notion of the neurotic symptom. Lacan's argument pivots around the controversial and paradoxical phrase *pantoporos aporos* which, in his view, designates at once humanity's technical agility in the face of a hostile natural world and its utter helplessness before the scandal of its finitude. "[Man] meets nothing in the future without resource," praises the chorus, in full high-theoretical mode, appending nonetheless a qualification: "Only from Hades shall he apply no means of flight." There then follows the crucial, ambiguous passage which forms the crux of Lacan's intervention in the controversies surrounding

Antigone's translation. After putting its finger on what limits man's control over destiny, the chorus adds, in the language of Lloyd-Jones's rendering, that he has also managed to "contrive [an] escape from desperate maladies."[26]

Now it must be left to the classicists to assess the merit of the references to Greek grammar with which Lacan justifies his new translation of one of the most celebrated passages in all Greek tragedy. For my purposes here, however, what is important is to grasp the gist of Lacan's claim, and this will require backing up a few lines before we consider the crucial final phrase. Lacan replaces Lloyd-Jones's rendering "he meets nothing in the future without resource" with the markedly less optimistic "he advances toward nothing that is likely to happen, he advances and he is *pantoporos*, 'artful,' but he is *aporos*, always 'screwed.' " Lacan substitutes an altogether more paradoxical and suggestive rendering for Lloyd-Jones's sunny statement about man's fitness with respect to his condition: It is precisely through his cleverness, Lacan suggests, that man sets himself up for disaster. Consider now the disabused, slightly bitter Sophoclean irony for which Lacan wants to argue: "[Man] knows what he is doing. He always manages to cause things to come crashing down on his head" (275).

The more scholastic details of Lacan's reading of the ode fail to dull the sting of its message. This lauded, wonderful creature for whom so much of Greek culture sang the praises, who would suffer, in the vicissitudes of Judeo-Christian culture, several centuries of self-abnegation before rising once more to his rightful, lofty position, acquires an element of pathos if we consider how he disguises from himself, through the gauzy obfuscation of fantasy, a destructive drive he experiences as a tendency toward self-obliteration. This strange, speaking being, caught in a web of symbols over which he has limited control, and deprived of the capacity to represent to himself his own end, is so resourceful that he devises "an absolutely marvelous gimmick" (275), one which allows him to prolong his self-satisfied complacency and to disavow the intrinsic implication of his desire in death. In the Lloyd-Jones translation the crucial line which follows "only from Hades shall he apply no means of flight" is rendered as "and he has contrived escape from desperate maladies." One cannot fail to remark that this last line lends a confusing schizophrenic note to the ode. At the precise moment when the chorus evokes the limits of humankind's ingenuity before the reality of its condition, a smug comment is thrown out apparently referring to its accomplishments in the fields of medicine and health. So resourceful is this being, the meaning goes—certainly still familiar in the New Age which is ours—that he can even heal himself.

The chorus's comment about desperate maladies is traditionally interpreted as just another item on the ode's long list of human achievements. But Lloyd-Jones unwittingly comes close to conveying what Lacan claims is the authentic Sophoclean meaning. All that is required to discern the other sense is a substitution of the preposition "with" or "through" for the translator's "from." An altogether different sense emerges: Man, this wondrous creature, has contrived escape from his condition through—by means of—desperate maladies. Because the subject cannot come to terms with its own mortal limit, Lacan offers, it requires a symptom. The symptom's purpose is to install a barrier between the subject and the intolerable ego-dystonic excess of jouissance, a symptom which, as we have seen, has a tendency to take the form of a properly aesthetic experience. Offering further references to Heidegger and Heraclitus, Lacan links these *mechanoen*—the self-fabricated maladies which shield humanity's gaze from death—with the Greek sophistic tradition and the philosophical concept of the Good. The mechanism of the neurotic symptom and the ancient art of sophistry have in common, Lacan subversively suggests, their shared strategy of dissimulating the immanence of the limit of death. And crucially, a disavowal of this limit— an unlimited extension of the Good across the social field, the very same extension at which Creon's *kerygma* aims—blinds man morally, directing him "sometimes toward evil and sometimes toward the good" (276). Only by recognizing the inviolable limit signified by death, Lacan contends, may the subject avoid the temptation of such an erroneous, fleshed-out universalism, one which causes him to do evil in the name of the Good.

It is precisely through his avoidance of this encounter with life's limit that Creon adopts his properly perverse, pseudoethical stance. The preeminently rationalist reference to the good of the polis functions as one of the Sophoclean mechanisms and works to deny the implication of Creon's own desire in death. As Lacan sees it, the suicide of Haemon, Antigone's fiancé, is the entirely logical, indeed necessary, outcome of Creon's enslavement to his untainted construction of the Good. This tragic event is an external manifestation—a return in the real, one could surely say—of Creon's own disavowed desire. Here we encounter the full significance of the difference between Creon's tragic *hamartia* and Antigone's entirely different ethical position. According to Lacan, "[T]he mortal fruit that Creon harvests through his obstinacy and his insane orders is the dead son he carries in his arms. He has been *hamarton*; he has made a mistake." And drawing the contrast with Antigone, Lacan continues, "[I]t's not a question [in the case of Creon] of *allotria atè* [going beyond *atè*]. *Atè* concerns the Other, the field of the Other, and it doesn't belong to Creon. It is, on the other hand, the place where Antigone is situated" (277). Dispensing with the philosophy of the Good with which Creon and the chorus are associated, Lacan suggests that Antigone situates herself in the field of the Other, at the point of the cut or limit imposed by being's traversal by language. Antigone's relation to atè therefore has something to do with the signifier, something to do with the way in which she positions herself with respect to the field of signification and its inherent, internal limit.

We recall that in a multiplicity of ways Lacan's theory is premised on the notion that the field of language is marked by its lack of completion, its internal limitation or incapacity to fill a central gap of nonmeaning. The signifying cut which inaugurates the subject's relation to desire therefore requires the emergence of a kind of absolute signifier—a "signifier for the lack of a signified"—which carries different names at different points of Lacan's teaching: "Name-of-the-Father," "phallic or master signifier," the "unary trait," or, in his later teaching of the early 1970s, the suitably and satisfyingly abstract "S_1." The function of this signifier of the absolute is to cover over the central gap which language cannot occupy, to set a limit to the order of signifiers in order that they might produce an effect of signification. Though this function indeed constitutes the signifying order as a totality, this totality includes its own internal negation, its own excess over itself. What becomes clear at the conclusion of Lacan's analysis of *Antigone* is that it is precisely by occupying this absolute position, by placing herself in the space of the emergence of the primordial signifier, that Antigone consolidates her uncompromising position vis-à-vis desire.

At this position of absolute, tautological Meaning—"My brother is my brother," Antigone, by word and deed, effectively states—no judgment can express what is at issue in this arena of radical freedom and pure desire. As such, Antigone's desire indexes an utterly singular but nonrelational and properly transcendental substance in her brother, one which belongs to him absolutely, and which therefore cannot be reproduced in any other subject, but which also remains unmodified by any of his attributes, by anything which could be uttered about him. As Lacan says, "[I]t can be seen that Antigone's position represents the radical limit that affirms the unique value of [Polynices'] being without reference to any content, to whatever good or evil Polynices may have done, or to whatever he may be subjected to" (279). The radical limit Antigone occupies or crosses over in acceding to the "beyond of atè"— Antigone is forced to cross over this limit in order to defend its legitimacy, according to Lacan—is the limit of the symbolic order itself: the place, in other words, where the signifier no longer slides across to the

next in the infinite, metonymical deferral of meaning, but instead refers
to nothing but itself, to nothing apart from its absolute, unconditioned,
eminently paradoxical meaning/lessness. Here it becomes possible to
link Antigone's position with the place of the father's name and with the
crime which it simultaneously designates and dissimulates. Indeed, it is
no coincidence that Lacan explicitly relates the atè in whose name Antigone
acts to the curse of the Labdacid family, whose point of origin Lacan
identifies with the incestuous epistemophilia of Antigone's father Oedipus,
and to the transgressive enigma of her mother Jocasta's desire.

The sombre, tragic cast of this evocation of the function of the father's
name suggests a crucial qualification of Judith Butler's nonetheless
sensitive appreciation of Lacan's reading of Sophocles. Butler's suspicions concerning Lacan's argument about the implication of Antigone's
desire in death are based on the assumption that the symbolic order
whose limit she defends constitutes a normative totality premised on the
incest taboo, the exchange of women, and the prohibition against homosexuality. As a result, she interprets Lacan's various formulations of the
unintelligibility of Antigone's act—her position outside of, or irreducible
to, the structure of the signifying order—as confirmation that it can
have no effect, that it in effect constitutes an exception which proves the
rule of the symbolic order's normative power. "If the symbolic is gov-
erned by the words of the father," Butler asks, "and the symbolic is
structured by a kinship that has assumed the form of a linguistic structure, and Antigone's desire is insupportable within the symbolic, then
why does Lacan maintain that it is some immanent feature of her desire
that leads her inexorably toward death?"[27]

In my view, however, Lacan makes clear in his seminar that it is not
the paternal law as such that Antigone defends, but rather the law's
estrangement from itself; its dependence on its own violation. The clos-
ing off of the symbolic order through the function of the paternal name
constitutes a veritably perverse totality in the precise sense that it guarantees the emergence of an illicit, criminal desire. In fact, Lacan wants
to suggest that desire *as such* is criminal, that it manifests itself as the
transgression of the normative laws to which Butler's references to Lévi-
Strauss refer. It becomes clear in this way that by linking Antigone with
what he calls "pure desire" Lacan is defending the symbolic order not
on the level of a normative efficacy which it does not have, but rather
on the level of its self-subversion, of its dissolution at the hands of the
real. Lacan reminds us that the paternal function which constitutes the
symbolic order's peculiar totality is always redoubled: The reassuring
father who would guarantee the effectiveness of symbolic exchange is
always haunted, indeed supplanted, by the real father of incestuous

enjoyment—what Lacan called the *père-version*. It is in the name of this father—the perverse father of enjoyment in whom Oedipus at Colonus recognized himself at the moment of his self-blinding and his desire "never to have been born"—that Antigone acts, not in the name of a symbolic father whose design would be to uphold the sociosymbolic status quo.[28] In the end, Lacan's desire with respect to *Antigone* is uncannily close to Butler's: Both wish to acknowledge how the heroine's act insists on the necessary failure of the elementary structures of kinship, and by extension the manner in which any attempt to impose family values inevitably results in its own subversion.

Lacan is not the only one to have traced the law of love which binds Antigone so unconditionally to her brother to the fact that they emerged from the same womb and share the Labdacid name. It has been suggested that the sacredness of the brother-sister bond in the ethos of Sophoclean tragedy therefore stems not from some sentimental notion of a shared familial substance, but rather from the purely formal, radically antipsychological nature of the relation. Hegel, for example, argued that a sister's relation to her brother is the purest, most disinterested of all kinship relations, the one least distorted by sensuous-empirical motivations. Lacan, however, adds an important twist to this observation: Just as the absolute disinterest which is supposed to characterize Kantian aesthetic experience finds its truth in the gory cruelties of Sade's torturer, the pristine sibling love Antigone expresses for her brother is strictly correlative to the illicit passion of incest. This is indeed the paradox of Lacan's evocation of Antigone's desire: Its purity corresponds to the impure shame of her family's troubled criminal history, and this shame must be affirmed in order to make manifest the sins of the true criminal, who is of course Creon.

Lacan's key suggestion is therefore that the region beyond atè which Antigone occupies exists in the space which results from the emergence of the symbolic order itself, a space neither inside nor outside of language, neither before nor after it, but rather at the point of its externality to itself. Antigone places herself, ethically, in the real: Not yet physically dead, yet neither properly alive, Antigone adopts a position which may only be articulated within language as negation, as transgression. A final, crucial quote from Lacan's seminar conveys the consequences of this position: "[The value represented by Antigone] is essentially of the order of language. Without language it is not even conceivable, and the being of he who has lived could not be detached in this fashion from all that he represented [*a véhiculé*] as good and evil, as destiny, as consequences for others, and as self-regard [*comme sentiments pour lui-même*]. This purity, this separation of being from all the qualities of the historical drama he lived through, it is precisely that which is the limit, the *ex nihilo* around which Antigone stands. It is nothing other than the cut that the presence of language inaugurates in the life of man" (279, TM).

The nature of language is such that it leaves open a space for the insertion of an absolute which corresponds to the infinity of the subject's desire. This absolute depends on what Lacan refers to as the "separation" of the subject's being—its nonphenomenal or transcendental essence—from the various communicable attributes with which it might be evoked. Desire, in its most radical formulation, therefore corresponds to that aspect of the subject which cannot be described, which resists the forms of knowledge, and which consequently may never be articulated within the terms of language. The character of Antigone is exemplary in that she clung to this absolute of desire more than she held on to life itself. Indifferent to the communitarian and integrationist illusion of a determinate, universal Good, Antigone stands out as the figure who arrived at that most perfect variety of knowledge, the kind which defends its inviolable limit and acknowledges the scandalous immanence of what presents itself to us as the accursed share of our destiny. Antigone's defiance of Creon's interdiction is an ethical act which defends the innate value of that which is excluded from the terms of the Good, that which appears outside the very conditions of possibility of life as mobilized in any particular sociopolitical formation.

When Lacan spells out what irritates him most about Hegel's interpretation, he argues that it is the "conflict of discourses" the philosopher stages between Antigone's and Creon's respective laws and the "form of reconciliation" toward which this conflict moves (249). What Lacan appears to object to most vehemently is the notion of tragic reconciliation Hegel developed most consequentially in the *Lectures on Fine Art*. Tragic reconciliation, Hegel there argues, "depends on the advance of specific ethical substantive powers out of their opposition to their true harmony."[29] As we recall, Hegel reproaches both Antigone and Creon for the "one-sidedness" with which they cling to their respective laws, and it is this unswerving steadfastness which blinds them to the interimplication of the opposing ethical systems to which they adhere. Reconciliation occurs, in Hegel's view, as a result of the cancellation of this one-sidedness through the destruction of the two protagonists and the unmediated ethical substance they embody together.

It is quite clear that nothing could be further from the spirit of Lacan's intervention. Antigone remains radically unreconciled at the conclusion of her ethical journey, preferring death to a blind acceptance of Creon's version of the political good. It is precisely this notion of a lack of reconciliation, I would suggest, this identification of the spirit of the ethical with the impossibility of the real, which makes Lacan's position so noteworthy in its properly political consequences. One must guard the being, Lacan suggests, of that which appears as evil or impossible within the terms of any given sociosymbolic formation, and one can hardly imagine a stronger call to arms than that.

The paradox of Lacan's ethics is thus that within its framework the purity of desire corresponds to that most impure aspect of psychic life—the traumatic scandal of our personal destiny—which Sophocles designates with the term *atè*. What Kant's universalizing formalism dissimulates, in its moral, ethical, and aesthetic modes, is the manner in which the anonymous purity of the ideal of disinterest correlates to the most intimate, scandalous, and disavowed element of our psychic lives. Ultimately, Antigone is able to adopt a purely nonperverse ethical stance—one which, by grounding itself in the impossible real, negates or transgresses all socially sanctioned, symbolically inscribed criteria for moral conduct—*precisely by assuming her own perversion*, by elevating the curse of her family history (incest, fratricide, betrayal) into the very sign of her own (and Polynices') inviolable human dignity. Through her ethical act, Antigone qualifies the recognition of this perversity as the very condition of properly nonperverse psychic life as such. Antigone becomes heroic, to put it aphoristically, by taking her own personal evil as her Good.

It is in this sense that Lacanian ethics is, by definition—as an ethics not of the symbolic, but of the real—always destructive of conventionally accepted mores as well as, one might add, necessarily political in the sense that it takes as its point of reference, acts on behalf of, what remains unsymbolized, unacknowledged within any given sociosymbolic order.[30] In *Antigone*, Jocasta's and Oedipus's incestuous union "split into two brothers," Lacan claims, "one of whom represents power and the other crime. There is no one to assume the crime and the validity of crime apart from Antigone" (283). But it would be a grave mistake to equate Lacan's impassioned plea for the defense of the validity of crime with the cynical postmodern cult of transgression which, in its very compulsion to flaunt the law's creation of a subterranean world of its own negation, effectively works to reconcile the law to itself, thereby aspiring to render it effectively normative. In this sense, perversion is an attempt to realize the power of a law which would be capable of conforming to its own command. As Lacan concludes with respect to Sade, "the apology of crime only pushes him toward a backhanded admission of the law."[31] The psychoanalytic point is precisely that, in the field of ethics, *crime coincides with duty* in its most categorical, disinterested, and absolute manifestation. Consequently, we should hardly be surprised when, in our efforts to achieve the conformity of our actions with desire and duty, the entire sociosymbolic framework giving body to our existence suddenly comes crashing down.

Chapter Six

Concluding (Un)Queer-
Theoretical Postscript

Perversion and Its Discontents

For reasons which I think are quite manifest, the emphasis in queer theory discourse since its inception has been placed overwhelmingly on the identification and critique of the way perversion, the concept and the signifier, has been used to pathologize particular sexual practices and the identities—personal styles and behaviors, the phenomenal appearance of subjects—associated with them. Within psychoanalytic theory and practice, of course, there is a long history of phobic misuses of the concept; these usually take the form of the assumption that homosexual desire is, in and of itself, an attribute of perversion in the strong, structural sense I identified in the first chapter. That there might be a downside to the casting off of the concept of perversion in its totality, however, has not to my knowledge been a subject for contemplation within queer theory itself.

As I tried to stress in the first chapter, Foucault was absolutely correct to link the properly obsessional, and now quite familiar, categorization, medicalization, and criminalization of sexuality in modernity with a prurient ambition of sexual surveillance and control. To be sure, this ambition in its most extreme forms allied itself with the horrific eugenicist ideologies of Nazi fascism, and links up with more recent projects of moral and ethnic cleansing, from the various religious fundamentalisms, to Kosovo, Rwanda, and the occupied Palestinian territories. In my view, however, what the Foucault of *The History of Sexuality* fails to grasp is that the dizzying taxonomic crescendos of sexology bespeak the ultimate futility of its project, indeed its inevitable self-subversion. More precisely, the increasing resemblance of mechanisms of sexual prohibition and surveillance to the practices and discourses they are designed to control is a function not of some essential perversion which would inhere in power as such, but rather of the unacknowledged dependence of instances of sexual normalization on the violation of these norms. This is indeed the paradox to which the dual understanding of perversion in psychoanalysis gives form: The very doggedness of the effort to secure a realm of sexual normality from an increasingly long list of deviations soon acquires the traits of fixity and sadism associated with perversion itself. Taken to its logical conclusion, the Foucauldian contention that discourse/power is essentially perverse is effectively a form of the pervert's disavowal of the essential perversity of desire: its constitutive deviation from its "proper" genital aim. The pervert unconsciously desires that power take on the instrumentalizing omnipotence Foucault wants to attribute to it; his psychic structure features the design of fusing power to knowledge, of becoming the support, the vehicle of a will which would know exactly what it wants. In other words, the pervert refuses to envisage the traumatic contradiction between what power knows and what it effectively does, between its self-justifications and what it actually puts into practice.

In the light of these observations, I wish in what follows to examine a number of the most far-reaching attempts available within contemporary discourse to theorize the relation between power and desire, and to problematize the Freudian antinomy of "civilization and its discontents" in the context of the homosexual experience. In these sections I will be interested in exploring what I will argue are the three fundamental weaknesses of contemporary queer theory, each of which appears to devolve from an overinvestment in Foucault's aim to historicize the unconscious: First, its latent regression to an emancipatory notion of perversion explicitly distinguished from, but effectively very similar to, the midcentury post-Freudian liberationist paradigm Foucault sought to critique; this perspective tends to feature the related assumption that homosexuality is or can be in some fashion political or subversive in itself. Second, its knee-jerk tendency to characterize an unspecified notion of the state as an agency of sexual normalization, and then to seek recourse to a minoritarian framework of community-based activism which severs its relation to the state. And third, its general failure to recognize the limits of sexual politics, in other words the way in which the variously formulated sexual-minority communities are themselves traversed by the same sociopolitical antagonisms which fracture the socius as a whole. In a strong sense each of these drawbacks of queer discourse results from the same Foucauldian premise of the determinative production of the subject by power as discourse.

I will then reflect on the nexus between recent work in Lacanian criticism and the queer theory problematic, providing my own perspective on the question of psychoanalysis and (the limits of) the politics of sexuality. And finally, I will propose that it may be time to accept in queer theoretical circles a difficult truth: Though indeed in a number of ways the gay movement has been and continues to be a valuable, though limited, political project, the familiar New Left-derived assumption that it was part of a desirable general rearticulation of socialist politics in the context of new postwar social and cultural realities is ultimately flawed. It must therefore be replaced by a decisive insistence on linking the problematic of sexuality to wider, global socioeconomic paradigms for cultural analysis.

A Dynamic Perversion

Jonathan Dollimore's *Sexual Dissidence* is a cogent, wide-ranging examination of the problematic of sexual deviance in Western culture. Emerging from the British intellectual field in 1991, the book aims to advance a history of sexual nonconformity on the basis of close, admirably nuanced readings of a set of cultural texts spanning the early modern to the postmodern period. Dollimore's larger project aims at tracing the development of properly sexual formulations of perversion out of earlier, moral and theological understandings which were at work in the culture of early modernity. One important portion of Dollimore's project involves an attempt to adjudicate between Freud's and Foucault's theories of the perverse, and on this level it anticipates many of the key trends in queer theory in the 1990s. My consideration of Dollimore will be much narrower than the admirably broad approach of the book itself; the aim will be to focus more intently on its theoretical presuppositions than on the breadth of its literary and cultural content.

In many ways *Sexual Dissidence* is emblematic of the concerns of the British New Left critical tradition, one which was interested in, among other things, finding ways to balance a properly materialist interest in cultural politics with an appreciation for the specificity of the notion of unconscious desire in psychoanalysis. In consequence, Dollimore's work stands out with respect to the mainstream of the American queer theory tradition in both its implicit assumption concerning the productive centrality of Freudian discourse to the theory of sexuality, and in its greater sensitivity to the implication of instances of homophobic discrimination in dynamics of social power and class. Though the sophistication and nuance with which Dollimore traces common links between Freud's and Foucault's theories of perversion is not in question, my sense is that his work is insufficiently aware of the full consequences of Foucault's mobilization of his concept of power. The uncommon rigor which Dollimore brings to his identification of what he terms a "perverse dynamic" in Freud ironically highlights the problematic aspect of his recourse to Foucault's reconsideration of perversion as power. Dollimore's Foucault reference retrospectively casts an unfortunate historicist shadow over his readings of Freud, and bespeaks a wider confusion of psychoanalytic and Foucauldian premises which in my view characterizes queer theory in general. As I will try to show, Dollimore only inconsistently comes to terms with the nonhistorical essence of the discontent Freud identifies within the dynamic of civilization.

In light of the available discourses on sexuality emerging from the psychoanalytic and sexological traditions, Dollimore distinguishes his own attempt at formulating a subversive agency associated with perversion from those attempts which seek, via a certain reading of Freud, to cast the liberation of a presocial "polymorphous perversity" in a revolutionary light.[1] Dollimore's readings of Freud highlight those instances which not only dissect the mechanisms through which the ideals of civilization depend on the perverse desires they are meant to repress, but also subvert themselves by reproducing these same perversions. This aspect of Dollimore's conception of the relation between civilization and perversion is therefore much more complex and intimate than the one presupposed by those who would posit that the liberation or desublimation of repressed instincts would find a straightforwardly emancipatory result. "There is something counter-effective in the very mechanism of repression," Dollimore asserts, "and indeed within the entire civilizing process: instead of transforming perverse desire into civilized achievement, it counter-productively coerces the subject into a perverse or neurotic existence."[2] Dollimore clearly finds much subversive insight in Freud's insistence that an overly zealous adherence to the renunciations civilization imposes produces subjects who impede the very project of civilization, disrupting even its capacity to reproduce itself.

This facet of Dollimore's reading of Freud therefore presents the view that civilization is a kind of superstructure built upon a base of repressed, perverse instincts. This construction guarantees that perversion will reemerge within the official domain of culture, destabilizing its traditions, unsettling its hierarchies of value, and introducing an element of conflict and antagonism which cannot be resolved or surpassed.

The implicit social theory Dollimore attributes to Freud thereby provides a method for tracing the social processes through which civilization effectively produces that which is antagonistic to it through the imposition of its own norms. This sociopolitical aspect of Freud, in Dollimore's view, is the one most conducive to the materialist analysis he wishes to advocate.

Dollimore uses his appropriation of Freud's theory of civilization to advance and develop his own concept of the perverse dynamic. This notion subtends that civilization may only reproduce itself through the pressure it exerts on the sexual instinct in the form of the renunciations and sublimations it requires. At the same time, culture[3] draws upon the perverse energies it suppresses in order to perpetuate its prohibitions. As a result, Freud accords to perversion, according to Dollimore, a certain logical priority over civilization. "It is sexual perversion," writes Dollimore, "not sexual 'normality,' which is the given in human nature" (176). Because the demands of the instincts are perpetually at odds with the constraints of civilization, culture is inherently unstable, prone to disruption. In effect, civilization works against itself; it undermines its own normalizing efforts. By forcing the conversion of perverse energies into the sublimations of cultural achievement, civilization guarantees for itself a minimum level of neurotic discontent which threatens to resurface, clamoring for a more direct satisfaction. "The pain of normality," states Dollimore, "is not just the consequence of a more or less successful renunciation, but the effect of a radical contradiction, an extreme dysfunction" (177).

In his 1908 essay "'Civilized' Sexual Morality and Modern Nervous Illness," Freud discusses the ambivalence of the instinctual renunciation civilization requires in transparently social terms, and Dollimore makes this essay the key to his formulation of the agency of perversion. His reading of this often overlooked text advances that the forms of sublimation sexual morality requires are damaging both to the individual subject and to the social order because of the high cost in neurosis which renunciation forces the subject to pay. According to Dollimore, Freud "speaks of desublimated perversions as not merely alternative to civilized sexuality, but actively hostile toward both it and the social order which that sexuality shores up" (186). Whereas elsewhere it insists that perversion inheres in civilization itself, implying therefore the impossibility of a desublimation which would not at the same time be repressive, Dollimore's argument here attributes to psychoanalysis a less paradoxical logic, one which would allow for a straightforwardly subversive libidinal release. Though this perversion capable of a subversive desublimation is no longer situated before or outside of civilization, as

it tends to be in the less sophisticated liberationist current, it nonetheless retains its capacity to disrupt dominant norms, indeed to act against
the social order as such. In this way, Dollimore's analysis wavers between its desire to distance itself from a straightforward liberationist
paradigm and its aim to attribute a certain subversive agency to a notion
of the perverse.

This ambiguity becomes more apparent in Dollimore's interpretation of Freud's one-time definition of neurosis as "the negative of perversions."[4] On the one hand, repressed perverse desires support the
neuroses associated with the ideals of civilization and its sexual morality.
For example, Dollimore quotes Freud's observation that the analysis of
neurotics never fails to uncover currents of repressed homosexual desire, and proceeds to comment that "the repression of perverse desire
actually generates neurosis" (177). On the other hand, however, Dollimore
attributes to these repressed perversions a potential "disruptive power"
which threatens to sabotage "the whole process of normative psychosexual development (or subjection) upon which civilization depends"
(181). Dollimore's argument is that the activation of this disruptive power
through desublimation causes civilization to produce the perversions it
wishes to repress, disrupting through its action the coherence of the
norms by which civilization is imposed.

It is here that Dollimore goes so far as to posit a conceptual parallel between Freud's theory of sexual morality and Foucault's notion
of power's production of sexualities both normative and deviant. But
before we embark on a closer examination of Dollimore's reading of
Foucault, I wish to make explicit what is at stake in Dollimore's understanding of perversion's agency. For if, as one facet of Dollimore's
argument indeed acknowledges, the production of perversion is endemic
to the terms of civilization—if, in other words, perversion is simply a by-
product of civilization's means of perpetuating itself, of reconstituting its
own ideals—then the strategy of desublimation, of undoing the repressions which constitute the experience of acculturation, will not necessarily produce the emancipatory result Dollimore appears to expect.
There is a strong sense in which Dollimore's interpretation of Freud's
concept of civilization assumes it is complicit with an agency of sexual
normalization whose effectiveness Freud's work calls into question,
though not without inconsistency. Dollimore's contentions thereby
reproduce the ambiguity of Freud's own notion of civilization. This
notion cannot decide whether it wants to designate a neurotic bourgeois sexual morality or rather the function of repression proper, in
the sense of Freud's contention that repression is a general a priori
condition of desire, one which *resists* the historicist reduction at work

in all notions of sexual morality, from the most stiflingly bourgeois to the most purportedly emancipatory.

It will be helpful here to turn to the theme of the repressed homosexual desires of Freud's neurotics, and to Dollimore's suggestion that the desublimation of these desires would constitute an example of the political agency of his perverse dynamic. Dollimore's argument assumes in this instance that the agency of repression concerned is expressed socially, in other words that the terms of civilization to which these neurotics need conform effectively enforce a prohibition against homosexuality. As I will explore at a later point, this assumption is akin to Judith Butler's concept of the "heterosexual matrix." What should be remarked is that Dollimore's claim—that the lifting of this repression carries a subversive or emancipatory agency—is based on the premise that these neurotics are what one might term "repressed homosexuals"; that their authentic desires are effectively pushed underground by the force of culture. Dollimore's questioning of a presumed heterosexual norm within the very terms of culture is consequently shown to rely on the imposition of a homosexual norm for desire, and in this way it loses sight of Freud's fundamental argument about unconscious desire, namely that it violates whatever norm works to prohibit it. Moreover, Dollimore's contention also implicitly qualifies the homosexual attribute of the repressed desire as perverse, thereby assuming the necessary or essential link between perversion and homosexuality Dollimore elsewhere wishes to problematize in his readings of Freud.

Of course, there existed in Freud's time, as there exist today and always have existed, subjects whose homosexual inclinations are neither "repressed," as Dollimore sociologically understands the term, nor particularly unconscious. What leads Dollimore to attribute subversive potentialities to desublimation and to qualify perversion as potentially transgressive is finally his confusion of what Freud terms "sexual morality" with the agency of repression as such. Repression, strictly speaking, is not coincident with the sexual norms created in the social world in its attempt to police desire. Freud's musings on the dynamic of civilization stress how desire is essentially perverse, how its deviation from the law is constitutive of desire as such. If civilization decides it wants to ensure that desire will express itself heterosexually, in other words, then it is abundantly clear that this attempt necessarily fails. Freud's dialectic of civilization is therefore not to be situated between a regime of sexual normalization and a field of repressed, perverse sexuality, but rather on civilization's cultivation of an inherently transgressive, inexhaustible desire. In other words, desire is by definition a desire for transgression.

Dollimore's argument comes very close to appreciating this paradox when he notes the following: "[I]t is when [the perversions] become an instance of the (in)subordinate entirely displacing the dominant (for which read heterosexual, reproductive, genital intercourse)—when they oust it completely and take its place in all circumstances—that Freud is prepared to regard them as pathological" (181). It becomes clear that Dollimore's claim that his perverse dynamic "begins to undermine key aspects of the psychoanalytic project" is already understood in Freud's own concept of desire. In consequence, Dollimore's dynamic subverts only psychoanalytic projects which misattribute to the Freudian texts a notion of *die ganze Sexualstrebung*: a libidinal drive which would be fully reconciled with its presumptive genital aim. Though Freud himself occasionally deviates from his own position, his theory's latent coherence, as I argued in the first chapter, asserts that the libido's deviation from this genital aim is constitutive, that desire is fundamentally a missed encounter with the aim it sets itself. The "pathological" element to which Freud refers therefore devolves not from desire's displacement of the dominant norm—a displacement which has always already taken place—but rather from the desire to normalize insubordination, to transform deviation into a new consistent law which does not latently work toward its own subversion.

To his credit Dollimore concisely extracts from Freud's writing the full subversive impact of his universalizing thesis about the inherently perverse nature of human desire. In the terms of my own analysis, in other words, he uncovers the way Freud's texts identify an essential perversity in desire which links the highest ideals of civilization to the base truth of its repressions and exclusions. But if desire is already antinormative, then Dollimore's attribution to Freud of a "continuum" between perversion and normality is not entirely correct: If normal sexuality always misses its presumptive aim, then it is the very ambition of normality which becomes perverse, an insight which Dollimore himself intuits when, paraphrasing Freud, he claims that "the real conservative is the pervert" (176).

In spite of his endorsement of Freudian theory's unsettling implications for bourgeois sexual morality, Dollimore finally accepts Foucault's claim that sexuality is a construction of discourse under the aegis of power. Though he bears witness to this claim's "strange" character and, citing Jeffrey Weeks and Michael Ignatieff, mentions without further elucidation that it "remains vulnerable to the charge of functionalism,"[5] Dollimore's analysis conveys with relative consistency how he situates the problematic of sexuality, along with the agency of his perverse dynamic, on the level of history and social relations, thereby sidestepping the specificity of Freud's concept of desire. The related assumption—it remains to some degree implicit in Dollimore's text—that nonnormative sexual activity is in some unspecified sense transparently political is of a sort with the tendency, characteristic of queer theory in general, to attribute in an undernuanced way a politically progressive quality to gay subjects and gay culture. For example, Dollimore makes the vague claim that "the homosexual ... in historical actuality" has "embraced both cultural and racial difference" (250). While it must certainly be recognized that the homosexual experience has a tendency to produce a greater sense of distance from familial or social acculturation than might otherwise, though by no means necessarily, be the case, there remains in my view something unsettlingly hubristic in the assertion that such a love of difference is a reliable outcome of an avowed homosexual orientation. Indeed, I would venture to say that such instances of gay self-privileging are dangerous in that they conjure the fantasy of the homosexual as the pure and innocent beautiful soul immune to xenophobia, misogyny, and the other politically incorrect crimes against difference.

Generally speaking, then, Dollimore's method ultimately falls back on two basic assumptions intrinsic to the historicist approach to sexuality theory. First, sexuality is constructed by productive and regulatory categories which act in the name of social relations of power. And second, this production of hegemonic sexual norms also gives rise to their own contradictions or transgressions. The productive agency of power creates a conflicted social space in which the possibility for the rearticulation of sexuality is ambivalently produced and controlled. The norm and its deviation bear the same determinative relation to the instance of abstract power. The specifically Freudian contention which Dollimore also identifies, however, was rather that the norm effectively inaugurates a perverse desire for its own transgression, and that this desire is properly unconscious, in the sense of unavailable to knowledge. Thus, Dollimore in the last instance endorses Foucault's view of sexual desire as coextensive with the forms of knowledge which effect its social construction; moreover, he reads the interdictions of civilization as a properly social agency which acts upon the subject through power from outside. In this way Dollimore erases the conceptual specificity of psychoanalysis, and is able erroneously to identify its analytic work with the deconstructive and historicist logics of poststructuralism.

In my view, then, the weaker points of Dollimore's negotiation of Freud and Foucault run as follows. First, Dollimore demonstrates a tendency to transpose what Freud delineated as properly psychical conflicts—as conflicts internal to the logic of desire—onto the social, thereby encouraging us to view social conflict as unrelated to the fundamentally split structure of consciousness, from the subject's separation from itself. If we are to take Freud seriously, to negotiate psychoanalysis on its own terms, it must rather be acknowledged that the real of social antagonism is the same real which accounts for the splitting of subjectivity; the subject's intrapsychic antagonism results from the same impasse which occasions the fundamentally antagonistic nature of social life itself. In consequence, there can be no workable concept of a social field which does not take account of its properly psychical apprehension by a subject of desire who does not appear within its terms. In the more specific terms of Dollimore's argument, a perverse dynamic inheres in social relations because this dynamic structures the psychical realm as such.

Further, even though Dollimore is careful not to glorify the subversions of a presocial polymorphous perversion, he nonetheless maintains that the activation of perversion through the perverse dynamic carries inherently political and unambiguously subversive significance. Though what Dollimore means concretely by the agency of his perverse dynamic remains ambiguous due to the abstract terms through which he articulates it, it appears that perversion, for Dollimore, may act oppositionally against the cultural order through a desublimation which destabilizes cultural categories. The suggestion appears to be that non-reproductive sexual acts undermine the normative (that is, genital) organization of sexuality. On the level of culture, the perverse dynamic effects a disruption on a more properly conceptual level, in other words by messing deconstructively with binary oppositions which impose a separation between the valued and devalued terms structuring a sociocultural field. In my view, both of these arguments in favor of the subversive potentialities of perversion require more careful consideration.

According to Freud himself, for instance, the genital organization of sexuality is an ideal to which subjects necessarily fail to conform. As a result, it is not entirely clear what constitutes the oppositional agency Dollimore wishes to attribute to desire's inherent perversion. Insofar as Freud, at not simply his most radical moments, but at his most theoretically consistent ones as well, maintains that the full genitalization of the instinct is a theoretical fiction, a residue of perversion—an abnormal fetishization of a body part, an undue preoccupation with an aspect of foreplay, a strange fantasy script without which enjoyment becomes impossible—remains active in even the most normative heterosexual encounter.

Insofar as Freud characterized the repressed perversions as intrinsic to the dialectic of civilization, it would appear that the disruptive force they may periodically level against the norms that civilization itself imposes actually constitutes an essential element of the system's stability. Momentary disruptions in the smooth regulation of sexuality's repression consolidate, rather than jeopardize, the authority of sexual norms, indeed constitute the experience of sexual desire as such. Dollimore's argument finally retracts from its recognition of the profoundly paradoxical nature of the dialectic of civilization. Recalling the Möbius strip, the most severe sublimations of civilization, as one follows their trajectory, turn into their opposite and become indistinguishable from the most forcefully disavowed and scandalously taboo aspects of the libidinal drive.

Dollimore's work suffers in this way from its inability to distinguish between the two latent understandings of perversion in Freud: perversion as characteristic of desire in general; and perversion as a problematic psychic structure designed to evade the traumatic enigma of desire. As a result, Dollimore claims for his perverse dynamic an agency which is already at work in normal sexuality itself. This assumption causes Dollimore to overstate the political consequences of the activation of his perverse dynamic. In addition, Dollimore's argument features the almost universally rehearsed queer-theoretical assumption that Freudian psychoanalysis presupposes that a homosexual object choice is necessarily perverse, not in the first, but in the second, sense. If this is not the case—if, in other words, theoretical coherence requires us to read at least some of the assertions about the perversity of homosexuality on the banal level on which Freud asserts that all sexuality is perverse—then Dollimore's arguments in favor of a residual psychosexual-developmental teleology in psychoanalysis are deprived of their political bite.

Moreover, if we assume that homosexuality, in particular the male kind, has no necessary relation to the structure of perversion properly speaking, then queer theory is required to abandon its smug tendency to assume that the mere choice of a same-sex object operates politically or oppositionally in some straightforward or objective fashion. For if anything has become clear in the past three decades since the alleged liberation of nonnormative sexualities, it is precisely that the profusion of images and lifestyles at one time considered beneath the threshold of social tolerance has been utterly subsumed by the forces of capital: There is at present perhaps no sexier commodity than the mobilization for commercial purposes of a certain male homosexual libidinal style. One would in fact want to suggest that the social deterritorialization, to borrow a term from Deleuze and Guattari, effected by the increasing liberalization of global capital has in fact enabled the increasing visibility and social acceptance of male homosexuality, but at the expense of its virtually seamless integration into the logic of the market. Though clearly the social acceptance of homosexuality must be valorized at all costs and the recognition of homosexual relationships defended unconditionally, the premise of a sexual liberation appears to have been colonized mercilessly by capitalist interests. It is almost as if the full globalization of capital required the fantasy of a male homosexual desublimation—likely merely a species within a larger genus of sexual desublimation—in order to attain its current, overwhelming and unprecedented, command over the engineering of social relations.

The Minoritarian Temptation

The full political consequences of Foucault's premise of a discursive sexuality are to my mind made intriguingly clear in Eve Kosofsky Sedgwick's *Epistemology of the Closet*. Indeed, in retrospect it has become apparent that Sedgwick's book featured an enabling and inaugurating function for queer theory within the American intellectual field in many ways comparable to the function Dollimore's book performed for the British. Moreover, Sedgwick's rigorously argued book has been without question among the most influential to have shaped the disciplinary transition from lesbian and gay studies properly speaking to the more theoretically ambitious queer discourse. From among the discourses which have shaped Sedgwick's project, psychoanalysis is conspicuously absent. Professing to an early interest in psychoanalysis, Sedgwick expresses the view that it became, as she puts it, "the sleekest of metatheoretical disciplines, sleeked down to such elegant operational entities as the mother, the father, the preoedipal, the oedipal, the other or Other."[6] One of the results of Sedgwick's skepticism, I will suggest, is an inconsistency between her theoretical project and its concrete political program. While the former seeks to uncover an incoherence of definition in modernist discourse linked with its conception of sexuality, the latter sets as its task the discursive accommodation of a minoritarian sex identity. More precisely, *Epistemology of the Closet*'s methodological gambit is to shift the focus of discourse analysis from history to form; but instead of marking the limits of an identity-predicated politics, Sedgwick's work ultimately demonstrates how both Foucauldian historicism and deconstruction's reading strategies as Sedgwick formulates them rest upon the same problematic immanentist idea of discourse.

Sedgwick acquires from Foucault's later work a number of assumptions about the complicity of discourse with power. For example, she endorses the view that sexuality is "so intimately entangled" with "historically distinctive contexts and structures" that knowledge is not "a transparent window onto . . . sexuality," but rather "constitutes that sexuality" itself (44). For Sedgwick, sexuality can be reduced to the forms of knowledge which create it at a given historical juncture; it is therefore coextensive with Foucault's knowledge/power paradigm or, more precisely, knowledge is "the magnetic field of power" (4). Sedgwick's full adoption of the historicist framework is apparent even where she attempts to distinguish her argument from Foucault's. Sedgwick first credits Foucault for refuting two "positivist assumptions": a) that homosexuality has a "transhistorical essence", and b) that the history of discourse on sexuality provides "an increasingly direct, true knowledge or comprehension of that essence" (44). But quoting a passage from *The History of Sexuality* which addresses the nineteenth-century creation of the homosexual as a "species," Sedgwick then accuses Foucault of making "an overarching point about the complete conceptual alterity of earlier models of same-sex relations," a point which works in tandem with a tendency to presume a "commonsense, present-tense conceptualization of homosexuality" as "we currently understand it" (46–7). In my view, however, Foucault does in fact allow for the simultaneous coexistence of contradictory sets of sexual categories; coherence is not a requirement of the notion of a "regime" of knowledge. The Foucauldian point is rather that all of these conflicting discourses are equally productions of power; power produces even its own forms of resistance. My intention in bringing out this seemingly arcane point is to show how deeply Foucauldian are Sedgwick's assumptions about sexuality; indeed, they are Foucauldian even when she tries to argue against Foucault. In order to attribute a degree of subversive agency to her notion of "performative contradiction," Sedgwick is required to gloss over Foucault's insistence that dissident or oppositional knowledges are as much a product of power as those with hegemonic pretensions.

This notion of performative contradiction is outlined as Sedgwick announces *Epistemology*'s project, which is to take the two dominant models of homosexuality in modernity—the minoritizing and the universalizing—and to provide the tools required to show how their mutual and contradictory interimplication dissimulates the agency of power in the control of what Sedgwick calls "modern homo/heterosexual definition" (47). The minoritizing model presents the problem of homosexuality as one which concerns "a small, distinct, relatively fixed homosexual minority"; the universalizing model, in contrast, approaches it as "an issue of continuing, determinative importance in the lives of people across the spectrum of sexualities" (1). Advancing that these two contrasting views structure not just the theory of homosexuality, but also the entire conceptual framework of the modernist cultural project in which it takes shape, Sedgwick's book wants to demonstrate "how issues of modern homo/heterosexual definition are structured, not by the supercession of one model and the consequent withering away of another, but instead by the relations enabled by the unrationalized coexistence of different models during the times they do coexist.... [This project] requires a reassignment of attention and emphasis within [historical narratives of sexuality]—attempting, perhaps, to denarrativize them somewhat by focusing on a performative space of contradiction that they both delineate and, themselves performative, pass over in silence" (47–8).

The strategy at work is therefore based not on an analysis of the permutations of sexual knowledge through time, but rather on its conflicting contentions at specific historical moments. More precisely, Sedgwick's method inquires after "how certain categorizations work, what enactments they are performing and what relations they are creating, rather than what they essentially *mean*" (27). In this manner Sedgwick inaugurates what I would call a synchronically discursivist approach to sex: synchronic in its curiosity about the "performative contradictions" between elements of discourse at a given historical juncture; discursivist in its reduction of sexuality to the discourses which attempt to describe or produce it.

The merit of Sedgwick's approach is surely that it insists on identifying a conflict or tension in sexual knowledge which is not properly historical, which is intrinsic to the forms of knowledge at a specific moment in time. Yet by reducing this conflict to the means of expression of antagonistic power interests, Sedgwick reintroduces the historicist assumption of knowledge's saturation by power. From a psychoanalytic perspective, however, sexual knowledge does not merely divide itself into competing claims expressing contradictory political interests; in addition, it encounters an inherent impasse, a structural knot where knowledge lacks. The incoherence of definition Sedgwick skillfully identifies in modernism's discourse on sexuality is therefore not the result of a faulty or incomplete appreciation of a (homo)sexual reality or identity, but rather a necessary symptom of the inherent disjunction between knowledge and sex. Though it could be argued that on the level of theory Sedgwick's sophisticated methodology occasionally accepts the immanence of the definitional incoherence her cultural readings bring out, there is a strong sense in which her concrete political pronouncements reflect an ambition of redressing a deficiency in sexual discourse, of finally constructing a home in discourse for the marginal, oppressed homosexual subject.

As a result, sexuality in Sedgwick's work becomes just another descriptive category which locates the subject as a presence in discourse (albeit a potentially self-contradictory one), as a composite of multiple knowledges on the social map. Sedgwick thus defines the subject as the sum total of its multiple and conflicting discursive determinations. Indeed, it is interesting to note that despite its psychoanalytic skepticism Sedgwick's definition of the subject bears a close resemblance to the pseudopsychoanalytic concept of subject position, much utilized not too long ago in cultural studies on the Left, in that it locates the subject precisely where it is not, namely among the sociosymbolic inscriptions through which the subject attempts to represent itself. The truly psychoanalytic concept of subject, in contrast, defines the subject through its absence from the symbolic landscape; its presence may only be discerned negatively, as the impossibility or limit of representation, as the negative excess which remains when all attempts at positive description have failed.

A consideration of two examples of Sedgwick's concrete political positions on homosexuality betrays their dependence on the historicist formulation of the subject. First, Sedgwick voices opposition to all attempts, particularly those of a scientific nature, to interrogate homosexuality's origins. She is concerned more precisely that "there currently exists no framework in which to ask about the origins of development of individual gay identity that is not already structured by an implicit, transindividual Western project or fantasy of eradicating that identity" (41). For example, one can argue in favor of the extermination of homosexuals regardless if one considers homosexuality genetically or culturally determined. Though the vagueness of the notion of exploring the origins of an identity only underscores the fundamentally problematic identitarianism of her understanding of sexuality (and surely also symptomatizes a misreading of deconstruction), it appears that Sedgwick wishes to stifle any critical interrogation of the causation of homosexual desire for fear that it jeopardize the very lives of those subjects who experience it. Indeed, for Sedgwick, any exploration of homosexual origins cannot be extricated from "gay-genocidal nexuses of thought" (40).

This argument conflates so completely attempts at understanding the factors at work in homosexuality with the political uses to which these understandings are put that Sedgwick is willing to dismiss outright the present value of any such attempt. The relation between Sedgwick's view of discourse and this particular political opinion is not arbitrary: Why seek after disinterested, scientific information about homosexuality if this information has no value outside of its potential political uses? The point here is clearly not that disinterested, purely scientific information about homosexuality actually exists, actually or potentially, in any straightforward way. Rather, the fact that each scientific datum about homosexuality carries no necessary political consequences, that its interpretation is always and necessarily a point of discussion subject to ideological articulation, means that research, for example, into the possible biological factors associated with homosexuality can, will, and should go on.

Moreover, with respect to the recent controversy surrounding evidence linking brain anatomy to male homosexuality, one should decry the faulty presupposition that usually informs discussion of this relation, namely that such biological evidence justifies the hypothesis that certain characteristics of the cerebral structure, in this instance, cause homosexuality. This argument conflates correlation with causation. In other words, it is just as legitimate to make the opposite claim, namely that it is homosexual object choice (or, to put it more psychoanalytically, a particular experience of castration) which causes the differential anatomical development, and not vice versa. This observation adds to the pressure mounting against Sedgwick's argument. For if the enlarged hypothalamus does not cause homosexuality, then the surgical alteration of the brain would have no necessary effect on the male homosexual's orientation. This of course in no way ensures that campaigns of this sort for surgical intervention would not arise from the most virulently homophobic of today's political constituencies. The point remains, however, that Sedgwick paranoically overstates the stability and coherence of the relation between a scientific finding and its ideological articulation. There is no gap between knowledge and power for Sedgwick: All knowledge is immediately concretized into an instance of the normative exercise of power; knowledge already contains—in itself—a determinate (potential) political meaning.

A further example of the concrete effects of Sedgwick's sexual historicism is linked to the genealogical aspect of her project. More specifically, the strategy offered for countering the noxious influence of all those "institutions whose programmatic undertaking is to prevent the development of gay people" is to provide "gay or proto-gay children" with the identity a homosexual discourse might create (43). The argument proposes that the development of homosexually inclined youth would proceed more smoothly if there were secure cultural identities available to them. One might legitimately wonder here what Sedgwick means by the "development" of gay people and how it would be decided what constitutes a desirable form of such development. Notwithstanding the vagueness of this formulation, however, Sedgwick's project concretely implies "recognizing and validating the creativity and heroism of the effeminate boy or tommish girl of the fifties (or sixties or seventies or eighties)" (43). It could of course be argued that the stereotypical examples Sedgwick provides for her project are arbitrary, that one could multiply these identities in order to account for variations in personality and self-presentation among homosexually inclined youth. It should also be said in support of Sedgwick that there is an authentic heroism in behaviors which visibly thwart rigid gender norms. But my concern lies rather with the assumption that the development of a sexuality or sexual identity may be ensured by the securing of a position in discourse designed to accommodate it, that the best way of facilitating, if one can put it this way, the experience of homosexual desire is to create a desirable or accurate discourse of homosexuality through the tracing of its historical development.

If the subject is a product of discourse, so the logic goes, then it is necessary to create a discourse of homosexual identity in order to safeguard the homosexual subject. The surest way to counter homophobia, in this view, is to create modes of being homosexual, rather than to address homosexuality—the practice of homosexuality—itself. Though it may indeed be the case that the creation of sociosymbolic points of identification for same-sex oriented subjects carries some psychological benefit, it also features, in my view, some consequential, properly normative, drawbacks. If one departs instead from a psychoanalytic understanding of sex, one which recognizes the limits of discourse's capacity to contain or express it, one is more likely, for example, to turn to projects such as frank, value-neutral, safer-sex education programs, initiatives which are geared less toward normative cultural initiatives than toward health and safety concerns. Indeed, the question of homosexual *sex* does not appear to figure prominently in Sedgwick's program. A shift in emphasis from the discursive construction of an oppositional homosexual identity to the incorporation of basic health information about same-sex relations into public education, for example, has the benefit of allowing queer youth to decide for themselves how, indeed if, their sexuality will define them—how it will inform, in other words, the manner in which they view themselves with respect to the wider social world.

It is difficult to conceive how Sedgwick's program would not inevitably reinstall identitarian norms which thereafter work to exercise a conformist pressure on the more impressionable. Moreover, such a program also becomes deeply problematic in the context of today's complex ethno-cultural realities. Consider for example the familiar argument against sex education which avers that homosexuality does not form part of this or that culture. Surely it is more strategic from the point of view of progressive public education policy to premise one's approach on the assumption that homosexuality is something one does as opposed to something one is. Indeed, an emphasis on the construction of a homosexual identity sets up a larger and more tempting target for those who argue that safer-sex education is part of a larger project of Western cultural imperialism. The alternative I am proposing introduces a disjunction between the problematic of sexuality and the negotiation of cultural, ethnic, and religious differences, one which is surely more likely to facilitate the negotiation of homosexuality in non-Western and non-Christian communities, perhaps especially in the West. To be sure, Sedgwick's apparent reluctance to conceptualize homosexual desire outside Anglo-American or Western European contexts is a symptomatic consequence of the sex-as-discourse view. The silent assumption is perhaps that the discourse on homosexuality elsewhere, insofar as it is held to exist, is so radically different and culturally specific that the American queer critic can have nothing to say about it, cannot even offer information and expertise on safer-sex practices, for example. In this connection it should be noted that the project of developing a determinate homosexual culture features the same underlying assumption detectable in the various forms of cultural and religious homophobia it seeks to oppose, namely that the experience of sex is a function of culture, that there is no disjunction, no lack of continuity, between a culture's attempt to regulate sex desire and the sexual relations which actually occur.

Hysteria in the Shadow of the State

In general terms Judith Butler's seminal work in queer theory makes the same assumption apparent in *Epistemology* concerning the discursive or cultural construction of sex. Unlike in Sedgwick, however, psychoanalysis has played a crucial role in the development of Butler's theories; indeed, it has clearly left its mark on Butler's more sophisticated adjudication of the problem of identity as it is viewed through the lens of sex. As is the case in Sedgwick's work, however, Butler's attachment to Foucault's premise of power's production of subjectivity occasionally detracts from her consideration of the Freudian and Lacanian discourses. The assumption that power structures the very conditions through which discourse produces sexuate subjects, in my view, forces Butler's argument to the conclusion that what resists these conditions remains outside of them, in an unconscious or imaginary realm at a remove from the means of political intervention.

Consequently, in order to retain a dialectical framework which allows for a degree of agency for the nonnormative or oppositional subject, she is required to make two contradictory statements about culture's conditions, about the norms which legislate subjective possibilities. On the one hand, these norms positively determine subject production in their role as material conditions; on the other, they constitute ideal discourses which individual subjects may never perfectly concretize in their actions or speech acts. This problematic ambiguity about the material or ideal character of discourse's normative command leads Butler to the premise that what limits the subject's agency, what renders it opaque to its own desire, is a positive condition of discourse enforced by power, rather than an immanent feature of the sociosymbolic system as such. For psychoanalysis, in contrast, the subject is not opaque to desire because power prevents it from being so; rather, this nontransparency is the very condition of subjectivity itself. This lack of clarity concerning the operation of normative power in Butler's work is not unrelated to the difficulty of reconciling from among her premises heterosexism's saturation of discourse with the actuality of same-sex desire. If the subject is a product of conditions coextensive with discourse, and discourse enforces a heterosexual matrix, then one is left wondering how and why discourse produces homosexual subjects in the first place.

The aim of Butler's *The Psychic Life of Power* is to describe in more detail than in her previous work how power impacts the dynamics of psychic life by placing psychoanalysis in dialogue with Foucault. Indeed, this text represents Butler's most ambitious attempt to synthesize the psychoanalytic concern for the unconscious with Foucault's emphasis on the productive agency of power. Butler seizes upon the description of subject production—Foucault's term is *assujetissement*—in *Discipline and Punish*, in which Foucault analyzes the history of incarceration in France to theorize how, in Butler's words, "one inhabits the figure of autonomy only by becoming subjected to power, a subjection which implies a radical dependency."[7] As Butler reminds her reader, Foucault advances that the production of the subject through discourse gives rise to the illusion of a soul: a truth or essence of subjectivity which power then mobilizes as an instrument for discipline, surveillance, and normalization. Nineteenth-century legal and medical discourses, for example, attempted to describe the physical attributes of criminality in an effort to make undesirable individuals identifiable to the authorities. In this way Foucault suggests that power disciplines the body through discourse's production of the illusion of the soul.

It is in relation to this notion of subject formation that Butler attempts a rapprochement between Foucault and psychoanalysis. She claims that the terms "soul" and "body" as used in *Discipline and Punish* parallel "subject" and "psyche" when we understand these words, as she states, "in the psychoanalytic sense" (86). Though no reference is offered to any particular psychoanalytic tradition or text, Butler provides in a footnote her definition of these two latter terms: Psyche "includes the notion of the unconscious," she asserts, whereas subject is formed "by the exclusion of the unconscious" (206). Butler's reading of Foucault's account of *assujetissement* is therefore based on the assumption that power produces the subject through the enforcement of discursive norms. In contrast to the subject, then, the psyche is "what exceeds the imprisoning effects of the discursive demand to inhabit a coherent identity, to become a coherent subject"; the psyche, in consequence, has the capacity, at least potentially, to resist "the regularization that Foucault ascribes to normalizing discourses" (86). Though Lacan insisted on associating the subject with the unconscious, and psyche is not technically a psychoanalytic concept for Lacan, it is nevertheless clear that Butler wishes to evaluate the antinormative potential of an agency she associates with the psychoanalytic concept of the unconscious.

These definitions reveal that Butler understands the unconscious to be an aspect of the psyche which remains to an extent outside the reach of power's normalizing grasp. But she then proceeds to make two criticisms of this theory she attributes to psychoanalysis (inaccurately, I will suggest), a theory of an unconscious which would be immune to power's effects. First, the unconscious may be just as "structured by power relations" as the other parts of the psyche; put differently, the source of what Butler calls the subject's "attraction to subjection" could be the unconscious itself. Second, if power does not occasion the unconscious, then the unconscious "cannot redirect the law in its effects." Butler then proceeds to the expected conclusion that "psychic resistance presumes the continuation of the law in its anterior, symbolic form and, in that sense, contributes to the status quo" (98).

It becomes apparent here that Butler has imported the Lacanian terms "law" and "symbolic" into her reading of *Discipline and Punish*, and in my view this results in a distortion of Lacan's position. In Lacan, the law designates the form of an agency of interdiction associated less with the father than with the notion of paternity (Lacan's seldom understood point being that the effort at representing this paternal agency necessarily fails), which marks the experience of loss with which the subject experiences its relation to the order of language and desire. Butler attributes to this notion of the law a binding regulative power with which she associates a heterosexist normativity. Butler argues that if psychoanalysis situates resistance to power in the unconscious, psychoanalysis offers no means of altering the terms through which the subject accedes to the symbolic domain. Forms of resistance to power allied with, or situated in, the unconscious are without recourse, Butler claims, before power's complicity with the law. "Where Lacan restricts the notion of social power to the symbolic domain and delegates resistance to the imaginary," Butler writes, "Foucault recasts the symbolic as relations of power and understands resistance as an effect of power" (99).

This last statement brings to the surface Butler's motivation for turning from psychoanalysis to Foucault. The notion of a productively normative symbolic law she attributes to Lacan causes her to view Foucault's identification of a resistance within the discourse/power nexus as a desirable corrective for queer theory. But in my view it becomes apparent here how Butler predicates her criticism of Lacan on a faulty understanding of the psychoanalytic argument. Indeed, it would seem that Butler derives this mistaken understanding from Foucault's revisionist critique of the psychoanalytic theory of subjectivity in *The History of Sexuality*. It should also be said that Butler's move is generally emblematic of queer theory's reception of Lacan, and it largely accounts, as I will go on to suggest, for the limitations of queer theory's grasp of the political. Butler in effect projects Foucault's idea of discourse's production of the subject onto Lacan's notion of the symbolic order. This conflation of the two theorists has the effect of hypostasizing the concept of the Lacanian symbolic by attributing to it a particular content of normative kinship relations which effectively polices the very process of subject production, indeed determining the very desires of the subjects thereby produced.

Moreover, Butler's qualification of the imaginary—which for Lacan was unambiguously a zone of fruitless rivalry and frustration for the subject—as a means of resistance and subversion provides further evidence of the way her argument makes faulty attributions to Lacan, who at this point in her argument becomes very much a straw figure. In essence, Butler reproaches Lacan, and psychoanalysis in general, for upholding a conservative complicity with patriarchal and heterosexist privilege, a privilege she believes—or she believes Lacan to believe—to be ingrained in the very conditions of subject production. Butler extracts from Foucault the idea that relations of power inhere in the very fabric of the symbolic order itself. Though Foucault himself, likely under the influence of Deleuze, came to reject entirely the baggage of the semiotic–linguistic paradigm with which he was earlier involved, Butler's work enacts an original but misleading fusion of the concept of the symbolic with the Foucauldian premise of a discourse shot through with vectors, as opposed to differential relations, of power. Whereas Foucault's *check*

?

late work rejects the premise of a linguistic paradigm for discourse, substituting for it a vocabulary of force derived from the physical sciences, Butler reintroduces through her reference to "the law" the semiotic framework of Lacan's reading of psychoanalysis. As a result, Butler's politicization of the symbolic assumes that the signifying order which the subject is forced to negotiate carries determinate political meanings fully enforced by a normative agency of power. From this perspective, it is only possible to interpret psychoanalysis as a doctrine with conservative and heterosexist political implications, in particular on the level of kinship relations and familial structures, since by implication it would jettison resistance to power to the unconscious or the imaginary, registers which both, in their isolation from social effectiveness, inevitably end up propping up power's normative command.

This is an challenge to it

My suggestion is as follows: The premise that power saturates the symbolic order, that its law succeeds in implanting on subjects the norm it seeks to uphold, does not accurately reflect the psychoanalytic argument. For example, Lacan's concept of the Other—the sociosymbolic apparatus legislating social relations, the very nexus of the psychical and social realms, the very point of entry of the social world into the subject's very subjective intimacy—is precisely characterized by the lack of knowledge at its center: Power, in this view, not only does not but cannot know what it wants. The properly semiotic, as opposed to political, logic with which Freud interpreted his patients' dream recollections—in which he explicated, more precisely, the mechanisms of condensation and displacement through which the signifiers constituting the dream narration betray traces of an unconscious desire—fails to express determinate and normative power relations. That a criminal, transgressive unconscious desire leaves evidence of itself in spite of the enforcement of the "father's law" demonstrates this law's noncoincidence with itself, its production of a desire which displays the law's failure to legislate against all exceptions. In short, Butler's argument makes its fatal mistake where it attributes a determinate political meaning or content to what in Lacan—even, though less clearly perhaps, from the days of the earliest published seminars—was always first and foremost a differential, properly semiotic order. Crucially, this order is always haunted by an internal inconsistency which rebounds upon the subject, causing the emergence of a desire which takes the form not of a normative assertion, but of a troubling, finally unanswerable, question.

To anticipate the obvious Foucauldian rejoinder, one should state that a symbolic system is not politically neutral, angelically immune to ideology. The Lacanian point is rather that the sociosymbolic order features a central void which makes necessary the addition of a political master signifier, as well as multiple imaginary contents, which attribute a false coherence to the system and constitute the semblance of reality we require to navigate the social world. Butler situates ambivalence and undecidability on the level of power's determination of the subject, power here understood as concrete and normative in a positive, legislative sense: Power is unlocatable, unidentifiable, but nonetheless always already realized. Lacan, in contrast, instead locates these qualities on the formal, negative, symbolic level of language. Because meaning is unverifiable and necessarily hypothetical, it becomes possible to act, to exploit power's nonsimultaneity with itself. While it is indeed the case that, for Lacan, the condition of possibility for nonpsychotic forms of subjectivity (that is, neurosis and perversion) is the subject's introjection of the paternal signifier, the entire clinical practice of analysis, indeed the very notion of the cure is, in Lacanian terms, viewed precisely as the means by which the subject accesses a zone from which the contingency of the relation between the *function* of the interdiction which makes the symbolic possible and the *order* it inaugurates may be apprehended. It is in this sense that Lacanian psychoanalysis affirms the possibility of a nonpsychotic contestation of any given sociosymbolic formation. Lacan's ethics is formulated precisely as the defense of such a utopian possibility of impossible sociosymbolic transformation; indeed, Lacan identifies this possibility as the subject's very duty, as the goal of psychoanalysis considered as a clinical, cultural, and political project.

It is therefore crucial to underline how Lacan, at various stages of his teaching, formulates his idea of the symbolic order with reference to theories describing the differential relation of forms—from post-Saussurean linguistics, to Frege's theory of numbers, to post-Cantorian set theory—to theories of differential systems, in other words, which have no determinate relation to power, no absolutely normative command over psychic life as Butler wants to theorize it. What these systems hold in common is their eventual confrontation with an internal incoherence, one which forever separates the differential system of relations from any determinate relation to an outside, to a final referent. The coherence of Butler's argument therefore requires the attribution to the law marking our dependence on these formal structures a normative meaning which obfuscates its properly psychoanalytic significance. More precisely, the law of castration is not a law which legislates positively; it does not make determinate, unambiguous prescriptions, and thus does not articulate power in any straightforward way. Rather, the law attempts to give substance to the subject's inescapable sense, to which fantasy gives form, of having lost a mode of enjoyment, a direct brand of satisfaction. Hence the law's properly paradoxical status: It

[handwritten margin notes: "mark dominant discourse", "where does this arise from except"]

serves to prohibit a structural impossibility; it proscribes a lost mode of enjoyment which the subject never possessed to begin with. The corollary of this is that the form of the law's prohibition—the incest taboo, to call it by its anthropological name—is necessary, transhistorical, noncultural; its content, in other words the concrete subjects, symbolic positions, or imagoes with whom or with which fantasized or real sexual commiseration is forbidden is, by contrast, contingent, historical, and indeed cultural, as anthropological research has consistently uncovered. The content of the law is therefore subject to change.

Indeed, in my view Lacan's framework is ironically much more open to a properly political intervention than is the one presented in *The Psychic Life of Power*. Psychoanalysis does not assert that our dependence on language forces us to internalize social norms which then hinder the access of particular subjects to enjoyment. Though it bears consequences for subjectivity throughout the subject's life, and indeed acquires a backhanded brand of agency which grows in proportion to the subject's denial of its effects, fantasy—Butler's notion of the "attachment to subjection"—features no absolutely determinative consequences for subjectivity. It becomes clear in this way how Butler's statements about the traumatic, indeed tragic, consequences of the normative command of the discourse and power tandem retain an undesirable humanistic meaning which should be turned on its head. What is most traumatic, in other words, is not that the Other forces me to desire in this or that way, but rather that it refuses to tell me how to desire. This was indeed the message of Freud's hysterical analysands: not that their suffering was caused by a patriarchal, normative symbolic order, but rather that the lack, indeed the subversion, of normativity in the Other is itself traumatic. The corollary of this is that it is the very possibility of freedom which accounts for the attachment to subjection Butler wants to theorize, not some inherently disciplinary and normative feature of the sociosymbolic landscape. We internalize social norms simply because it is easier to do so than to confront the traumatic inconsistency in the Other: the fact that the Other refuses our demand for love, refuses to legitimate or recognize the way we choose to live.

From a Lacanian perspective, this desire for fixed political norms and meanings—structural sexism and heterosexism, in the case of the presuppositions of Butler's argument—is characteristic of the hysteric's relation to the Other.[8] To the extent that one proceeds from the presupposition that there is a consistent bias against women and homosexuals which transcends particular utterances or institutional practices—a bias ingrained, in other words, in the fabric of culture itself—one advances a hysterical argument. Since this is quite obviously a dramatic claim in

[handwritten margin notes: "not Butler", "Where is this argue."]

the queer theory context, I feel compelled to add that the properly uto-pian ethical ideal of psychoanalysis is predicated on the possibility of overcoming this inherent, hysterical feature of subjectivity, of traversing the fantasy fuelling one's passionate attachments, and heroically recon-ciling oneself with the lack in the Other, with the traumatic realization that there is, properly speaking, no end to desire. The proper psycho-analytic response to Butler's argument is therefore to turn back upon it the question of why the heterosexual matrix is already assumed, why the notion of symbolic order is attributed with such all-encompassing power, and then to recognize that the argument's very coherence (or at least that part of it which argues against a version of Lacan) depends on this unjustified assumption. Once the traversal of this fantasy is accom-plished, it seems to me, Foucault's concept of an all-encompassing exer-cise of power is revealed to rest on the politically debilitating, paranoid presupposition of an omnipotent Other, an Other it effectively conjures in response to its own desire.

In anticipation of perhaps the most obvious of queer theory's likely rejoinders, it should be stressed that the proper Lacanian understanding of the symbolic order does not imply that there is no such thing as sexism and homophobia, that these currents do not operate nefariously in the social world. What it does imply is that sexism and homophobia are not conditions of our very existence as viable subjects in culture, that there is no way of being a subject without being irremediably marked at the level of one's inmost psychical intimacy by its effects. And by extension, the psychoanalytic position does not imply in political terms that our agency is limited to theatrical performances designed to un-cover a history of citationality or to trace the genealogy of power's ef-fects. One is in fact tempted to suggest that the correct psychoanalytic position would characterize the performative aspect of Butler's version of political agency as a form of hysterical acting out, to be distinguished from the nonhysterical, properly ethical, act.

Butler's assumption concerning the symbolic order's simultaneity with power leads her to formulate a theory of the state apparatus which in my view features questionable consequences for political agency. As is the case in David Halperin's problematic work,[9] though in not so unnuanced a fashion, Butler's ideas about power's role in the determi-nation of subjectivity cause her to assume that the state structure car-ries a virtually seamless normative influence, to the extent that the political activities of nonheterosexual communities are best undertaken, in her view, outside its parameters. Quite clearly, state power generically conceived is normative to a significant extent. My difficulty stems rather from the lack of clarity concerning the concept of the state mobilized in

Butler's discourse. For example, if Butler were to use to the term "bour-geois state," then one could link her discourse up with the Marxist tradition and recognize a critique of the state's collusion with capital. In this scenario it would be possible to distinguish Butler's argument from the contentions of the anarchist tradition: The state is necessary, at least in the stages prior to the securing of the elusive communism, and should take the form of what orthodox Marxism calls the "dictatorship of the proletariat," or else at least a form less transparently supportive of the logic of capital. But in the absence of such a qualification the premise of discourse's production of the subject appears to lead queer theory down the political blind alley of a pseudodemocratic discourse entirely sev-ered from its relation to the state and its power.

The hyperpoliticization of the subject, the ultimate and paradoxical effect of which is precisely the depoliticization of the sociosymbolic order, claims that the state, by its very nature, robs its citizenry of their (sexual) freedom, of their right to enjoyment. The argument tends to proceed like this: If the state and its discourses embody and articulate power, and if power creates subjectivity, then the entire framework of "the as-sertion of rights and claims to entitlement," as Butler puts it, is premised on normative identity categories which power manufactures and enforces (100). The very category of citizen, in this view, is necessarily shot through with particular subjective determinations which deprive sub-jects of their rights to pleasure and autonomy. Instead of working with universal abstract categories such as that of citizenship in the interests, for example, of contesting the final attribution to them of any particular content or constituency, these categories are characterized as in them-selves working in complicity not with this or that specific political inter-est, but rather with an agency of power abstractly defined. This is precisely what I would characterize as the paranoid aspect of the Butlerian-Foucauldian position with respect to the state: One advances from the (legitimate) premise that the liberal-democratic vocabulary of citizenship is contaminated with illegitimate or problematic particular interests to the (illegitimate) conclusion that the most viable form of political action is an outright rejection of such categories and vocabular-ies as well as their substitution by more properly communitarian or minoritarian paradigms of political intervention.

An example from contemporary politics may prove helpful here. If the state's legal definition of marriage requires a couple whose mem-bers belong to different biological sexes, then it follows on hard late-Foucauldian logic that the entire legal-jurisprudential infrastructure associated with this state is inherently biased against homosexual sub-jects and remains irremediably resistant to any form of change. The

something dis causes maybe

only remaining authentic mode of political agency is therefore to be situated on the level of the minority community, which, it would seem quite apparent, must then be required to create for itself its own mode of political representation: its own substate. A conceptual distinction between, on the one hand, the state form on the level of its particular historical incarnation and, on the other, the problematic of political representation as such therefore needs to be introduced. The fact that Butler's argument does not make such a distinction has the consequence of assuming, in the form of a brand of deconstructive communitarianism, a kind of escape from sociosymbolic constraint. Queer antistatism is therefore premised on the bad utopian assumption that liberation from the shackles of the state apparatus somehow puts in abeyance the problematic of political representation, in other words the requirement that political desires be extraneated—alienated—in the terms of (some version of) a representational system. Such a gesture is not without a cynical dimension: In effect, by focusing on the presumed aspirations of an ill-defined minority community whose members share only a set of concerns related to an experience of discrimination, the communitarian argument tends toward foreclosure on the possibility of a radical overhaul of the political formation in its totality.

In contrast, if the citizen is defined as both indefinite and indefinable, as necessarily subjected to an abstraction from determinate content, then it becomes possible to argue in favor of the civil recognition of same-sex partnerships, however one may wish to define them, with reference to the universal category of citizen itself. The political goal becomes not the circumnavigation of the state apparatus in the name of the defense of a hermetic, isolated community, but rather the much more radical declaration that this apparatus must be viewed as, in mathematical terms, an infinite set which, by virtue of its very closure or limitation, lacks a final term, and is therefore open to an unlimited project of inclusion. To the criticism that the political goal of legalized same-sex partnerships simply extends an inherently exclusionary convention to a new constituency, one may respond by appropriating the standard homophobic "slippery slope" argument that if gay couples are allowed to marry, then nothing will prevent members of the same family, for example, from marrying as a means of securing its legal privileges. The point is that there is *no inherent, analytical (in the Kantian sense) limit to the political strategy of inclusion.* The notion of citizen should therefore be conceived as a negative universal category which, by the terms of its very definition, must be continually redefined with reference to that which it excludes. The radical political gesture, in other words, is not the abandonment of the category of the universal, but rather the

claiming of this category in the name of the subject who does not appear under it. Historically, of course, this subject has been called vassal, peasant, proletarian, African or African-American, woman or, to be sure, homosexual. Indeed, the ultimate statement of political hubris in Western history carries an unanticipated effect of subversion when uttered by the victim of state power: What happens to queer politics when its subject, cowering in the shadow of the state, dares to declare, "L'état, c'est moi!"?

Butler's argument reiterates Foucault's premise that the state, through power, sets the terms of the psyches of its citizens. This premise suggests, for Butler, the corollary that the "remaking of subjectivity" must occur "beyond the shackles of the juridical law" (100). Butler cites the first volume of *The History of Sexuality*: "[T]he simultaneous individualization and totalization of modern power structures," Foucault there offers, requires us to liberate ourselves "from the state and the type of individualization which is linked to the state" (101). Clearly, by this time in his career, Foucault's views concerning the state's necessary complicity with power's techniques of normalization had led him to give up entirely on the possibilities for democratization within the state apparatus itself. But in what sense, we might wish to ask, does the state "individualize"? If the subject, as psychoanalysis maintains, is very precisely unrepresentable, then what does it mean to talk about a subject of the state, a subject subjected, to use Butler's term, to the state apparatus? As is commonly acknowledged, this strong antistatist stance led to Foucault's interest, in the latest stages of his career, in Stoic discourses of self-regulation and self-stylization, discourses with strong elitist, aristocratic, and hyperindividualistic undercurrents which in my view have an extremely compromised relation to models of radical-progressive collective struggle. In contrast to more strident enthusiasts of the later Foucault like David Halperin, however, Butler's contentions do indeed feature an element of ambivalence concerning Foucault's qualification of the state as an oppressively normalizing agent, not because she disagrees with the argument which posits the state's power to produce subjectivity, but rather because she believes that Foucault's position fails to explain the subject's attachment to subjection: "How are we to understand," she asks, "not merely the disciplinary production of the subject, but the disciplinary cultivation of an attachment to subjection?" (102).

A closer look at Butler's idea of the attachment to subjection allows us to identify how her hyperpoliticization through Foucault of the psychoanalytic argument fuels her suspicions about the normative agency of state power. To be sure, Butler insightfully identifies a current in the dynamics of subjectivity which courts the ideological certainty that submission to a master can provide. She rightfully suggests in addition that the attachment to subjection is a function of the unconscious, of the subject's fantasmatic kernel, or "fundamental fantasy" in Lacanian vocabulary. But because Butler's argument assumes that power coincides with the very terms through which subjects are produced, there occurs an overstatement of the conclusion that a desire for authority, indeed the desire for normativity itself, is a more or less inescapable condition of subjectivity as such. This condition places severe limitations on Butler's conception of political agency. Her argument contends for example that though "subject formation—and reformation—cannot succeed" without "the passionate attachment to subjection," there exist "possibilities for resignification" which can "rework and unsettle" the forces which effectively subject the subject to social norms (105). In other words, Butler's argument starts off from the assumption of a successful production of the subject through norms of power, and then proceeds to the introduction of an ambivalence in the operation of power which allows for a modest degree of agency connected to a notion of "resignification." In contrast, Lacan's framework begins at Butler's endpoint, namely with the contention that the ambivalence Butler associates with the subject's agency is already an inherent feature of the subject, in other words that the subject's desire is in itself a manifestation of the failure of the normative instance of power. The agency available through the subject's traversal of the attachment to subjection therefore has the effect of entirely dissolving, though only momentarily, the normative efficacy of the symbolic order, thereby leaving open the possibility of a radical transformation extending well beyond the limits of resignification's comparatively modest purview.

The Paradox of Desublimation

The recent work of a newer generation of Lacanian critics has aggressively challenged the historicist, relativist, and deconstructionist assumptions which have overwhelmingly laid the foundations of Anglo-American antihomophobic criticism. These theorists have launched a wide-ranging cultural program which aims to rejuvenate psychoanalysis at a historical moment when the postmodern proliferation of identities appears to have inaugurated a strong sense of political and erotic cynicism and fatigue. From the perspective of my own project this new tradition in critical theory makes—or more precisely lays the foundations for—two fundamental arguments. First, the concept of sexual difference developed by Lacan redresses the remnants of heterosexism in Freud, thereby establishing the conditions of possibility for the clinical interrogation of the specificity of homosexual desire, and reeroticizing the inward subject of postmodernity at a remove from the atomizing deterritorializations of capital. And second, a Lacanian rereading of the critique of ideology allows for the imagination of a genuine social alternative which would run counter to the general degradation and short-circuiting of democratic process which has occurred through the expanding neoimperialisms and corporatisms we increasingly know today. In these final sections I will work out my view of the significance of aspects of this new Lacanian work for a genuinely political antihomophobic theory by stressing two points: First, how the Freudian dialectic of civilization imposes a limit on the politicization of sexuality; but second, how Lacan's theory of the sexuate subject implicitly includes the homosexual within a fractured, inherently antagonistic but unlimited social field open to the possibility of transformational change.

Slavoj Žižek's consideration of the dialectic of the libidinal drive and the civilizing constraints of the sociosymbolic order has tremendous consequences for the theory of sexuality. It also throws into relief Dollimore's argument about the dependence of civilization on perversion. We recall that Dollimore's "perverse dynamic" enjoined us first to illuminate civilization's dependence on the content of the repressed, and then to reclaim this content—desublimate it, in other words—as a means of sowing subversion by calling into question dominant sexual norms. Žižek for his part casts a critical eye on this notion of a liberatory desublimation through a reading of Theodor Adorno's seminal essay on psychology and sociology and a reference to Herbert Marcuse's concept of repressive desublimation. Žižek argues that in intellectual-historical terms the import of psychoanalysis lies partly in its refusal to decide between a theory of causality derived from the tradition of the natural sciences, and a theory of cultural interpretation that Žižek associates with what the Germans call the *Geisteswissenschaften*: the humanities or *sciences humaines*. The former asks: What causes phenomena such as neurotic symptoms and historical events? The latter poses the question: What do neurotic symptoms and historical events mean?

As Žižek elaborates, a theoretical approach focusing on the causal dimension of phenomena attacks psychoanalysis for "failing to formulate exact, verifiable causal laws," laws which identify positive, empirically determinate causes for particular psychical or social events.[10] Conversely, an exclusively interpretative method reproaches psychoanalysis with the charge of determinism: that it draws up a rigid theory of unconscious causality through its formulation of a subject at the mercy of libidinal urges, neglecting in this manner the subject's circumscription in, and determination by, social and political, cultural and historical, conditions of possibility. For Žižek, only two intellectual traditions since Freud have successfully avoided taking one or the other of these routes: psychoanalysis, in particular in its Lacanian incarnation, and the work of the Frankfurt School, more specifically its critique of so-called neo-Freudian revisionism. Žižek argues that Adorno resolved this conflict between causal and hermeneutic approaches by claiming that the meaning of psychic suffering lies in its causation by an alienated, historically specific social actuality which causes the subject to experience its life substance as an uncannily menacing interior force misrecognized as natural or biological. Lacan then effectively dehistoricizes this move by recasting the cause of the subject as a specifically psychical object of fantasy. In this latter view, the meaning of the subject's sociosymbolic universe stems from a fantasmatic distortion which occasions—causes—the fundamental symptom of its psychic structure.

Žižek underscores the importance of Adorno's and Marcuse's attack against Freudian revisionism's "socialization and historicization" of the unconscious.[11] Erich Fromm, for example, not unlike Judith Butler, argues in favor of the quasi-irremediable quality of consciousness's internalization of what Žižek calls "historically specified ideological agencies" through the structure of the superego, positing that the goal of analysis should therefore be the reconciliation of the subject's desire with a transformed, authentic sociocultural actuality.[12] In short, the revisionist tendency sought to minimize the transhistorical and noncultural bite of Freud's contention concerning the irresolvable tension between ego and id by resituating this antagonism on the level of the subject's negotiation of cultural meanings upheld through the structure of the superego. There are two logical possibilities here, both of which constitute aspects of the revisionist current: The rift between subject and society may be redressed either by the ego's reconciliation with social reality or with the transformation, possibly revolutionary, of social reality to make it conform to the subject's libidinal demand. Opting for this second possibility, Fromm's existentialist humanism rationalizes the persistence of psychic suffering through reference to concepts such as existential frustration, alienated labor, and intersubjective inauthenticity.[13] The Frankfurt School accusation against the type of Freudian revisionism articulated by Fromm targets how what Freud presents as a noncultural and properly irresolvable antagonism between the subject's egoic investments and the disruptiveness of unconscious desire is translated into an antagonism between the ego and a historically variable field of culture or civilization. A neopsychologism is admitted through the back door when the ego is redefined as a locus of agency achieved by means of a process of cultural mediation or harmonization which the human agent subjectively effects.

The Frankfurt School, however, modified this reduction of psychical antagonism by decisively situating the false or inauthentic element not on the side of the subject's psychological relation to reality, but rather on the side of history and social relations. In this view, the perception of inauthenticity becomes a properly historical symptom, an "adequate manifestation of a historical reality which is itself 'false'" (11). In this manner the focus of the revisionist current shifts from a concern for the individual's relation to a cultural reality to a model of a social reality distorted by socioeconomic alienation, and therefore in need of transformation to suit the subject's libidinal need. Psychic suffering, in this latter view, is not a function of the authenticity of the subject's manipulation of the social environment, but rather a symptom of the inadequacy of the social environment itself. If the libidinal drive appears to the subject as an externally imposed, alienated substance situated outside the field of consciousness and social relations, it is because the increased atomization of individuals in late capitalism has made it so. The permutations of bourgeois capitalism structure conditions of possibility for subjectivity which relegate the libido to a pseudonatural realm the subject falsely grasps as a transhistorical necessity. Where the psychological revisionist formulates the antagonism of civilization on the level of the subject's personal relation to historical actuality, Adorno's antirevisionism depsychologizes this relation by resituating the antagonism on the level of a distorted, neurotic—or indeed even perverse—sociocultural reality structured by capitalist relations of production and subject to radical historical change.

Žižek's rearticulation through Lacan of Freud's dialectic of civilization, however, allows us to add one further depsychologizing and antihistoricist move to the Frankfurt school's antirevisionist statement. For though he clearly considers the Frankfurt School revision of Freudian revisionism a move in the right direction, Žižek ultimately reproaches both Adorno and Marcuse for reintroducing a historical horizon at which the subject's reconciliation with social reality can be envisaged. Žižek's move allows us to situate properly the antagonism of civilization not on the level of the subject's psychological grasp of historical actuality, nor on the level of this actuality's socioeconomic qualities, but rather in what Lacan called the real. More precisely, Žižek credits Adorno and Marcuse for viewing the ambivalence of civilization—the fact that it is both repressive and necessary as a barrier against barbarism—as constitutive of the fabric of culture, at least in its present state, distorted or made dysfunctional by the workings of bourgeois capitalism. The Frankfurt School's critique of revisionism, in other words, acknowledged the truth of Freud's message about the impossibility of distinguishing between, as

Žižek puts it, "the repression of a drive and its sublimation"; failure necessarily awaits, therefore, "every attempt to draw a clear line of demarcation between these two concepts" (13) for the simple reason that no form of sublimation will fully compensate for the subject's sense of libidinal loss undergone as a consequence of acculturation and socialization.

As a result, psychoanalytic theory and practice cannot decide between liberating repressed drives and, in a gesture of resigned conservatism, counseling the subject to live with repression as a sacrifice to the development of civilization. But this ambivalence of theory, Žižek argues, is neither a form of agnostic fence-sitting nor a regressive antiutopianism; rather, it reflects a constitutive impasse within subjectivity as such. Because the ego mediates both the irrational libidinal drives and the repressive-sublimatory terms of civilization, the subject's sovereignty—over its libidinal urges, over its social duty—is compromised when the ego is both strengthened and weakened. Hence the properly irreducible quality of Freud's idea about the problematic impossibility of psychoanalytic practice. "The goal of psychoanalysis and its contradictory character," Žižek offers, "reproduce the fundamental social antagonism, the tension between the individual's urges and the demands of society" (13). In consequence, the notion of a full liberation of the drive only exacerbates the subject's sense of libidinal deprivation and short-circuits the relation between the ego and the unconscious, as Adorno suggestively argued through the example of fascist totalitarianism. Thus, argues Žižek, clinical technique must locate itself on the comparatively narrow terrain of the ego's manipulation of the symbolic field of social relations and the subversive pressures of the libido. Crucially, however, this manipulation is geared not toward social conformity, in other words toward the reconciliation of desire with the sociosymbolic order, but rather toward the subject's apprehension of desire's inexhaustible quality—to the necessary inadequacy of any sociopolitical actuality to individual and collective political aspirations.

The singular interest of Žižek's reading of Frankfurt school antirevisionism lies, in my view, in his appropriation of the notion of repressive desublimation in his effort to modify, or more precisely to nuance, Freud's theory of the superego to make it relevant to our postbourgeois, postrepressive and allegedly libidinally liberated historical moment. As we have already considered, Adorno strove to uphold the dialectical and paradoxical aspect of Freudian psychoanalysis by asserting against the revisionists that the subject's alienation is not a function of a faulty or inauthentic psychological relation to the social, but rather a constitutive condition of the subject's psychosocial existence as such. However, Adorno retained an element of "bad utopianism" in his

formulation by characterizing alienated social existence as fully historical, and hence as susceptible to a final, decisively redemptive reformulation.[14] In contrast, Freud viewed the repressive character of civilization
as a nonhistorical condition of subjectivity, "an anthropological constant"
(16), as Žižek puts it. For Žižek, then, fidelity to the bite of Freud's
dialectic requires one to denounce Adorno's residual belief in a
disalienated historical eventuality, and to reformulate the concept of
repressive desublimation—a liberation of libidinal impulses in the service of social domination—to update Freud's notion of the superego,
that psychic agency which the subject experiences as invasive, traumatic, and directed at its most intimately personal core.

For Adorno, Freud was a classical bourgeois thinker who theorized
the conditions of subjectivity in an atomized social grouping of self-
interested, narcissistic individuals. This view forcefully articulates what
remains the most trenchant Left, properly socialist, critique of psychoanalysis, namely that its presupposition of an a priori antagonism between desire and the social makes its premises difficult to reconcile with
any straightforward form of political progressivism. As Žižek presents
Adorno's view, the bourgeois subject in capitalism "represses his unconscious urges by means of internalized prohibitions and, as a result, his
self-control enables him to get hold of his libidinal spontaneity" (16).
The historical experiences of fascism and totalitarianism, however, provided a glimpse at a new, postliberal and postbourgeois principle of
social organization based on repressive desublimation. Žižek suggests
that repressive desublimation establishes a short-circuit in psychic structure in which the ego, viewed as an agency of repression, collapses,
thereby allowing for the full complicity of libidinal urges with the
superego's command. When the sociosymbolic structure's performative
interpellation of the subject fails—Adorno's famous example is fascist
mass spectacle—the direct expression of libidinal urges enters into the
service of ideology and propaganda; hence, of state control. "In postliberal societies," concludes Žižek, "we experience the superego not as
a demand for renunciation or self-control," but as "a hypnotic agency
that imposes the attitude of 'yielding to temptation,' that is to say, its
injunction amounts to a command: 'Enjoy yourself!' " (16) The superego
enjoins us, in other words, to fall asleep by mindlessly taking part in
collective ideological spectacle, by renouncing our repressive critical
rationalism in favor of an attitude of complicit, ludic amusement.

Žižek's point is that the Marcusean notion of repressive desublimation
illustrates how, in the era of Foucauldian analyses of regimes of power,
the interiorized agency of social repression takes the form not of a commandment to renounce satisfaction, but rather of an injunction to relax

and enjoy oneself, fully to corporealize one's pleasure as a means of allegedly subverting the sadomasochistic dynamics of power's production of an illusory subjectivity. Foucault's postsubjective ideal very much begins to resemble the totalitarian repressive desublimation itself: Call it the "Don't worry, be happy" brand of consumerist discipline and surveillance. But while Adorno's emphasis on the alienated conditions of social existence suggests a horizon of social-subjective integration through social progress, Lacan's teaching emphasizes, in contrast, the inherently repressive character of any attempt to resolve the psyche's irreducibility to the social field. The ethico-political ideal at work in Lacan is therefore not a neo-Marcusean rearticulation of the reality principle which professes to harmonize the subject with reconfigured egalitarian social norms, but rather a prolongation of antagonism, the perseverance of desire. Such an insistence on desire's perseverance in fact valorizes the irreconcilable element of the subject with respect to all possible sociosymbolic configurations. In effect, this is what the subject is for Lacan on the social plane: The subject is precisely this incommensurability between desire and its possible social actualization.

Where Adorno saw the practical limit of psychoanalytic theory in the historical disappearance of the self-disciplined bourgeois subject it allegedly theorizes, Žižek through Lacan uncovers the return in the real of the heterogeneous drives the consumerist, postbourgeois subject disavows. This return of the repressed manifests itself, in this view, in the concrete historical phenomenon of totalitarianism. Far from discounting psychoanalytic conceptuality, then, the Stalinist-fascist phenomenon simply renders the concrete social effects of the—alleged, of course—postideological liberation of the bourgeois subject. Here we apprehend Žižek's deep suspicion both of simplistic revolutionary resolutions of social contradictions—though this reservation has become noticeably more tempered in his most recent work—and cynical-relativist strategies which valorize ironic, performative citations of social norms as a means of establishing distance between the subject and its circumscription by social dictates. Both strategies tend to conform to the logic of repressive desublimation by seeking an escape from the inherent, properly insurmountable antagonism between psyche and society. But crucially, to state that this antagonism is insurmountable is not to disqualify in advance the possibility of radical social transformation. On the contrary, the implication for Left politics of the preservation in theory of the fundamental Freudian dialectic is that the emphasis of political strategy must shift from a symptomatic fascination with the world to come, which tends to inhibit concrete action for fear of failure or inadvertent repressive effects, to a recognition of the need for a continually reenacted

gesture of subversion aiming to reconstitute the sociosymbolic formation by means of the impossible articulation, through word and deed, of
the real. In this sense, Lacan's notion of the ethical act amounts to a
suspension of the political order as constituted in this or that particular
social formation, a suspension which makes visible the exclusionary
social violence on which that order depends.

Adorno's and Marcuse's critical appraisal of neo-Freudian revisionism highlights Žižek's desire to preserve the singularity of psychoanalytic discourse, in particular its stubborn insistence on desire's a priori
inadequation to the social world. Fidelity to psychoanalysis, more precisely, requires safeguarding from two erroneous gestures: a culturalist
reduction of the unconscious to social norms—from kinship structures
to sexual morality—whose subversion would allow for "the possibility of
a non-repressive sublimation," a possibility in favor of which Marcuse
himself argues in *Eros and Civilization,* and a hollow, falsely utopian
humanist-existentialist optimism, characteristic of Fromm's work, which
posits the "development of human creative potentials not paid for by the
mute suffering articulated in the formations of the unconscious." The
power of Adorno's antirevisionist statement therefore lies in its identification, as Žižek puts it, of a properly structural antagonism "between
the individual's self-experience and the objective social totality" (14–15).
The libido and civilization, the drive and the signifier, are in this view
nonsimultaneous and noncomplementary; they effectively split consciousness—the subject's very apprehension of the social world—from itself.
The civilizing constraints of society available to consciousness and the
unconscious psychical representations of the perverse partial drives
divide the subject against itself, and this separation defines the subject
as such. Perhaps the final word on the Frankfurt School reading of
Freud is that any sociopolitical consideration of psychoanalysis premised on the notion of a historical or political reconciliation of the
dialectic of drive and signifier necessarily leads toward an obfuscating
suturing of psychical antagonism, one which produces the kind of synergy between illicit libidinal satisfaction and strict social conformity
characterizing today's postideological world of branded social identities and hyperconsumerism.

But what, one might now wish to ask, do Žižek's gloss on repressive
desublimation[15] and his thesis about the transformation of the content of
the superego's hypnotic call have to do with theories of sexuality and
the objectives of an antihomophobic criticism? More specifically, how
might the psychoanalytic insistence on a subject split between a desire
which social experience refuses to satisfy and a libidinal drive which
produces a satisfaction beneath the threshold of consciousness

problematize the assumptions of hegemonic queer theory? In my view the discourse on repressive desublimation puts further pressure on the queer-theoretical assumption concerning the social or political agency of homosexual practices and identities. The emergence of the postliberation gay male identity—though it of course at some earlier point had real, concrete emancipatory effects—has been entirely subsumed by the logic of the market, and has allied itself with a predominatly white, professional, upper-middle-class constituency with a late Foucauldian lifestyle ethics of self-discipline and self-stylization which may no longer be held to retain even the slightest element of social opposition. The recent proliferation of gay male glossies such as *Genre* and *Out*, the homoerotic idealization of the male body in the image repertoire of advertising, and the radical dissociation of gay politics from the political and economic totality (but certainly there are further examples) all bear witness to the general mainstreaming of gay politics and the increasing difficulty in both the academic and general political spheres of politicizing homosexuality in any authentically critical manner.

These considerations lead me to formulate a number of propositions which run against the grain of the contemporary doxa of liberal political correctness and poststructuralist antihomophobic inquiry. First, queer theory's valorization of oppositional sexual identities—however performative, deconstructed, productive–affirmative, or postbinary—as inherently liberating or politically significant does little to address the difficulties of nonheterosexual quotidian existence, particularly that of the underprivileged and geopolitically marginal. Indeed, such difficulties usually bear no direct relation to sexual practices as such. It is still necessary to point out the obvious: Apart from the concrete juridical figurations of same-sex relationships in the various legal apparatuses, homosexuals are generally subject to the same sociopolitical dictates and macroeconomic vectors as their heterosexual confrères. Second, the cynical dismissal apparent in much poststructuralist queer theory of the importance of addressing the relation between homosexual experience and the general public sphere implicitly reaffirms the social marginality of homosexuality, a marginality which admittedly may not impede the homosexual subject's access to sexual pleasure—in fact, the reverse is likely true—but which re-asserts that most pernicious of homophobic axioms: Heterosexuality is the unacknowledged condition of full citizenship, political agency and social legitimacy. Indeed, by implicitly granting queer-identified subjects the right to a marginal identity, dominant political structures render the relegation of these subjects'—*our*—political ambitions to the abject realm of special interests all the more effortless and seemingly logical.

But it will be argued that such an assertion can also be made from Foucauldian premises. So where do the concrete political consequences of the Foucauldian and the psychoanalytic arguments go their separate ways? The ultimate consequence of Foucault's assumption concerning the production of subjectivity by power/knowledge is that the category of the subject as such is inherently repressive, normative, disciplinary. Therefore, the very paradigm of political representation, and at the limit the notion of the sociosymbolic order itself, must be abandoned in favor of a multitude of positive micropractices, a reformist politics of particular issues whose most actualized manifestation was perhaps the AIDS lobby emerging from the Anglo-American gay movement in the 1980s. In my view there are three proofs of the failure of this movement, each of which forms a symptom of the inherent limitations of micropolitics. First, it never managed fully to assume the consequences of its determination by U.S. heath-care policy, and therefore had no long-lasting impact on its negotiation. Second, it remained narcissistically fascinated with the tragic deaths of glamorous and privileged first-world gay men, and consequently reneged on its responsibility to ally itself with the global struggle against HIV transmission, whose most important means is of course not sexual relations between men. And finally, it became mired in a liberal ideology of sexual freedom inherited from post-Stonewell erotic vanguardism, which to a large degree sabotaged what should have been, but never effectively were its fundamental aims: first, to decisively curb rates of transmission of the virus among men who have sex with men, particularly in the institutions in the urban centers of Europe and North America designed to facilitate erotic contact, and, second, to build an institutional structure designed to transmit the culture of safer-sex to subsequent generations.

The Subject of Sex

In contrast to the most Foucault-inflected queer discourses, psychoanalysis steadfastly holds onto an idea of the subject, latently advancing, I will argue, that one may never legitimately presume the heterosexuality of the universal subject of modernity we have inherited from the Enlightenment. This subject is also, of course, the universal subject of the modern democratic state form, the subject assumed in the very concept of democracy. In order to explore this argument further, however, it will first be necessary to draw the fine lines of the psychoanalytic formulation of the subject.

Among the new generation of Lacanian theorists writing in English, Joan Copjec has put forth surely the most theoretically consequential attempt to distinguish the psychoanalytic concept of the subject and its political implications from Foucault's historicist reduction of the unconscious. We recall that Foucault argued that Freud's theory of the unconscious serves as an alibi for the covert workings of power by creating an illusion of subjective truth which normalizes the subject through discourse. From the perspective of Foucault's later work on sexuality, the Freudian paradigm of a subject of unconscious desire exacerbates our subjection to discourse by making us think that our own confessional production of discourse leads to ever greater levels of self-intimacy. As Foucault would have it, these disclosures mold us ever more perfectly to the normative dictates of power; the more we attempt to explain ourselves to ourselves, the more we appear in discourse as power's realization of its disciplinary goal. Any theoretical formulation of subjectivity premised on a notion of self-representation in discourse is necessarily complicit in power's perverse disciplinary command. Hence Foucault's emphasis on bodies, acts, and pleasures: The mechanism of representation, considered as a function of discourse and power, must, by definition, be normative, even where it produces nominally nonnormative effects of subjectivity. For Foucault power imposes itself upon us through language quite literally as we speak.

Copjec's work has forcefully argued, in contrast, that the subject is not a realization of discourse; in other words, the subject does not appear as a concrete manifestation of discourse's disciplinary desire. Foucault's ultimate reproach against psychoanalysis—that its incitement of the subject to produce a discourse about itself subsumes this subject under power's mechanisms of surveillance—is therefore premised on a faulty reading of the psychoanalytic argument. Freud's formulation of desire rigorously separates this desire from what is amenable to symbolic representation. If the truth of the subject strictly eludes symbolization, then under Foucault's very premise of the immanence of power in discourse, this subject remains invisible to power. The corollary of the fundamental Freudian premise of the subject's opacity to desire is that this subject may never fully see itself reflected in its own utterances. Far from molding it within perverse disciplinary power relations, then, discourse manifests only its own failure to produce the subject in positive terms, to articulate the subject in an objective, verifiable manner. The subject, as subject of the unconscious, always and by definition exceeds the normalizing efforts of discourse and power; it is, as Copjec summarizes, "unknowable, unthinkable, finally, of course, nonhistoricizable."[16] The impossibility of making the subject palpable by translating it into the terms of social relations redefines power's relation to the social field. Power, in short, is not copresent with the relations it structures. What is most problematic about Foucault's theory of power is thus, as Copjec succinctly puts it, "this notion of immanence, this conception of a cause that is immanent within the field of its effects." From this contention directly follows Copjec's concise definition of historicism: "the reduction of society to its indwelling network of relations of power and knowledge" (6). The Foucauldian concept of discourse as a disciplinary, territorializing force complicit with relations of power is therefore a faulty one: What language—considered within its wider sociosymbolic or institutional context—precisely cannot do is to create the subject as a realization, a concretization, of power's normative command.

Copjec's refinement of the psychoanalytic definition of the subject makes reference to the relation between the psychical and social realms. As we recall, Judith Butler's argument makes the assumption that one of the effects of power is the creation of an interior psychic space through the subject's interiorization of its instances. Through the agency of the conscience or superego, the subject constitutes its self-relation by incorporating dominant social norms, as is the case, for example, in Butler's development of Freud's theory of melancholia. For Butler, then, the social produces the psychic. Social discourses saturate psychic life, such that it is traversed by conflicting social discourses which battle for hegemony within consciousness. In Butler's Foucauldian theory of subjection, the interface between the psychical and social realms may be formulated as a relation of positive determination. Social relations, in other words, *cause* the subject. Copjec argues against this assumption by claiming that "it is the real," as she puts it, "that unites the psychic to the social" (39). The relation between psyche and society is thus fundamentally incommensurable, unformulatable, antagonistic to the premises of an empiricist or historical causality. Because the terms of civilization provide no satisfying norm for desire, no realizable promise of final satisfaction, the subject seeks existential completion through fantasy. By means of its relation to a properly fantasmatic object, the subject explains to itself its ontological lack, such that this lack—this nonsocial, noncultural "nothing"—logically assumes a causal function with respect to the subject and its desire.

Copjec's argument explores how Lacan traces the psychoanalytic concept of the subject—this properly modern subject who fails to appear within the terms of a given sociosymbolic constellation—back to the notion, much derided in postmodern discourses, of the Cartesian cogito. For Lacan, the subject of psychoanalysis bears an intimate relation to the empty, skeptical subject of modern science who paved the way, Copjec asserts, for the emergence for the modern revolutionary subject of bourgeois democracy. What twentieth-century linguistics has called the subject of enunciation—the subject, in other words, who remains the same, unmodified by all the statements it makes—was made possible by Descartes' elaboration of his quasi-paranoid epistemological subject. This latter subject, Copjec argues, correlates to the "*instance* of doubt" which "cannot be doubted," and hence "remains innocent of all charges of error" (145). The scientific method which underlies the paradigm of modernity therefore emerged when the subject paradoxically grounded its objectivity on its exclusion from the realm of phenomenal appearance, therefore guaranteeing its unverifiability. Copjec argues that Descartes' cogito, in its very contentless, indeterminate abstraction, was the condition of possibility—conceptual rather than properly historical—for the democratic revolutions of Enlightenment from which the promise of popular sovereignty, in short the radical horizon of authentic democracy, took form. As Copjec writes, "No one would have thought of fighting for the rights of a universal subject—a subject whose value is not determined by race, creed, color, sex, or station in life—no one would have thought of waging a war on behalf of liberty and justice for all subjects if Descartes had not already isolated that abstract instance in whose name the war would be waged: the democratic subject, devoid of characteristics" (146).

Now Foucault, and other followers of the historicist paradigm such as Eve Sedgwick, for example, would surely dismiss this concept of the universal subject as vague and unhistorical, as failing to take account of the self-evident empirical fact that all subjects are different from one another. Indeed, this last proposition is in fact the first axiom of Sedgwick's introduction to *Epistemology of the Closet*. Copjec responds to this counterargument with the claim that the concept of subject in psychoanalysis is not vague, but rather generic. All subjects, as subjects of unconscious desire, share the nonempirical "fact" that they do not coincide with their own statements, that they are not transparent to their desire. Copjec is thus able to state that the notion of the universal subject "does not poorly or wrongly describe a subject whose structure is actually determinate, but precisely indicates a subject that is in some sense *objectively indeterminate*" (147). To the pedestrian relativist argument that all subjects are different from one another, psychoanalysis adds the more conceptually consequential claim that each subject is also different from itself. Thus, since all subjects share a negative point of self-estrangement, one can proceed to make general claims—for justice, equality, well-being—in this subject's name.

The psychoanalytic subject is therefore beyond positive determination. The sum total of its positive differences, the full panoply of its discursive positions, does not qualify what in fact constitutes its essence, namely its opacity to desire. This psychoanalytic argument, in Copjec's view, suggests an ethico-political project. Because, contra Foucault, power is disjoined from knowledge, the renewal and deepening of the democratic revolution requires us to renounce the demand that the Other recognize the small differences we mistakenly hold to signify the deep essence of our being. The subject encounters not knowledge but ignorance in the sociosymbolic Other to which its political demands are addressed. The demand that the Other recognize our identity, be it ethnic, sexual, or otherwise, forestalls our recognition of genuine political desire, in other words our apprehension of the consequences of the fact that the sociosymbolic order—the very field of political intelligibility—separates us from ourselves, thereby preventing us from seeing ourselves adequately reflected in the sphere of democratic contestation. The cynical antistatism of the various communitarianisms and minoritarianisms can be viewed to stem from this political nontransparency. The more the subject resists its alienation in the state apparatus—the more it clings to the differences which fail to appear within it—the more the state acquires its Foucauldian guise as an alien abstract power of normalization and surveillance.

If the modern epistemological subject inaugurated by Descartes founds a universalizable subject situated at the limit of knowledge, the psychoanalytic inquiry into sexual difference forces the conclusion that this subject must assume one of two possible relations to this limit. For Copjec, the universal subject of democracy, by virtue of the very lack of determination by which it is characterized, requires us to think of this subject as sexed. The opacity which hinders every subject's effort to achieve a relation of intimacy with itself designates its properly sexuate dimension, the very principle of its desire. For even though the Lacanian concept of the real has been used to designate any sociopolitical actuality—global corporate capital, for example—which not only evades symbolic determination, but also violates it, any faithful reading of Freud must acknowledge that there is an irreducible sexual dimension to the real, one which paradoxically guarantees the inherently antinormative quality of sexual desire by allowing for only two possible types of sexuate subjectivity. Of course, the concept of sexual difference as formulated in the various psychoanalytic traditions has met with forceful resistance in numerous feminisms and queer theory (including Butler's), the assumption being that all formulations of sexual difference tend to assume a heterosexual norm. Because Copjec's consideration of Lacan's approach to sexual difference distinguishes itself through its explicit denial of this view, it will be useful to explore the parameters of Lacan's concept of sexuation. In so doing it will become possible to discern more clearly the theoretical implications of Lacan's work for antihomophobic theory and for the theory of sexuality more generally.

With reference to Kant's critique of the two common-sense responses to the conflict of pure reason with itself, Copjec distinguishes the psychoanalytic approach to sex from the dogmatist option which refers sex to immutable laws of nature, and from the Butlerian skeptical view which places sex (or gender, in Butler's vocabulary) on the level of cultural scripts the subject chooses to perform. Each of the two erroneous responses to the enigma of sexual difference leads to an obfuscating conclusion: the former to a positively determinate causal link between nature and sex, and the latter, despite its protestations to the contrary, to what Copjec calls a "confident voluntarism" of deconstructive-cum-performative subversion. Both responses fail to take into account the unconscious–real dimension of sex, that the subject is indeed subjected to a kind of real of sexuality. Putting a philosophical valence on the deeply entrenched sex/gender and nature/culture axes of Anglo-American feminist theory, Copjec proposes that the 'sex as natural (bio-physiological) substance' and the 'sex as cultural signification' paradigms do not exhaust the available theoretical options. More specifically, Copjec criticizes the underlying assumption of Butler's early book *Gender Trouble* that sex's division of all subjects into "two separate, mutually exclusive categories . . . serves the aims of heterosexism" (202). Sexual difference, as Lacan theorized it, is a real, not an imaginary, difference, and therefore the sexes do not entertain a reciprocal or complementary relation to one another. Lacan's axiom that "there is no sexual relation" implies that the two sexes do not combine to form a cosmic whole; there is nothing of the order of nature or necessity, in consequence, in heterosexual coupling. It also implies, however, pace the Deleuzo-Guattarian proponents of a utopian infinity of positive sex identities, that there are only two possible classes of sex.

Here we stumble over a number of terminological problems arising from the difficulty of translating the Continental, speculative, properly psychoanalytic vocabulary of sex, sexuation, and sexual difference into the predominantly Anglo-American behavioral or sociological terminology of sex, gender, and sexuality. This problem is linked to the fact that psychoanalysis does not divide the realm of sex into natural and cultural components. Sex is cultural to the extent that we have recourse only to the available terms of culture in our attempts to signify it. But the peculiarity of sex, Copjec argues through Lacan, lies in its emergence as culture's failure to signify, in culture's antagonism with itself. Sex remains stubbornly unpresented by all attempts at articulating it within discourse. This is not to say, however, that sex exists in some nondiscursive realm in excess of culture. The well-rehearsed scuffles over the natural or cultural determination of the nonappearance of sex within the terms of culture obscure the more crucial fact of sex's inherent hostility to sense and meaning, indeed to signification itself.

In essence, as Copjec argues, sex is "the impossibility of completed meaning," not "a meaning that is incomplete," a crucial nuance which forever separates sex from identity, from signified being (206). Whereas Butler's gender matrix assumes the coherence and completion of masculinity and femininity, the psychoanalytic position, in contrast, insists on the ruin of gender on the rock of the real. In this way the Lacanian argument shifts the emphasis from Butler's endless performative evocation and deconstruction of gender identities to a more emphatic pronouncement on sex's link to a fundamental failure of meaning. But again, the nonappearance of sex within the realm of signification does not imply that it exists concretely—as substance—outside of, or before, discourse. Sex, then, can only be represented by negation within the forms of knowledge or discourse; it marks the spot of the impossibility of meaning or identity, the place where sexual knowledge encounters its own internal subversion.

To take the psychoanalytic argument on its own terms is therefore to be forced to the conclusion that the sex-and-gender paradigm fails properly to describe the subject's sexuate dimension. But how does the concept of "sexuation"—Lacan's term for the two possible modes through which subjects may assume a relation to the real of desire—relate to the descriptive term "sexuality," a term introduced by the classificatory ambitions of nineteenth-century sexology, and one which still grounds the discourse of sexual orientation today? Copjec summarizes the fundamental tenets of Lacan's difficult late conceptualization of sexual difference, presented as part of his effort to render psychoanalysis transmissible by means of mathematical formalization. Copjec bases her philosophical gloss on Lacan's formulas of sexuation on four main propositions. First, sex negatively describes the subject: It qualifies "the mode of failure of our knowledge" of it; therefore sex does not describe any of the subject's concretely identifiable attributes. Second, the premise of the lack of relation between the sexes ensures that sexual difference remains incapable of enforcing a Butlerian heterosexual matrix. Third, "the principle of sorting" all subjects into two sexuate classes proceeds on enunciative, as opposed to descriptive, grounds; the subjects of each class of sex share, in other words, an "enunciative position" with respect to language, rather than an ensemble of positive characteristics. And last, each mode of sexuation is characterized by a relation between two mutually exclusive functions, the first an instance of a universal rule of castration, the second an exception to that rule describing a mode of enjoyment. It becomes apparent that in no manner may either sex qualify as an identity—as the form of knowledge expressing the totality of a whole, completed being (212).

If the antinaturalism of Lacan's concept of sexual difference emerges with uncommon clarity from these propositions, the link between sexuation and the identitarian framework of sexuality may not. For though Copjec insists on Lacan's disjunction of sex from knowledge in a way which renders illegitimate the reproach of heterosexual normativity which has been launched against it, the implications of the sexuation framework for the theory of homosexuality remain largely undeveloped. Indeed, if Lacan's attempt at formalizing Freud's confused statements on sexual difference is going to have any lasting antihomophobic effect, as Copjec seems to suggest it should, then it would be not only highly desirable, but effectively necessary, to underline not only the disjunction between sex and knowledge, but also the disjunction between the real of sex and the language with which we are condemned to signify it. Insofar as the sexes psychoanalytically understood are classes of the subject properly speaking, one presumes too much when one refers to them as "male and female." Nor will the interpellations "man and woman" (234) necessarily fail to stumble over a contradiction between what we might wish to call the subject's psychical and biological sexes. For surely a corollary of Copjec's third proposition is that biologically male and female subjects may find themselves belonging to the same sex, as Lacan conceives of this term, just as anatomically intersexed subjects will perforce be led to assume one or the other psychical sex.

It would likely be unfair to reproach Copjec's argument for reinforcing psychoanalytic heterosexism by making use of a vocabulary which reinscribes the properly sexual under anatomical difference. Still, in my view the point needs to be made explicit. As I pointed out in the first chapter, Lacan in *Encore* advances that what Copjec calls the male form of sexuation is available to women "if it suits them," as he puts it, since one ultimately aligns oneself with respect to the phallic function according to which the sexes are constituted "by choice."[17] Insofar as "male" and "female," "man" and "woman" usually denote in English the biological sex of the speaking subject, and insofar as the sexed pronouns almost invariably make reference to that same biological sex, these terms cannot be used in any rigorous manner to signify the sex of the subject in the properly psychoanalytic sense. If indeed sexual difference is real—if, in other words, sex is a function of language's failure to signify—then the terms which constitute the properly symbolic representation of sexual difference are unreliable when it comes to the question of psychical sex. The corollary of this is that it is manifestly possible for the subject to be cross-sexuated: Biologically male subjects may undergo a feminine sexuation, and female subjects a masculine.

Now it should be stressed that this is not a trifling argument whose relevance would be confined to the Lacanian, or even the psychoanalytic, worlds. In fact, our very ability to characterize the subject—the abstract universal subject of modernity borne of the Cartesian cogito; the support of the incomplete, and flagging, project for a properly radical democracy—as always potentially homosexual depends on it. Ultimately, Lacan's formulas of sexuation suggest that there is a fundamental lack of continuity between, on the one hand, language's division of subjects into two classes on the basis of the sexed body and, on the other, the real's categorical separation of all subjects regardless of anatomical sex, however self-evident or hermaphroditically indeterminate, into two enunciative classes according to the mode by which their speech stumbles over sex. It is precisely this gap between anatomical and enunciative determinations of sex which, when properly theorized, ensures the homosexual subject's status as a member of the universal genus "citizen," gestures toward this subject's centrality to the creation of an authentic democracy, and foreshadows a clinical horizon which would illuminate the specificity of male and female homosexual desires.

Though there is clearly some ambiguity concerning the implications of Lacan's sexuation framework with respect to the relation between sex and sexuality—the relation, in other words, between the subject's enunciative position and the biological sex of its object choice—it remains clear that sexuality, like sex itself, fails to qualify as a fully reliable indicator of knowledge of the subject. Indeed, it is likely that the indeterminacy of the relation between sex and sexuality is a necessary consequence of the psychoanalytic theory of sex. Sexuality as such may in fact be a pseudoconcept we are better left without.[18] Here Lacan would remain faithful to Freud's assertion that the attractions of the object, including perhaps most significantly its biological sex, remain, when all is said and done, independent from the aim of the drive.[19]

When theory ceases to view sexuality as a positively descriptive term which increases our knowledge of the subject, the subject who calls him- or herself queer or homosexual moves from the margins of the democratic structure to assume his or her rightful place as universal citizen whose interests are to be situated, in their inalienable legitimacy, at precisely the same level as every other subject's. The deep implication of psychoanalysis for antihomophobic criticism lies therefore in its insistence that the sexuate character of the political subject prevents us from assuming that this subject's desire will manifest itself heterosexually. In consequence, the revolution of our time must be fought in the name of a generic subject whose sexuality may not be predicted in advance, a sexuality which is finally indeterminate and unknowable. While this contention forces us to question the lasting political desirability of the entire ideological apparatus of sexual orientation, it also dissuades the nonheterosexual subject from confining itself to its community by placing it decisively at the center of contemporary political antagonisms.

Though the thoroughgoing consequences of these notions clearly await their definitive elaboration, I would suggest by way of conclusion that the psychoanalytic concept of sex both foregrounds and limits what is known as the politics of sexuality. For on the one hand it implies that it is illegitimate—a violation of the subject's very sovereignty—to link the privileges and responsibilities of citizenship to this citizen's assumed heterosexuality. Indeed, I would go so far as to claim that the refusal of marriage and adoption rights to same-sex couples on the basis of their homosexuality is a violation of the very spirit of Freudian psychoanalysis. On the other hand, however, the politicization of sex cannot justifiably lead to a coherent notion of a community defined by its members' sexual self-definitions. Such a community can only be the result of a deeply obfuscating misrecognition perpetuated by a class of queer-identified theorists and intellectuals who have almost without exception failed to recognize how the constituency they represent is shot through with the general sociopolitical antagonisms produced through the workings of capital.

Nonheterosexual subjects surely share a very specific and insidious, but also decreasing, mode of social discrimination, but that is about all. Though I write from Canada, which in 2005 became, after Holland and Belgium, only the third nation to legalize same-sex marriage (Spain may take issue—it was a photo-finish), and where everyone benefits from routinely effective antidiscrimination legislation, it occurs to me that the limitations of the liberal horizon of sexual politics is everywhere becoming increasingly apparent. The tremendous social gains made by the gay and lesbian movements of the past three decades must be valorized and defended at all costs. Yet the resistance sex insistently puts up to knowledge and agency surely limits the politicization of sexuality to a negative and properly symptomatic program, to one which focuses not on any putatively political meaning or significance which could be ascribed to sexual experience as such, but rather on the sexualization of politics—on how political antagonisms are shot through with the effects of unconscious, frequently plainly homophobic, fantasy. Now is the time to reintroduce social antagonism into the theoretical discourse on sexuality and to call into question the ersatz notion of community on which it is based.

Notes

1. Epistemologies of Perversion

1. For the gist of Copjec's argument against Foucault, see especially "Introduction: Structures Don't March in the Streets," in *Read My Desire: Lacan against the Historicists* (Cambridge, MA: MIT Press, 1994), pp. 1–14.

2. In an invaluable article Arnold I. Davidson traces the development of the idea of perversion in sexological and psychiatric thought during the late nineteenth century. Unfortunately, however, he reproduces the incorrect *lieu commun* of historicism when he confidently avers that there exist "underlying rules for the production of discourse" in each historical period. Nevertheless, Davidson's article does the necessary historical work of tracing how Freud's writings on sexuality absorb and modify the concepts belonging to the psychiatric vocabulary of the time. Davidson's analysis first stresses the radical epistemological break Freud inaugurated in the *Three Essays*. Not without justification, the author then regrets in a second moment that Freud did not live up to the ramifications of his own claims, reverting periodically to a heterosexually normative framework which casts a regressive shadow on the decisiveness of the psychoanalytic break with sexological doctrine. My own effort at tracing the history of the concept of perversion contrasts with Davidson's in two respects. First, Freud's attempt at defining perversion did not cease, as Davidson's article would imply through omission, with the publication and modification of the *Three Essays*. As I shall go on to show in the following section of this chapter, the seeds of the structural theory of perversion were planted in later writings on fetishism and sexual difference. Second, I do not believe that "perversion is no longer a legitimate concept." But I will ask the reader to continue further to find out why, to answer the author's climactic question, I will not go as far as he. "How to Do the History of Psychoanalysis: A Reading of Freud's *Three Essays on the Theory of Sexuality*," in *The Trial(s) of Psychoanalysis*, ed. Françoise Meltzer (Chicago: University of Chicago Press, 1988), pp. 41, 62.

3. Foucault, *The History of Sexuality: An Introduction*, trans. Robert Hurley (New York: Random House, 1990), p. 34. Further references are cited in parentheses in the text.

4. See for example R. D. Laing's *The Divided Self* (London: Tavistock Press, 1960) and Reich's *The Sexual Revolution: Toward a Self-Regulating Character Structure* (New York: Orgone Instutute Press, 1945). See also Juliet Mitchell's incisive analysis of the work of these two figures in *Psychoanalysis and Feminism* (New York: Vintage, 1975).

5. In a timely book Kristeva responds to the postmodern malaise—a decline in the richness and intensity of subjective experience—which media oversaturation and hyperconsumerism bring about. The explosive growth of image-intensive communication technologies, according to Kristeva, produces a new symptomatology characterized by negative narcissism, the somatization of symptoms, and the general decline in the quality of the representation of psychic life. The erasure of the category of the subject to which Foucault's logic leads participates directly, in my view, not only in the process Kristeva describes, but also in a general withdrawal of the subject from its implication in the public sphere of political antagonism. "A diagnosis imposes itself," Kristeva writes. "Hurried by stress, impatient to earn and to spend, to enjoy and to die, today's men and women spare themselves the representation of their experience we call a psychic life." *Les nouvelles maladies de l'âme* (Paris: Fayard, 1993), p. 16, my translation.

6. Deleuze, *Foucault*, trans. and ed. Seán Hand, foreword Paul Bové (Minneapolis: University of Minnesota Press, 1988), p. 75. I discuss in greater detail the conflation of the concept of the state with power in queer theory in chapter 6.

7. Indeed it is not at all a coincidence, in my view, that at the moment Foucault was developing his critique of the repressive hypothesis, he began to give interviews to such figures as Bernard-Henri Lévy, one of the main luminaries of the post-*soixante-huitard* neoliberalism of the so-called *nouveaux philosophes*. In these interviews Foucault very explicitly distances himself from the "totalizing" and "universalizing" ambitions of various Marxist models for radical social change. When Foucault claimed, for example, that "we are perhaps experiencing the end of politics," he meant the end of ambitious and utopian forms of politics which aspire to something more fundamental than an analysis of the micropolitics of specific oppressed groups; more wide-ranging than specific tactics of resistance which aim at modest, practical interventions in circumscribed contexts. "Power and Sex," in *Michel Foucault. Politics, Philosophy, Culture: Interviews and Other Writings 1977–1984*, ed. Lawrence D. Kritzman (Routledge: New York, 1988), p. 122.

8. Canadian social theorist and public intellectual John Ralston Saul has made a similar claim in defense of universalist notions of "disinterest" against the tradition, in his view principally economistic on the right and sociological on the left, which reduces the field of human sociality to pure interest abstracted from any individual or collective subject. Saul calls this tradition "corporatist." His analysis also implicitly warns against swallowing the antistatist tendencies discernable in Foucault's theory of power, tendencies advancing that the strategic response to power's extension beyond the channels of political representation into the corporate forms of civil society is not to relegitimate the state form as the true locus of the people's power, but to abandon the very distinction

between state and corporate forms of political legitimacy in favor of an analytics of abstract vectors of power. My own analysis implies that Foucauldian historicism and its related aesthetics of power and lifestyle ethics may be the most pervasive brand of corporatism currently at large in the human sciences. See *The Unconscious Civilization* (Concord, ON: Anansi, 1995).

9. The dedialecticizing gesture through which Foucault dissociates power from concrete efforts at hegemonization produces a profoundly deterministic view of the relation between power and those whom it affects. For example, claiming that a traditional analysis of the agency of decision makers in the execution of a particular policy fails fully to disclose how that policy "hurts a particular category of person," Foucault advances that one should instead study "all those techniques by which a decision is accepted and by which that decision could not but be taken in the way it was." All decisions are a priori decided by a technique of power, which implies that even forms of resistance are determined in the same manner by such techniques. "On Power," in *Michel Foucault: Politics, Philosophy, Culture*, p. 105.

10. Freud, *Three Essays on the Theory of Sexuality*. Further references will be cited in parentheses in the text. *The Standard Edition of the Complete Psychological Works of Sigmund Freud (SE)*, trans. James Strachey (London: Hogarth Press and the Institute for Psychoanalysis, 1953), 7:149.

11. Davidson argues, more specifically, that Freud played a crucial role in "the overturning of the theory of degeneracy" which heralded a new era in the history of psychiatry. "How to Do the History of Psychoanalysis," p. 51.

12. Jean Laplanche's and Jean-Bertrand Pontalis's gloss on Freud's use of the German term *Trieb* has justifiably become canonical. It suggests that the proper English translation should be "drive" and not "instinct," as Strachey chose to render it. The German *Instinkt*, also used by Freud, designates for Laplanche and Pontalis a "behaviour predetermined by heredity and appearing in virtually identical form in all individual members of a single species" or, in more modern terms, "the concepts of behaviour patterns, innate trigger-mechanisms, [or] specific stimuli-signals." *Trieb*, in contrast, refers more specifically to "the internal sources of a constant inflow of excitation which the organism cannot evade and which is the basis of the functioning of the psychical apparatus." *The Language of Psycho-Analysis*, intro. Daniel Lagache, trans. Donald Nicholson-Smith (London: Karnac, 1988), pp. 214–15. Drive, unlike instinct, is thus a properly psychoanalytic concept, indeed one of the four Lacan would in 1963 designate as fundamental.

13. Freud, "Instincts and Their Vicissitudes," *SE*, 14:122; further references cited in parentheses in the text.

14. Lacan, *The Four Fundamental Concepts of Psycho-Analysis*, ed. Jacques-Alain Miller, trans. Alan Sheridan (New York: Norton, 1981), p. 175. Further references are cited in parentheses in the text.

15. Freud, "Fetishism," *SE*, 21:157.

16. Ibid.

17. Ibid.

18. Ibid., p. 154.

19. I refer after Freud to the properly psychical meaning of these problematic terms, not to something akin to the poststructuralist notion of gender and its performance. Indeed, the impediments to queer theory's serious engagement with psychoanalysis stem largely, in my view, from its inability to distinguish between the properly psychoanalytic concept of sex or sexuation, which is reducible neither to nature nor culture, and gender, which is indeed understood to be a function of culture or the social. For psychoanalysis there is no necessary correlation, in other words, between the subject's unconscious sex and the manner in which he or she conforms to socially constructed gender norms.

20. Janine Chasseguet-Smirgel's scandalously homophobic work on perversion is emblematic of this tendency. It first reduces all forms of male homosexuality to the perverse structure, and then brutally links all legitimate forms of creativity and ethical viability on a libido organized by procreation and filiation. See *Éthique et esthétique de la perversion* (Paris: Presses Universitaires de France, 1984). Joel Whitebrook offers an excellent critique of Chasseguet-Smirgel's essentialist conservatism, as well as a nuanced appreciation of Joyce McDougall's contribution to the theory of sexuality, in *Perversion and Utopia: A Study in Psychoanalysis and Critical Theory* (Cambridge, MA: MIT Press, 1996). McDougall's most interesting book in this context is *The Many Faces of Eros: A Psychoanalytic Exploration of Human Sexuality* (New York: Norton, 1995).

21. See my "The Sameness of Sexual Difference and the Difference of Same-Sex Desire," *Umbra: A Journal of the Unconscious* (2002): 43–63. What follows is a brief summary of the discussion contained in this article. I return to the question of sexuation and homosexuality in the final chapter.

22. *Le Séminaire de Jacques Lacan, vol. 20, Encore*, ed. Jacques-Alain Miller (Paris: Seuil, 1975), p. 67; my translation.

23. André, *L'Imposture perverse* (Paris: Seuil, 1993), p. 170; my translation.

24. Freud, "Some Psychical Consequences of the Anatomical Distinction Between the Sexes," *SE*, 19:252.

25. André, *L'Imposture perverse*, p. 197.

26. Ibid., p. 425.

27. MacCannell, "Perversion in Public Places," *The Hysteric's Guide to the Future Female Subject* (Minneapolis: University of Minnesota Press), p. 35.

2. Confessions of a Medieval Sodomite

1. Thomas Wilson's *Bluebeard: A Contribution to History and Folk-Lore* (New York: Knickerbocker Press, 1899) provides a useful overview of the relation between the facts of the trial and the development of the Bluebeard motif in Breton folklore. Leonard Wolf's *Bluebeard: The Life and Crimes of Gilles de Rais* (New York: Clarkson N. Potter, 1980) elaborates on the differences between the events of Gilles's life and their distorted representation in the Bluebeard tradition.

2. Reinach's article "Gilles de Rais" is the best-known and most influential attempt to rehabilitate Gilles through the argument that the trial was the instrument of a political conspiracy which entirely fabricated Gilles's crimes. *Cultes, mythes et religions* 40, no. 8 (1912):267–99. None of the recent interpretations of the trial, however, subscribes to this thesis; Georges Bataille, among others, argues vehemently against it. Clearly, Reinach's article is to be placed in the context of a post–Dreyfus affair revisionist effort to comb French legal history for instances of abuses of power against political undesirables. Though Reinach demonstrates analytic acumen in his discussion of the political motivation for the trial, and in fact I draw significantly on his work in this chapter's conclusion, I agree with most commentators that the strength of the evidence against Gilles should not allow us to go so far as to question the authenticity of the witnesses' depositions.

3. The late nineteenth-century reawakening of interest in the trial of Gilles de Rais was largely due to the publication of Eugène Bossard's historical biography *Gilles de Rais, maréchal de France dit Barbe-Bleue* (Paris: Champion, 1886). Most of the subsequent studies which argue in favor of the influence of Gilles's biographical life on his criminality make reference to Bossard's pioneering text.

4. In Georges Bataille, *Le procès de Gilles de Rais* (Paris: Société Nouvelle des Editions Pauvert, 1979), pp. 189–338.

5. Georges Bataille, *The Trial of Gilles de Rais*, trans. Richard Robinson (Los Angeles: Amok, 1991), p. 150. Further references are cited in parentheses in the text; "TM" signifies that I have modified Robinson's translation.

6. It is not clear from the evidence of the trial documents of what exactly consisted this oft-evoked "sodomitic vice." Étienne Corrillaut, known familiarly as "Poitou" in the Gilles entourage, provided the most detailed account of what occurred during the rituals of abuse. According to Corrillaut, Gilles "first took his penis or virile member into one or the other of his hands, rubbed it, made it erect, or stretched it, then put it between the thighs or legs of the said boys and girls, bypassing the natural vessel of the said girls, rubbing his said penis or virile member on the bellies of the said boys and girls with great pleasure, passion, and lascivious concupiscence, until sperm was ejaculated on their bellies" (219). It is entirely possible, indeed probable, that anal penetration never featured among Gilles's practices with his young victims. Corrillaut's account also underlines the tremendously broad late-medieval understanding of 'sodomy,' extending as it did to any sexual activity which may not directly lead to conception.

7. Michel Bataille, *Gilles de Rais* (Paris: Mercure de France, 1972), p. 20, my translation. Though the author appears to want to present his text as a historical biography of Gilles de Rais, it indulges in novelistic evocations of situation and decidedly nondocumentary focalizations of his protagonists' consciousnesses which read more like fictionalized biography. As such, Michel Bataille's text is an unusual, generically unclassifiable work. Unfortunately, the author's assurances that he has read all the major works on Gilles de Rais does not compensate for the lack of standard scholarly documentation. In spite of these drawbacks, however, Michel Bataille's book is a serious attempt at

exploring the subjectivity of Gilles de Rais by analyzing what we know of his biographical life as a feature of his criminal motivation. In this way, in spite of its psychologizing limitations, the author begins the work of reattributing the status of subject to Gilles that is regretfully missing, I will contend in the next section, in Georges Bataille's analysis.

8. Bataille, *Trial,* p. 189; TM. Further references are cited in parentheses in the text.

9. For example, although it is impossible to detail this point here, the Gilles case cries out for comparison with mass media treatments of serial killers, in particular those whose cases involve child or adolescent victims and same-sex eroticism. As the Gilles phenomenon exemplifies, the prurient sensationalism surrounding cases of perversion says more about the anxieties and social antagonisms of the culture in which the crimes are committed than they do about the subjectivities of the perpetrators. The 1991 case of Jeffrey Dahmer in the United States, for example, provided an alibi for the venting of ugly homophobic prejudices. Further, media coverage of instances of child molestation and of the use of child pornography by public figures routinely expresses intense social discomfort at the reality of child and adolescent sexualities. Such coverage tends to conjure a traumatic yet fascinating fantasy of a virile, predatory pederastic male the concrete social consequences of which are clearly far out of proportion with the threat posed by actually existing child molesters and pornographers. For a lucid analysis of aspects of this dynamic in American popular culture, see Mark Seltzer's *Serial Killers: Death and Life in America's Wound Culture* (New York: Routledge, 1998).

10. It is crucial to distinguish this idea of subjective sovereignty from any erroneous voluntarist, psychologistic interpretations. The subject is sovereign in the precise sense that it remains unexpressed through its utterances; the subject, in other words, remains undetermined by "discourse" in its historical, Foucauldian sense. The notion of the sovereign subject features a noteworthy application to the Gilles case. The infanticides are the means by which Gilles attempts to express the inexpressible, to occlude the traumatic real of desire, to transfer the necessary splitting constitutive of subjectivity onto his Other. In order to assert that Gilles fails to become a sovereign subject, the subject must of course first be defined as sovereign in the manner here described.

11. Hollier, *Against Architecture: The Writings of Georges Bataille* (Cambridge: MIT Press, 1989), pp. 36–7.

12. Gilles claimed that he was led to a life of crime "on account of the bad upbringing he had received in his childhood" (189, TM). There is indeed some evidence of the traumas the young Gilles suffered, enough to persuade us to take seriously the effects of these experiences on his future criminality. When Gilles was eleven years old, his father, Guy de Rais, was gored by a wild boar on a hunting expedition and died four years later. It was at this point that Gilles's maternal grandfather, Jean de Craon, assumed Gilles's guardianship after successfully appealing Guy's deathbed attempt to accord responsibility for the boy to a distant cousin. Evidently, Gilles's father had little confidence in his father-

in-law's merits as a parental figure, and Gilles's own testimony reveals that Craon allowed his ward to indulge his most savage tendencies. Further, only months after the death of his father, Gilles's mother appears to have abandoned her two boys, due either to sudden death or to remarriage. See Michel Herubel, *Gilles de Rais et le déclin du Moyen-Age* (Paris: Perrin, 1982), pp. 49–73. This (somewhat speculative, to be sure) biographical information supports my claim about the psychodynamic significance of Craon's death for Gilles; given that the figure of Craon recalls the Freudian figure of the primal father, his demise could only have exacerbated what was very likely Gilles's already fragile relation to the paternal function of prohibition. The other standard-issue view concerning the influence of lived trauma on Gilles's criminality presents the execution of Joan of Arc as the source of an extreme disillusionment which causes Gilles, in essence, to lose faith in humanity. For a suggestive, though again highly speculative, account of this angle, see Michel Bataille, *Gilles de Rais*, pp. 92–105. Michel Tournier turns this insight into a compelling novella entitled *Gilles et Jeanne* (Paris: Gallimard, 1983).

13. Goldberg, *Sodometries: Renaissance Texts, Modern Sexualities* (Stanford, CA: Stanford University Press, 1992), pp. 9, 19.

14. Reliquet, *Le Moyen-Age. Gilles de Rais : maréchal, monstre, martyr* (Paris: Pierre Belfond, 1982), pp. 244-45.

15. Indeed, we can revisit the problem of historicism via the theme of homosexual desire. A historicist conception of homosexuality is one which subsumes same-sex desire under the discourses through which it is represented. This way of thinking about homosexuality features the absurd corollary that one cannot conceive of homosexual desire in the absence of a discourse about it. A second corollary would be that late-medieval sodomy and late-modern homosexuality are utterly distinct phenomena featuring no properly subjective or psychosexual kinship whatsoever.

16. Another clear indication of Bataille's troublesomely symptomatic relation to the idea of homosexuality occurs in a bizarre passage of his interpretation in which he imagines the decadent orgies Gilles allegedly organized as a prelude to the staging of his bloody scenes of torture. Gilles apparently had a particular fondness for the voices of young choirboys and, in reference to two of Gilles's musical recruits, André Buchet and Jean Rossignol, Bataille avers that they "undoubtedly had the voices of homosexual angels" (38). Elsewhere, with reference to the increasingly self-destructive nature of Gilles's comportment leading up to his arrest, Bataille refers to Gilles's enclosure in "the solitude of crime, homosexuality, and the tomb" (45). Clearly, homosexuality appears to bring out in Bataille a peculiar taste for the oxymoronic. Finally, evoking toofamiliar images of plague and contagion, Bataille makes reference to the Florentine origin of Gilles's favorite necromancer when he claims that François Prelati "came from a city where homosexuality was widespread" (57).

17. Lacan, "Intervention sur le transfert," *Écrits* (Paris: Seuil, 1966), p. 225; my translation.

18. Freud, *SE*, 2:303.

19. Lacan presents this notion of *agalma* as a manifestation of the function of *objet petit a* in his reading of Plato's *Symposium*. See *Le Séminaire de Jacques Lacan, vol. 8, Le transfert*, ed. Jacques-Alain Miller (Paris: Seuil, 2001), pp. 167–182.

20. I develop this theme in relation to the Christian concept of original sin in the next chapter.

21. Freud, *Group Psychology and the Analysis of the Ego, SE,* 18:105.

22. Ibid., p. 106.

23. Ibid., p. 110.

24. Denis Hollier has shed some light on the question of Gilles's intentionality in his development of the theorization of crime in Bataille's work. "Crime escapes from justice," Hollier offers, "precisely through its lack of reasons. Without the nakedness of his avowals offered without explanation Gilles de Rais would not have been a 'pure' criminal. In the last instance his crime was to have had no reason." As I shall go on to develop, it is incumbent upon any interpretation of Gilles's motivation to define more carefully than Hollier what is meant by what he refers to as a "reason." For it is not that Gilles had no reason to commit his criminal acts; indeed he makes it perfectly clear that he killed the children because the murders gave him pleasure. What is crucial about the Inquisition's reaction to Gilles's avowal is that it needs to attribute to the criminal a principle according to which he acted, a principle beyond mere empirical-sensuous interest. "Gilles de Rais au 'Théâtre de la Cruauté,'" *L'Arc* 44 (1971):77–86, my translation.

25. Immanuel Kant, *Religion within the Limits of Reason Alone* (Chicago: Open Court Press, 1934), pp. 63n–64n.

26. Ibid., p. 28.

27. Ibid., p. 21.

28. Ibid.

29. Ibid., p. 32.

30. Ibid.

31. Lacan, "Kant avec Sade," *Écrits*, p. 774; my translation.

32. This is precisely the moral tradition against which Pascal would launch his famous polemic in the *Lettres provinciales*.

33. A comment on my use of the term "moral": I am not arguing in favor of moralism or a moralistic perspective on Gilles de Rais, which I would define as a structure of judgment or action which takes as its point of self-legitimation ambient, commonly acknowledged criteria inherent in any particular historical discourse. The word "moral" as I am using it here in a vaguely Kantian fashion refers instead to the manner in which a subject rationalizes its thoughts and actions to itself in the context of a dialogue not between the subject and society, but rather between the subject and his or her Other, defined psychoanalytically as the sociosymbolic network from the perspective of which every subject views itself as worthy and unworthy, innocent and guilty. The moral realm, in other words, indexes the very nexus of the psychic and the social at which the subject pays the price for its narcissism. The psychical agency which allows us to view ourselves approvingly, in other words, is the selfsame agency through which we

reproach ourselves for our inadequacies. The movement from morality to ethics may be defined as coinciding with the subject's ability to liberate itself from such egoic dependencies and to self-legislate—to rationalize its act ex nihilo, with reference to nothing other than the sacred legality of desire. Obviously, it is precisely this movement which Gilles, as well as his auditors and the trial authorities, failed to effect.

34. One may suggestively juxtapose the tremendous comfort and pleasure with which Gilles seems to adopt the role of the moral pedagogue with the serenity of the fetishist who, according to Freud, shows himself "quite satisfied" with his fetish. It is also possible to compare the paradox of Gilles's idea of his empirical guilt and metaphysical innocence with the fetishist's ability to entertain two contradictory propositions concerning his psychical experience of castration: " 'the woman has still got a penis,' " says the fetishist at the same time that he admits " '[his] father has castrated the woman.' " Freud, "Fetishism," *SE*, 21: 152, 157.

35. Reinach, "Gilles de Rais," pp. 269–70.

36. Michel Bataille, *Gilles de Rais*, p. 175.

37. Heers, *Gilles de Rais. Vérités et légendes* (Paris: Perrin, 1994), p. 12.

3. Cleopatra's Nose

1. Goldmann, *The Hidden God: A Study of Tragic Vision in the* Pensées *of Pascal and the Tragedies of Racine*, trans. Philip Thody (New York: Humanities Press, 1964), p. 5. Further references are cited in parentheses in the text; "TM" signifies that I have modified the Thody translation.

2. For a more detailed account of Pascal's reception, which includes an analysis of Voltaire's and Nietzsche's readings of him, see Henri Lefebvre, *Pascal*, 2 vols. (Paris: Nagel, 1949).

3. Among the emblematic examples of the critique of postmodernism, one can mention Fredric Jameson, *Postmodernism: Or the Cultural Logic of Late Capitalism* (Durham: Duke University Press, 1990); Terry Eagleton, *The Illusions of Postmodernism* (Cambridge, MA: Blackwell, 1996); Alain Badiou, *Ethics: An Essay on the Understanding of Evil*, trans. Peter Hallward (London: Verso, 2002); Alex Callinicos, *Against Postmodernism: A Marxist Critique* (Cambridge, UK: Polity Press, 1989); and Peter Sloterdijk, *Critique of Cynical Reason* (Minneapolis: University of Minnesota Press, 1988), which will be of concern in the following chapter.

4. Lacan, *Television: A Challenge to the Psychoanalytic Establishment*, ed. Joan Copjec, trans. Denis Hollier, Rosalind Krauss, and Annette Michelson (New York: Norton, 1990), p. 22.

5. *The Seminar of Jacques Lacan, Book 7, The Ethics of Psychoanalysis*, trans. Dennis Porter, ed. Jacques-Alain Miller (New York: Norton, 1992), p. 313.

6. Though we should not reduce Pascal to this context, neither can we ignore it. We might say of Pascal what Kant, with reference to the voice of God,

said of the Pietists in *Conflict of the Faculties*: "They may be excused, those who, disoriented by the incomprehensibility of this power, mistake what is supersensible, precisely because it is of the practical order, for supernatural." Quoted in Olivier Reboul, *Kant et le problème du mal* (Montréal: Presses de l'Université de Montréal, 1972), p. 162. In Kantian terms, Pascal's religiosity transgresses "the limits of reason alone" both in its consideration of Christianity as revealed and in its reference to miracles performed by Jesus Christ as historical, as opposed to spiritual, proofs of Christianity's truth. Nonetheless, I will maintain throughout this chapter that Pascal's concepts anticipate with uncanny accuracy future developments in the Kantian metaphysics of morals and Freudian psychoanalysis. In my view it is highly unlikely that Kant was not intimately acquainted with Pascal. Further, with reference to the fraternity between Pascal and Kant, one should not underestimate the effects of the debt Jansenism (Pascal's religious sect) and Pietism share to the work of St. Augustine.

7. Though I strongly endorse Goldmann's decision to place Pascal in the tradition of tragic thought, I feel obliged to object to the premise underlying the entirety of *Le Dieu caché* that the tension between the relative and the absolute which tragedy locates outside history as a condition of human nature (what would now more commonly be referred to as "subjectivity") is later corrected by historical materialism through its idea of a resolution within history of this constitutive antagonism. For tragedy, human imperfection and the divine-supersensible demand for the absolute are inherently irreconcilable. For the Marxist Goldmann, dialectics—in its historical, or perhaps more accurately historicist, version—supersedes tragedy through its reinterpretation of this irreconcilability as a human construction which may be undone in a classless social formation. The pseudoconclusion to be avoided at all costs within the tragic perspective is clearly that the ahistoricity of the structure of social contradiction either disallows the possibility of social change *tout court* or makes irrelevant the concept of class struggle. One should also mention in passing that Goldmann's sociologism has him tie Pascal's concepts too perfectly to the class interests of the *noblesse de robe* of mid-seventeenth-century France.

8. In *Pensées* Pascal speaks anthropologically either of humanity in general or of a particular individual as representative of this humanity in general. Goldmann uses the term "man" very much in this sense. It is primarily for this reason that I have occasionally adopted this usage myself, which in my text is intended to be sex inclusive. Generally, however, I have preferred the psychoanalytic term "subject," which is not always perfectly appropriate when discussing texts such as Goldmann's.

9. Georg Lukács, "The Metaphysics of Tragedy," in *Soul and Form*, trans. Anna Bostock (Cambridge, MA: MIT Press, 1978), p. 153.

10. I have consulted the Brunschwicg edition of *Pensées*, trans. W. F. Trotter, intro. T. S. Eliot (New York: Dutton, 1958), p. 48, TM. References are to page numbers in the Trotter translation; "TM" signifies that I have modified this translation. I have refrained from referencing fragment numbers due to continuing updates of the Brunschwicg edition, which occasionally depart from strict correspondence with the edition on which the translation is based.

11. Olivier Reboul helpfully underscores how this theme of the Old and New testaments—that sin is original and universal, that it exceeds the power of free will or earthly redemption—leads to the two reactions I have just identified. The former Jesuitical position opts for a version of responsibility resting upon an idea of individual merit: "Each is born, like Adam, innocent and capable, by his own actions, to earn or lose divine grace." Saint Augustine inaugurated the contrasting, radically tragic, interpretation more closely related to Pascal's: "Adam's fault affects each of us like a hereditary evil, and . . . our freedom, corrupted at the origin, has a necessary tendency toward evil." *Kant et le problème du mal*, p. 21. For the Augustinian Pascal, we are born in sin, unworthy of God's grace, incapable of acquiring the knowledge which would indicate how it might be earned. Yet man is nonetheless capable, as we will see, of an act of faith which succeeds in bringing him closer to the divine. Joan Copjec's introduction to her edited volume *Radical Evil* (New York: Verso, 1996) made me aware of Reboul's invaluable book and also prompted me to think about the concept of grace in the context of Pascal's work (see the last section of this chapter).

12. Freud, *Totem and Taboo*, *SE*, 13:125.

13. Ibid., p. 158.

14. Ibid., p. 159.

15. Freud describes this paradox of a desire for absolution which exacerbates the sense of guilt in the terms of a logic of sacrifice, a logic which emblematizes the strong structural understanding of perversion in Lacan. Because the unconscious memory of the primal father's murder cannot be eradicated, its "undistorted reproduction emerged in the form of the sacrifice of the god," Freud claims. "Totem and Taboo," *SE*, 13:151–2. In Lacanian terminology, disavowed guilt "returns in the real"; the crime which cannot be acknowledged is committed anew in the form of a sacrificial offering to the "totemic" God/Father.

16. For a much fuller yet accessible account of belonging and inclusion in set theory see the seventh meditation of Alain Badiou's *L'Être et l'événement* (Paris: Seuil, 1988), pp. 95–107.

17. Louis Althusser, "Ideology and Ideological State Apparatuses (Notes towards an Investigation)," in *Lenin and Philosophy and Other Essays*, trans. Ben Brewster (New York: Monthly Review Press, 1971), pp. 167–8.

18. Ibid., p. 168.

19. Goldman, *Hidden God*, p. 287; TM.

20. Slavoj Žižek, whose references to the wager originally led me to Pascal, puts it this way: The "short-circuit between the intimate belief and the external 'machine' [automaton] ... is the most subversive kernel of Pascalian theology." *The Sublime Object of Ideology* (London: Verso, 1989), p. 43. This section's argument is indebted to Žižek's account of ideology.

21. In his own historical and ideological situation, Pascal combined an attitude of utter submission to the church hierarchy with devastating, acerbic critiques, best exemplified by the *Lettres provinciales*, of those elements in the church that he considered inimical to the spirit of Christianity. In this sense Pascal embodies the paradox whereby one is more likely to question the legitimacy of authority if one considers oneself bound by it, forced to comply with its command.

22. That the meditating subject, according to Buddhist thought, must focus on the breath only underscores the truth of Pascal's claim: Meditation presupposes that the subject's attention is directed, if not on the breath itself, then on its mantra. Even the experienced practitioner of meditation is not entirely reconciled to the fundamental void underlying subjectivity.

23. Pascal, *Pensées and The Provincial Letters*, trans. W. F. Trotter and Thomas M'Crie (New York: Random House, 1941), p. 336.

24. Ibid., p. 363.

4. This Whole World of Perversion

1. One hesitates to translate *philosophe* as "philosopher" because the English term fails to convey the specificity of the French. For the philosophe is no generic philosopher: He exhibits that peculiar combination of rationalism and materialism—that faith in the innateness and universality of the human faculty of reason combined with a conviction in the self-evidence of empirical fact—which characterized Enlightenment thought in its French incarnation. However, I have occasional recourse to the general English term to forestall irritating repetition.

2. G. W. F. Hegel, *Phenomenology of Spirit*, trans. A. V. Miller, intro. J. N. Findlay (Oxford: Oxford University Press, 1977), ¶486. Further references, denoting paragraph numbers in this edition, are cited in parentheses in the text. I have on occasion added to Miller's translation, where necessary, the original German term.

3. Quoted in Jean Hyppolite, *Genesis and Structure in Hegel's* Phenomenology of Spirit, trans. Samuel Cherniak and John Heckman (Evanston, IL: Northwestern University Press, 1974), p. 406–7.

4. Charles Taylor describes utilitarianism, as Hegel considers it, as a manifestation of the more materialist, anti-Kantian tendencies of Enlightenment: It is "an ethic in which acts are judged according to their consequences, that is, their relevance to some extraneous end, hence their usefulness." In contrast, ethical schemas featuring what Taylor calls "intrinsic properties" judge acts on the basis of the extent to which they can embody "a given virtue" or conform to a "moral law." *Hegel* (Cambridge, UK: Cambridge University Press), p. 181.

5. Peter Sloterdijk, *Critique of Cynical Reason*, trans. Michael Eldred, foreword Andreas Huyssen (Minneapolis: University of Minnesota Press, 1987), p. 6. Though Sloterdijk's definition of cynicism is of tremendous use to my discussion of Diderot and Hegel, and, indeed, presciently diagnoses a tendency of postmodernism I find deeply troubling, I wish to point out that I do not consider his larger argument unproblematic. In effect, Sloterdijk's effort to reconcile body and affect with the tradition of ideology critique falls back, in my view, on a number of the postmodern assumptions against which his book sets out to argue. Further, it advances an underconceptualized, speciously populist, and rather too ad hominem polemic against the Kantian critical tradition.

6. Ibid., p. 5.

7. Indeed, *Rameau's Nephew* is mentioned in the early pages of Sloterdijk's book as an example of the desirable Greek cynical tradition of political critique, and is in fact offered as a counterexample to the presumably more modern or proto-postmodern cynicism of Machiavelli. I agree with Sloterdijk's implication that the Nephew's low social position on one level allies him with the "declassed" cynicism of Diogenes; still, the Nephew's discourse is much more complex and contradictory than this statement would imply, and indeed features the fearful, desperately conformist drive which Sloterdijk associates with the postmodern moment.

8. Denis Diderot, *Rameau's Nephew*, in *Rameau's Nephew and D'Alembert's Dream*, trans. and intro. Leonard Tancock (Harmondsworth, UK: Penguin, 1984), p. 81, TM. Further references are cited in parentheses in the text; "TM" signifies that I have modified Tancock's translation.

9. Sloterdijk, pp. 3–4.

10. Ibid., p. 7.

11. I borrow the term from Slavoj Žižek's consideration of the Frankfurt School concept of repressive desublimation; I offer my own discussion of these questions in the context of contemporary queer theory in chapter 6. Žižek, *The Metastases of Enjoyment: Six Essays on Woman and Causality* (London: Verso, 1994), p. 16.

12. Should the reader wish to compare, the extremely British Tancock translates Diderot's "en linge sale" as "in dirty linen" and the original "bien vêtu" as "well shod."

13. Freud, "Negation," *SE,* 19:235.

14. Quoted in Émile Benveniste, "Language and Freudian Theory," *Problems in General Linguistics*, trans. Mary Elizabeth Meek (Coral Gables, FL: University of Miami Press, 1971), p. 68.

15. A. V. Miller translates Hegel's *Reichtum* as "wealth"; Charles Taylor prefers the term "riches." In this section I will alternate between Miller's term and a third term, "capital," which makes explicit the link between Hegel's analysis and the development of the Marxian theoretical edifice. Beyond its particular meaning in the context of the late stages of ancien régime France, it is clear that Hegel's analysis also helps illuminate the contemporary antagonism between, on the one hand, the state form of liberal democracy in its (theoretical) representation of the public interest and, on the other, what has now long since become a transnational form of capital.

16. The relation between the dialogical structure of Diderot's text and the dialectical conceptuality of Hegel's reading is considered in depth in a noteworthy article by H. R. Jauss, *"Le Neveu de Rameau*: Dialogue et dialectique," *Revue de métaphysique et de morale* 89 (1984):145–181. Jauss proposes that Hegel's analysis imposes a final resolution of a metaphysical character on an open text which dialogically problematizes the fundamental presuppositions of Enlightenment. Contra Jauss, my premise of departure does not acknowledge such a philosophical gap between the original text and Hegel's interpretation. Indeed,

I will argue that the speculative resolution Hegel proposes articulates the terms of the psychical process, the analytical work, which the dialogue itself performs. Jauss thus overestimates the allegedly metaphysical character of the concluding, "invisible" step of dialectical reason. The moment of the return of Spirit to itself in fact further alienates self-consciousness from itself and therefore may not be said to involve a return to the same which represses or abjects difference in the way Jauss suggests.

17. Benveniste, "Subjectivity in Language," in *Problems in General Linguistics*, p. 226.

18. Lacan, "Subversion of the Subject and the Dialectic of Desire in the Freudian Unconscious," *Écrits: A Selection*, trans. Alan Sheridan (London: Norton, 1977), p. 313.

19. Deleuze and Guattari, *Kafka: Toward a Minor Literature*, trans. Dana Polan (Minneapolis: University of Minnesota Press, 1986), p. 22.

20. Lacan, "The Function and Field of Speech and Language in Psychoanalysis," *Écrits: A Selection*, p. 67.

21. Ibid.

22. The German reads *Verkehrung* where A. V. Miller translates "inversion." "Perversion" appears for *Verkehrung* in other instances of Miller's rendering. It is not clear to me what distinction, if any, Miller wishes to communicate through this choice, which in my view is not necessary.

23. It would seem likely that Hegel here singles out Diderot's use of the term *espèce* because it succinctly articulates the dialectic of the universal and particular in *Rameau's Nephew*. Tancock problematically renders the singular form of the word as "race" and the plural as "characters." For the philosophe, the term represents what is appealed to in order to inspire the individual to extend the horizon of its interest: "Let us forget for the moment the point we occupy in time and space," he urges, and "think of the good of our species" (42). The Nephew, in contrast, uses the term to designate the already particular class of court jesters, "fools" and swindlers from which he insists on further distinguishing himself (91).

24. Hyppolite, *Genesis and structure*, p. 415.

5. The Guardian of Criminal Being

1. Gearhart, *The Interrupted Dialectic: Philosophy, Psychoanalysis, and their Tragic Other* (Baltimore: Johns Hopkins University Press, 1992), p. 1.

2. Jacques Lacan, *The Seminar of Jacques Lacan, Book 7, The Ethics of Psychoanalysis 1959–1960*, ed. Jacques-Alain Miller, trans. Dennis Porter (New York: Norton, 1992), p. 277. Further references will be cited in parentheses in the text. "TM" indicates that I have modified Porter's translation.

3. For those readers unfamiliar, or requiring reacquaintance, with the action and convoluted kinship relations featured in *Antigone*, the tragedy begins after the two sons of Oedipus, Eteocles and Polynices, have killed one another in a conflict over succession to the throne of Thebes. Eteocles had assumed control

of the city after the death of his father Oedipus in spite of being the second-born son. After the deaths of Eteocles and Polynices, Creon becomes king by virtue of being brother of Jocasta, mother (and of course wife) of Oedipus. As the tragedy begins, we learn that Creon has issued an edict against the exercise of burial rights on the body of Polynices, justifying his decision on the grounds that Polynices usurped the public order by attacking Thebes at the head of the Argive army. Antigone is arrested and imprisoned after defying Creon's command. When Antigone hangs herself, Haemon, fiancé of Antigone and son of Creon, commits suicide in a gesture of solidarity with his intended. Upon hearing of the death of her son, Creon's wife Euridyce also kills herself, causing Creon to recognize the inhumanity of his actions and to suffer the tragic loss of his relations.

4. G. W. F. Hegel, *Phenomenology of Spirit*, trans. A. V. Miller (Oxford: Oxford University Press, 1977), ¶ 448. Further references to paragraph numbers in this edition are cited in parentheses in the text.

5. Sophocles, *Antigone*, in *Sophocles, vol. II, The Loeb Classical Library*, trans. Hugh Lloyd-Jones (Cambridge, MA: Harvard University Press, 1994), p. 41.

6. Freud, *Totem and Taboo, SE,* 13:151.

7. "Through pity and fear [tragedy] achieves the purgation (catharsis) of such emotions." Aristotle, *Poetics*, in *On Poetry and Style*, trans. and intro. G. M. A. Grube (Indianapolis, IN: Hackett, 1989), p. 12.

8. Aristotle, *The Politics*, ed. Stephen Everson, trans. Jonathan Barnes (Cambridge: Cambridge University Press, 1988), p. 195.

9. Freud, *Beyond the Pleasure Principle, SE,* 18:63.

10. Ibid., p. 42.

11. Freud and Breuer, *Studies on Hysteria, SE,* 2:8–10.

12. Freud, *Beyond, SE,* 18:18.

13. *Sophocles vol. II,* pp. 77, 79.

14. Ibid., p. 79.

15. Lacan, "Kant avec Sade," *Écrits* (Paris: Seuil, 1966), p. 776; my translation.

16. Kant, *Critique of Judgment*, trans. and intro. Werner S. Pluhar (Indianapolis, IN: Hackett, 1987), p. 43. Further references are cited in parentheses in the text.

17. In "Kant with Sade" Lacan points out how this strange, objectless subjective relation obtains in moral as well as aesthetic experience. The moral law, more precisely, has no object; it fails to materialize in any form on the level of experience. "Let us retain the paradox that it should be at the moment when the subject is no longer faced with any object that he encounters a law, one which has no other phenomenon than something which already signifies [*quelque chose de signifiant déjà*], which is obtained from a voice in the conscience, and which, in articulating itself as a maxim, proposes [there] the order of a purely practical reason or of a will." *Écrits*, p. 767, my translation. See also Slavoj Žižek, "Kant with (or against) Sade?" *New Formations* 35 (Autumn 1998): 93–107; and Jacques-Alain Miller, "A Discussion of Lacan's 'Kant avec Sade,'" in *Reading Seminars I and II: Lacan's Return to Freud*, ed. Richard Feldstein, Bruce Fink, and Maire Jaanus (Albany: State University of New York Press, 1996), pp. 212–240.

18. Freud, *Beyond, SE,* 18:55.

19. Antigone's stance with respect to the second death is nicely articulated by Jane B. Malmo in reference to a Miltonian hero: "It is [the] suspension of the symbolic order that returns us to the domain between two deaths, since 'the second death' is always that of the symbolic universe itself. In his drive toward annihilation, Samson becomes a subject who, in suspending the symbolic fictions that support daily life, confronts us with the radical negativity upon which these fictions are founded. As a transgression of the symbolic order, Samson's destructive violence throws us back into the trauma of the real out of which our symbolic reality struggles to emerge." "Towards a Limitless Love: From Symptom to Sinthôme in Milton's *Samson Agonistes,*" *New Formations* 23 (Summer 1994): p. 94.

20. Reinhardt, *Sophocles,* trans. Hazel Harby and David Harvey (Oxford: Blackwell, 1979), pp. 3–4.

21. Rohde, *Psyche: The Cult of Souls and the Belief in Immortality among the Greeks,* trans. W. B. Hillis (Freeport, NY: Books for Libraries Press, 1972), p. 426.

22. Reinhardt, *Sophocles,* p. 77.

23. Richard E. Doyle, *Atè: Its Use and Meaning. A Study in the Greek Poetic Tradition from Homer to Euripides* (New York: Fordham University Press, 1984), p. 4.

24. Doyle cites W. S. Barrett's *Euripides: Hippolytus* (Oxford: Clarendon Press, 1964), who in turn quotes from E. R. Dodds' classic *The Greeks and the Irrational* (Berkeley: University of California Press, 1963).

25. *Sophocles, vol. II,* pp. 35–7.

26. Ibid., p. 37.

27. Butler, *Antigone's Claim: Kinship between Life and Death* (New York: Columbia University Press, 2000), p. 54.

28. For a more detailed response to Butler's appreciation of *Antigone* see my "(Queer) Theory and the Universal Alternative," *Diacritics* 32, no. 1 (2004):1–18.

29. Hegel, *Aesthetics: Lectures on Fine Art,* 2 vols., trans T. M. Knox (Oxford: Clarendon Press, 1991), p. 1217. Though no specific source is mentioned in the ethics seminar, Lacan's reproach against the Hegelian reading would seem to be more closely informed by the interpretation featured in the *Aesthetics.* As I argued earlier, however, the reading Hegel offers in the *Phenomenology* is the one which lends itself best to comparison with Lacan's.

30. Alenka Zupančič's *Ethics of the Real: Kant, Lacan* (London: Verso, 2000) provides an excellent book-length discussion of Lacanian ethics in the context of Kant's intervention in moral theory.

31. *Écrits,* p. 790, my translation.

6. Concluding (Un)Queer-Theoretical Postscript

1. The texts Dollimore analyzes as instances of the project to theorize the liberating desublimation of perversion are the following: Norman O. Brown's *Life against Death: The Psychoanalytic Meaning of History* (London: Routledge,

1959); Herbert Marcuse's *Eros and Civilization: A Philosophical Inquiry into Freud* (Boston: Beacon Press, 1966); Guy Hocquenghem's *Homosexual Desire*, trans. Daniella Dangoor (Durham, NC: Duke University Press, 1993); Mario Mieli's *Homosexuality and Liberation: Elements of a Gay Critique*, trans. David Frenback (London: Gay Men's Press, 1980); and John Rechy's *Sexual Outlaw: A Documentary* (London: W. H. Allen, 1978).

2. Dollimore, *Sexual Dissidence: Augustine to Wilde, Freud to Foucault* (Oxford: Clarendon Press, 1991), p. 177. Further references will be cited in parentheses in the text.

3. Following Freud's own recommendation in *The Future of an Illusion*, I will use the terms "culture" and "civilization" synonymously throughout this section. *SE*, 21:6.

4. "Symptoms are formed in part," writes Freud, "at the cost of abnormal sexuality; neuroses are, so to say, the negative of perversions." *Three Essays on the Theory of Sexuality, SE*, 7: 165. "The neuroses," Freud elsewhere contends, "contain the same tendencies, though in a state of 'repression,' as do the positive perversions." "'Civilized' Sexual Morality and Modern Nervous Illness," *SE*, 9:179.

5. Dollimore's text neither presents Ignatieff's and Weeks' arguments against Foucault nor explains of what this charge of "functionalism" might consist. Since they generally accord with my own reservations, it will be useful to provide an account here. In an overview of Foucault's work on the history of incarceration in France, Ignatieff reproaches the Frenchman for providing a "cloudy" answer to the question of agency, and for speaking "passively" of power, making it "impossible to identify who, if anyone, was the historical agent of the tactics and strategies [Foucault] describes." Contrary to Dollimore's insinuation, then, Ignatieff argues that Foucault opposes the functionalist view of the prison system, a view which would claim that the prison actually "is the designated punitive instrument within a social division of labour," and not itself an instrument of power forces coming from elsewhere. Ignatieff, "State, Civil Society, and Total Institutions: A Critique of Recent Social Histories of Punishment," *Social Control and the State*, ed. S. Cohen and A. T. Scull (Oxford: Robertson, 1983), p. 92.

Weeks, for his part, advances four arguments against Foucault, one of which does accuse him of a "latent functionalism." By this Weeks means that Foucault's view of power's normalization tends "towards a necessary social equilibrium . . . particularly as both the resistances and the individual internalisations are not specified: social control seems to be absolute." In other words, the adjective "functionalist" here designates a power apparatus of perfect effectiveness, a system which accords seamlessly with its self-professed function. *Sex, Politics, and Society: The Regulation of Sexuality Since 1800* (London: Longman, 1981), p. 9.

6. *Epistemology of the Closet* (Berkeley: University of California Press, 1990), pp. 23–24. Further references are cited in parentheses in the text. I would also point out that Sedgwick's qualification of "Marxist, feminist, postcolonial, and other engagé critical projects" as "more familiar" than psychoanalysis problem-

atically identifies the implicit addressee of her work: "we" American queer and queer-friendly academics to whom the vocabulary of psychoanalysis appears strangely exotic.

7. Butler, *The Psychic Life of Power: Theories in Subjection* (Stanford, CA: Stanford University Press, 1997), p. 83. Further references are cited in parentheses in the text.

8. See for example Lacan, "Le maître et l'hystérique," *Le Séminaire de Jacques Lacan, vol. 17, L'Envers de la psychanalyse* (Paris: Seuil, 1991), pp. 31–42; and Juliet Flower MacCannell, *The Hysteric's Guide to the Future Female Subject* (Minneapolis: University of Minnesota Press, 2000).

9. See Halperin, *Saint Foucault: Towards a Gay Hagiography* (New York: Oxford University Press, 1995) for the best—or worst, depending on one's perspective—example of the use of late Foucauldian politics for queer theory.

10. Žižek, *The Metastases of Enjoyment* (London: Verso, 1994), p. 8. Further references are cited in parentheses in the text. It should also be noted that Žižek's discussion of Freudian revisionism is mediated by Russell Jacoby's essential *Social Amnesia: A Critique of Contemporary Psychology* (New Brunswick, NJ: Transaction Publishers, 1997); my own commentary will refer more directly to the primary texts.

11. Though he refers to Marcuse as a participant in the Frankfurt School's antirevisionist current, Žižek's reading is based mainly on Adorno's essay "Zum Verhältnis von Soziologie und Psychologie," translated by Irving N. Wohlfarth in *New Left Review* 47 (Jan.–Feb. 1968):79–97.

12. For the most important examples of Fromm's arguments in this context, see *Man for Himself* (New York and Toronto: Rinehart, 1947), and *Psychoanalysis and Religion* (New Haven, CT: Yale University Press, 1950). Marcuse's classic attack against Fromm, Karen Horney, and other revisionists is articulated in "Critique of Neo-Freudian Revisionism," *Eros and Civilization: A Philosophical Inquiry into Freud* (Boston: Beacon Press, 1955), pp. 238–274. It is useful to spell out here the shortcomings of Marcuse's nonetheless deeply admirable essay, given that it is predicated on the notion of the possibility of a historical rearticulation of the reality principle, one which would enable a kind of perverse equivalent of the full genitalization posited by the most normative strands of psychoanalytic theory. In my view, Marcuse, in this particular essay, subverts his own intention to rediscover the properly critical dimension of Freudian theory by positing a harmonization of the libido with the constraints of civilization. In contrast to the essay on revisionism, then, Marcuse's later notion of repressive desublimation is a more rigorously critical concept, although even this notion rests on the premise of a possible historical reconciliation of civilization and drive.

13. Of course, this is not to say that labor conditions, for example, cannot be a source of legitimate social alienation. The point is that by solely committing all forms of alienation to sociohistorical causes, revisionism, in agreement with the orthodox Marxist tradition, posits the possibility of a social formation capable of effectively reconciling the subject with its uncon-

scious. Yet I would also argue that the psychoanalytic hostility to the concrete possibility of a positive social utopia does not require that we eliminate the utopian ideal from theory as, precisely, an object-cause of desire, as a conceptually necessary construction required to instigate thoroughgoing social transformation.

14. I would suggest that it is necessary to distinguish between two forms of utopianism. The "bad," strictly positive utopianism of revisionism posits the subject's libidinal alienation as the determinate effect of a historically specific mode of the relations of production and reproduction, rather than as an effect, more simply, of the human condition, of the nonhistorical conditions of desire. This psychoanalytic claim does not discount, however, the desirability of any model for social change. On the contrary, a nuanced utopianism acknowledges the political necessity of models for possible social arrangements which do not, and may never, exist. In contrast to the other brand, however, this one refuses to succumb to the ideological illusion of a transparent society without antagonism constituted by subjects reconciled to desire and to the social field. We can briefly qualify this assertion with reference to the idea of the psychoanalytic act, which by definition resists symbolic formulation in any given sociohistorical arrangement, and may therefore only be considered as decisively negative with respect to the social status quo. One must bear in mind, however, that this negativity may have radically transformative, albeit indeterminate and unpredictable, concrete effects. Antigone's "negative" ethical heroism, as I tried to describe it in the last chapter, would serve to emblematize the structure of this alternative utopianism.

15. Žižek does not in fact fully endorse the Frankfurt school's treatment of repressive desublimation, which he eventually dismisses as a "pseudo-concept." For where Adorno interpreted fascist mass spectacle as an ideological performance orchestrated by the state to disguise its actual, rationally self-interested designs for manipulating the masses, Žižek prefers to interpret this phenomenon as protopsychotic, in other words as a failure of the subjects concerned to find themselves interpellated by the sociosymbolic network. This failure therefore masks no hidden, rationally conceived plan. However, Žižek does agree with Adorno that Freud's circumscription by bourgeois ideology prevented him from seizing the significance of the superego's transformation from an agency of interdiction to an incitement to enjoyment. It is this last observation which is most significant to my own argument.

16. Copjec, *Read My Desire* (Cambridge, MA: MIT Press, 1994), p. 3. Further references are cited in parentheses in the text.

17. Lacan, *Le Séminaire, vol. 20, Encore* (Paris: Seuil, 1988), p. 67; my translation. Further references are cited in parentheses in the text.

18. See on this point Tim Dean's *Beyond Sexuality* (Chicago: University of Chicago Press, 2000) for a path-breaking discussion of Lacan and queer theory with somewhat different political and conceptual investments.

19. "It has been brought to our notice," Freud comments, "that we have been in the habit of regarding the connection between the sexual instinct and

the sexual object as more intimate than it in fact is. . . . We are thus warned to loosen the bond that exists in our thought between instinct and object. It seems probable that the sexual instinct is in the first instance independent of its object; nor is its origin likely to be due to its object's attractions." *Three Essays on the Theory of Sexuality, SE,* 7:147–8.

Index